SAINT,
SITE,
AND
SACRED
STRATEGY

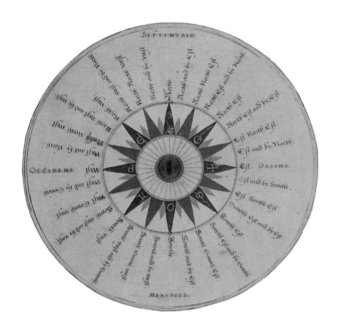

SAINT
SITE
AND
SACRED
STRATEGY

IGNATIUS ROME AND JESUIT URBANISM

CATALOGUE OF THE EXHIBITION
BIBLIOTECA APOSTOLICA VATICANA
EDITED BY THOMAS M. LUCAS S.J.

Contents

Welcome 7
S.R.E. Cardinal Antonio Maria Javierre Ortas S.D.B.

Presentation 11
V.R. Father Peter Hans Kolvenbach S.J.

Acknowledgements 13

Apparatus 15

Saint, Site, and Sacred Strategy:
Ignatius, Rome, and the Jesuit Urban Mission 16
Thomas M. Lucas S.J.

"A Noble Medley and Concert of Materials and Artifice"
Jesuit Church Interiors in Rome , 1567-1700 46
Evonne Levy

The Catalogue 63

Bibliography 226

Photographic material used with permission from other sources:

Bibliotheca Hertziana, Roma, pp. 49, 55
Bibliothèque Nationale, Paris, Cat. 82
Felice Bono, p. 30, Cat. 64
Thomas Lucas S.J., p. 11, Cat. 49, 50, 52, 105, 106, 128
Franco Marini, pp. 4, 24, 46
Musei Vaticani, Vatican City, Cat. 31, 121, 124, 141
Museo del Palazzo Venezia, Rome, Cat. 134
John Wm. Nagle, pp. 52, 57(r),
Thomas Rochford S.J., pp. 38, 57(l)
Oscar Savio, Cat. 109

Published and distributed by
The Biblioteca Apostolica Vaticana
Vatican City

ISBN: 88-210-0625-5

Edited & designed by Thomas M. Lucas S.J.
Typeset *in aedibus Societatis Iesu Romae et Californiae*
Filmset, printed, and bound in Italy by So.Gra.Ro., Rome - Via I. Pettinengo, 39

Cover illustration: Detail, "Roma Ignaziana," ca. 1609 (Cat. 71)

Title Pages: p. 1, Details of the Casa Professa and St. Ignatius, Francesco Villamena, 1604, (Cat. 84); p. 2, Compass with Illuminated Rose of the Winds, Studio of Battista Agnese, ca. 1542 (Cat. 8); p. 3, Seal of the Society of Jesus recently discovered in the restoration of the rooms of St. Ignatius, Rome, ca. 1600

Frontispiece: Statue of St. Ignatius, Chapel of S. Ignazio, Church of the Gesù, Rome

Welcome

His Eminence
Antonio Maria
Javierre Ortas S.D.B.,
Cardinal Librarian and
Archivist of the
Holy Roman Church

I embraced with great fondness the project of an Ignatian exhibition at the Biblioteca Apostolica Vaticana from the very beginning. It would not be fair to hide the personal satisfaction with which I welcome Iñigo of Loyola to our Roman home on the anniversary of dates which were so important and in the city for which he held great affection in his Life and Works. The title of the celebration —"Saint, Site, and Sacred Strategy: Ignatius, Rome, and Jesuit Urbanism"— is praiseworthy due to its well-chosen theme, the context of the exhibition, and the importance of the event.

It is not an easy task to choose the right perspective through which to evoke the past. Fortunately for us, points in space and time leave us with no doubt. After a spiritual itinerary which begins at Loyola and which takes him to Montserrat, Manresa, Salamanca and Paris, the fully mature Ignatius ends his pilgrimage in Rome, the Eternal City. It was in Rome that he lived without any interruptions the last and most decisive stage of his life. It was always from the city of Rome that he saw the Society of Jesus rise, grow, and flourish, always from the very beginning at the service of the Church and at one with the wishes of the Roman Pontiff. Thus, the particular focus of this period of growth, intensely lived in the center of Rome and at the heart of the sixteenth century, is well justified. It could be said, therefore, that "Ignatius and sixteenth-century Rome" represents a theme which is not only legitimate, but also obligatory. Ignatius' personality cannot possibly be sketched if one forgets that he was a man of his time. Likewise, Roman history in the sixteenth century would be incomplete if it did not include one of its most outstanding protagonists.

The environment which contextualizes the Ignatian exhibition is felicitous indeed. The quality of its historical documentation harmonizes with the characteristics of the *Biblioteca Apostolica Vaticana*.

The *Biblioteca* is the ideal place in which to remember the past. We cannot think of a more appropriate environment in which to evoke Ignatius' situation in sixteenth-century Rome. It must be kept in mind that he did not find support in his intention to come to the city of Rome: "Do you wish to go to Rome?" (*Autobiography*, no. 36) It seemed like a warning, which Ignatius shared with his companions years later: "Coming to Rome he told his companions that he saw all doors closed, meaning to say that there would be many contradictions" (*Autobiography,* no. 97). However, Rome remained the goal of his pilgrimage. Rome was his definitive goal, since, despite his previous plans, he remained there because "the Roman Pontiff's will was that we would not move from here, since the mission in Rome is plentiful" (*Obras,* p. 669).

The *APOSTOLIC* dimensions of this library are congruent with the ambitions of the "urban mission" which fed the zeal of the small group of men gathered around Ignatius. They were apostles of the city through the word proclaimed from the university, whispered in the confessional, and spelled out in catechesis. They were also apostles of the world. Ignatius' heart beat simultaneously with Xavier's, who had recently entered Japan—"We have rejoiced in the Lord that you have arrived with health and that doors have opened to have the Gospel preached in that region" (*Obras,* p. 809). Between the city and the world, Ignatius' apostolic desires reveal themselves in his letters to Cardinal Pole (*Obras,* pp. 848-849, 895-896), to Fr. Canisius (*Obras,* pp. 710-711, 880-887) and to the Fathers who worked in places where there were Catholics and Protestants (*Obras,* pp. 765-771).

Finally, our library, besides being apostolic, belongs to the *VATICAN*. Its name indicates its allegiance. The fact that it is in the Vatican Palace reveals its adherence to the Pope and his charitable desires. It is precisely why Ignatius would have found himself comfortable here. Historically, the Society of Jesus structured itself around the Pope's desires through the fourth vow which Ignatius and his companions took. Ignatius knew four Roman Pontiffs during his years as general of the Society of Jesus in Rome: Paul III (1534-1549), Julius III (1550-1555), Marcelus II (April-May, 1555) and Paul IV (1555-1559). "All of them," according to Villoslada, "esteemed Ignatius' contribution in reforming Christianity and evangelizing the world" (1986, p. 516).

I have already alluded to the importance of this anniversary celebration. It should not be limited to a brief and erudite evocation. It is up to history to continue teaching us. As Ortega y Gasset said while celebrating the University of Granada's centenary: "It was neither the past nor the memories which were important. Life is a task which takes us forward." And Ignatius' monumental work must always move forward indeed. It would be suicidal merely to contemplate the past, no matter how glorious. Living beings must always move forward and "recharge their batteries." Ignatius' project is as contemporary today as it was in the middle of the sixteenth century.

To realize the Pope's mission to the Society of Jesus means to fight under the banner of that "modern evangelization" which John Paul II insistently preaches. Centuries cannot erase harmony of ideals.

I have nothing more to add but to welcome Ignatius familiarly: "Eres en tu casa, You are at home." The Biblioteca Apostolica Vaticana is part of the Rome which you knew and preserves details from the life of your century. I pray that your stay here be a pleasant one: for you and for yours. And that it be fruitful for all of us, since your lessons as formator of formators is still very contemporary. May the Lord wish that the reading of your projects and the evaluation of your results promote a renewal of ideals which become historic reality and remain open to the future.

Rome, July, 1990

Presentation

Very Reverend Father
Peter-Hans
Kolvenbach S.J.,
Superior General of the
Society of Jesus

Cat. 61

The "Ignatian Year" which is the occasion for the exhibit commemorated by this book marks the 500th anniversary of the birth of St. Ignatius of Loyola and the 450th anniversary of the Society of Jesus. The year began on September 27, 1990 in memory of September 27, 1540, when Pope Paul III approved the Society. It will end on July 31, 1991, recalling that day in 1556 when Ignatius could at last contemplate face to face his Creator and Lord. For Jesuits, the Ignatian Year has no other goal than renewal in the Spirit of their apostolic life, individual and communitarian. The Jubilee will be useful and fruitful to the degree it succeeds in deepening the Society's fidelity to its mission.

But Ignatius belongs also to the history of the entire People of God. So it is fitting to associate in the celebration all those men and women who are inspired by Ignatian spirituality in their following of Christ, and all those who would like to know Ignatius better. This exhibit is one way of doing that.

It is a fact that St. Ignatius is a person whose true figure is not always clearly perceived at first sight. Ignatius has to be discovered. He reveals himself, not to superficial observation, but only to a profound and persistent search. Discovering him, of course, must never become an end in itself; it inspires us, rather, to share the experience which Ignatius himself had. For the person of Ignatius is overshadowed by the spiritual adventure which, from Pamplona to Rome, the Lord wished to live with him.

This exhibit is an attempt to study a facet of Ignatius' life not yet adequately explored: his interaction with the urban world of his time. It seeks to show how the Society he designed was a response to the exigencies of a world where what had been stable was now shifting—in its physical and cultural horizons, and in the relationship of the Church to the world. The practical imagination which is the hallmark of Ignatius allowed him to try various options, to invent new models of service which incorporated the best of the tradition he came from, while at the same time adapting old, and creating new ways of serving the People of God.

In the sixteenth century, as now, Ignatius' Society and the Papacy were "next-door neighbors" in both the physical and spiritual sense. Chapter Seven of the *Constitutions* of the Society of Jesus sees in the Vicar of Christ the focus of the apostolic life of the Church, the person who best comprehends what it is that Jesuits ought to do in addressing the needs of the Church Universal. It is appropriate, then, that this exhibit about Ignatius and Rome be mounted in the Apostolic Library.

It is particularly fitting that the host of this exhibit is the Biblioteca Apostolica Vaticana, with which the Society of Jesus has many vital links. It was almost a century ago that Father Franz Ehrle, S.J. served as Prefect of the Library (1898-1912), and contributed greatly to the shape it has taken in modern times. It was Father Ehrle who set up the restoration laboratory—the first of its kind in Europe—and systematized the photographic reproduction of manuscripts. He was ultimately made a cardinal after his successor as Prefect, Achille Ratti, became Pope Pius XI.

In the name of the entire Society of Jesus, and of all those people whose knowledge and understanding of Ignatius and of the Church he served will be deepened by their exposure to this exhibit, I wish to express gratitute to the Cardinal Librarian, His Eminence Antonio Mario Javierre Ortas, S.D.B. to the Prefect, Rev. Leonard Boyle O.P., and to all those in the Library without whose generous help this exhibit would not have taken place.

Rome, The Feast of St. Ignatius, 1990

Acknowledgements

THOMAS M. LUCAS S.J.,
CURATOR

In the name of all involved with the planning and execution of this exhibit, I wish to express our sincerest thanks to our host, HIS EMINENCE, CARDINAL ANTONIO MARIA JAVIERRE ORTAS, S.D.B., Cardinal Librarian and Archivist of the Holy Roman Church, and to VERY REVEREND FATHER PETER-HANS KOLVENBACH S.J., Superior General of the Society of Jesus who supported this Ignatian initiative from its inception.

The expert professional administration and staff of the Biblioteca Apostolica Vaticana most generously shared their enthusiasm as well as their expertise. REV. LEONARD BOYLE O.P., Prefect, kindly shepherded this project from its conception. MONSIGNORE PAOLO DE NICOLÒ, Secretary of the BAV and lover of things beautiful, opened many doors. DR. ALFREDO DIOTALLEVI, Curator of Prints and Drawings, and DR. GIOVANNI MORELLO, Curator of the BAV Museum and Galleries were friendly and patient guides to the wonders of the Vatican Collections. DR. GIANCARLO ALTERI, Director of the BAV Medagliere, the entire BAV circulation and photographic services staff were most cooperative. A personal word of acknowledgement goes to PIERO TIBURZI, CARLO MATT, ELVIO BURIOLA, GIOVANNI LATORELLA, ANGELO POMPILI, and FRANCO MARINI for many extraordinary services.

Thanks also to Jesuits JOHANNES GERHARTZ, Secretary General; JOHN O'CALLAGHAN and GIUSEPPE PITTAU, Assistants to Father General; EUGEN HILLENGASS, Treasurer; The General Curia of the Society of Jesus, Rome; the staff of the Archivium Romanum Societatis Iesu (ARSI), Archivist WIKTOR GRAMATOWSKI, JOS. DECOCK, FRANCIS EDWARDS; HUGO STORNI, Librarian of the Istitutum Historicum S.I., Rome; LIVIO PAGELLO, THOMAS KOLLER, of the General Curia of the Society of Jesus, Rome; FEDERICO LOMBARDI, Provincial of Italy; GIULIO CESARE FEDERICI, Rector of the Chiesa del Gesù; GIULIO LIBIANCHI, Rector of the Church of S. Ignazio; VINCENZO PELLICCIOTA, Archivist of the Church of the Gesù; PAUL BELCHER, Provincial of California; GILLES PELLAND, Rector of the Pontificia Università Gregoriana; WERNER GÖTZ, Rector of the Collegium Germanicum-Hungaricum.

A word of remembrance for many Jesuits—both living and dead—whose love of history and beauty have inspired this project: CLAUDIO AQUAVIVA, GIOVANNI TRISTANO, GIUSEPPE VALERIANO, ORAZIO GRASSI, ANDREA POZZO, GIANPAOLO OLIVA, GIACOMO CORTESE, PIETRO TACCHI VENTURI, FRANZ EHRLE, WILLIAM V. BANGERT, PIETRO PIRRI, WALTER KROPP, AUSTIN FAGOTHEY, EDMOND LAMALLE, NORRIS CLARKE, ANDRÉ RAVIER, MANUEL MARTINEZ-FAZIO, GEORGE GANSS, JOHN PADBERG, JARED WICKS,

GERARDO ARANGO, AURELIO DIONISI, UGO DAMIANI, EUGENIO BRUNO, JAMES EMPEREUR, THOMAS MCCORMICK, CARLOS SEVILLA, CARLO DI FILIPPI, MICHAEL BREAULT, and M. PIO HILBERT.

DOTT. CARLO PIETRANGELI, Director General; DOTT. FABRIZIO MANCINELLI, Director of Medieval and Modern Art; DOTT. ALESSANDRA UNCINI, General Inventory of the Musei Vaticani, generously expedited the loan of paintings from the Pinacoteca Vaticana.

AVV. FERDINANDO FACCHIANO, Minister, and PROF. FRANCESCO SISSINI, Director General, Ministero per i Beni Culturali e Ambientali della Repubblica d'Italia; DOTT. EVELINA BOREA, Soprintendente per i Beni Artistici e Storici di Roma e di Lazio, ARCH. ROBERTO DI PAOLA, Segretario del Comitato del Settore del Consiglio Nazionale per i Beni Culturali; DOTT. MARIA PIA D'ORAZIO, Funzionaria per la Soprintendenza per i Beni Artistici e Storici di Roma; DOTT. CLAUDIO STRINATI, Director, Galleria Nazionale d'Arte Antica, DOTT. MARIA LETIZIA CASANOVA UC-CELLA, Director, Museo Nazionale del Palazzo di Venezia, DOTT. ROBERTO CANNATA', Director, Galleria Spada, Rome generously cooperated in organizing the loan of several important pieces.

Colleagues, teachers, and friends have offered much valuable counsel, advice and support: THOMAS ROCHFORD S.J., ING. FRANCESCO NOVELLI, LUCIANO CALDIROLI S.J., ENRICO DONATONI, MASSIMO TAGGI S.J., PRISCILLA GRAZIOLI MEDICI, JOHN BALDOVIN S.J., SPIRO KOSTOF, JOSEPH CONNORS, FRANCIS HASKELL, MSGR. CHARLES BURNS, DOROTHY LINDSEY, MARIETTA CAETANI, DANIELE SPANICCIATI, JOSÉ BADENAS, LUIGI TUROLLA, MARCELLO AND BEATRICE SACCHETTI, WILLIAM and ROSANNA MONTALBANO, FRANK LUCAS, DENNIS and JUSTINE BARNARD.

The collaborators on this catalogue produced heroic work in an impossibly short time: RICHARD BÖSEL, Curator of the Graphische Sammlung Albertina, Vienna; ALAN CEEN, Cornell University, Rome; GUIDO CORNINI and MAURIZIO DE LUCA of the Musei Vaticani; ALFREDO DIOTALLEVI and GIOVANNI MORELLO of the Biblioteca Apostolica Vaticana; MARIA PIA D'ORAZIO of the Soprintendenza per i Beni Artistici e Storici di Roma; JOHN PADBERG S.J., Director, and GEORGE GANSS, S.J., Director Emeritus of the Institute for Jesuit Sources, St. Louis, MO; MANUEL RUIZ-JURADO S.J., Pontificia Università Gregoriana; VINCENT DUMINUCO S.J., Secretary for Education for the Society of Jesus, PIETRO TOGNI S.J., GTU, Berkeley, CA. A special acknowledgement and thanks to EVONNE LEVY of Princeton University who labored mightily both in the organization of the exhibit and the preparation of the catalogue. Her bibliographic and editorial acumen, good counsel, and profound knowledge of the seventeenth century greatly enriched this exhibition.

Apparatus

Commonly used abbreviations in footnotes and catalogue citations

AHSI: *Archivium Historicum Societatis Iesu.*

ARSI: Archivium Romanum Societatis Iesu (General Archives of the Society of Jesus, Borgo Santo Spirito 5, Rome).

ASV: Archivium Secretum Vaticanum, Vatican City.

Autobiography: The "Acta Patris Ignatii" dictated to Luis Gonçalves da Cámara by St. Ignatius between 1553 and 1555, found in *Fontes Narrativi de S. Ignatio de Loyola et de Societatis Iesu* (Monumenta Historica Societatis Iesu). I, Rome,1943, pp. 323-507. For easier crossreferencing to other editions, the standard paragraph number is given instead of page numbers.

Chron: POLANCO, J. *Chronicon seu Vita Ignatii Loiolae et rerum Societatis Iesu Historiae.* 5 vols. Madrid, 1894-1898.

Const.: *Constitutions of the Society of Jesus.* Translated by G. Ganss, St. Louis, MO, 1970. For easier crossreferencing to other editions, the standard paragraph number is given instead of page numbers.

DALMASES: The standard modern biography of Ignatius available in English (richly footnoted with references to the Monumenta Historica Societatis Iesu sources) is Candido Dalmases' *Ignatius of Loyola, Founder of the Jesuits, His Life and Work.* Translated by Jerome Aixalá, St. Louis, MO, 1985.

EppIg.: *Epistolae et Instructiones S. Ignatii de Loyola* (Monumenta Historica Societatis Iesu). 12 vols. Madrid, 1903-1911. References are given to volume and the number of the letter cited.

FD: *Fontes Documentales de S. Ignatio de Loyola* (Monumenta Historica Societatis Iesu). Rome, 1977.

FN: *Fontes Narrativi de S. Ignatio de Loyola et de Societatis Iesu* (Monumenta Historica Societatis Iesu). 4 vols. Rome, 1943-1965.

Obras: *Obras Completas de San Ignacio.* Madrid, 1982.

SpEx: *Spiritual Exercises of St. Ignatius.* Translated by L. Puhl. Chicago, 1951. For easier crossreferencing to other editions, the standard paragraph numbering is given instead of page numbers. Note that when the words "Spiritual Exercises" appear in *italic* type they refer to the book of the Exercises; when they appear in roman type, they refer to the entire dynamic or process of prayer, meditation, contemplation, and activity sketched out in the book.

Contributors to this catalogue are identified by their initials at the end of their entries.

RB:	RICHARD BÖSEL
AC:	ALAN CEEN
GC:	GUIDO CORNINI
MDL:	MAURIZIO DE LUCA
AD:	ALFREDO DIOTALLEVI
MPD'O:	MARIA PIA D'ORAZIO
VD SJ:	VINCENT DUMINUCO S.J.
GG SJ:	GEORGE GANSS S.J.
EL:	EVONNE LEVY
TL SJ:	THOMAS LUCAS S.J.
GM:	GIOVANNI MORELLO
JP SJ:	JOHN PADBERG S.J.
MR-J SJ:	MANUEL RUIZ-JURADO S.J.
PT SJ:	PIETRO TOGNI S.J.

"BERNARDUS VALLES, MONTES BENEDICTUS AMABAT;
OPPIDA FRANCISCUS, SED MAGNA IGNATIUS URBES."[1]

"BERNARD LOVED THE VALLEYS, BENEDICT THE MOUNTAINS,
FRANCIS THE TOWNS, BUT IGNATIUS THE GREAT CITIES."
— A PROVERB

Romanæ urbis ſitus, quem hoc Chriſti anno 1549 habet.

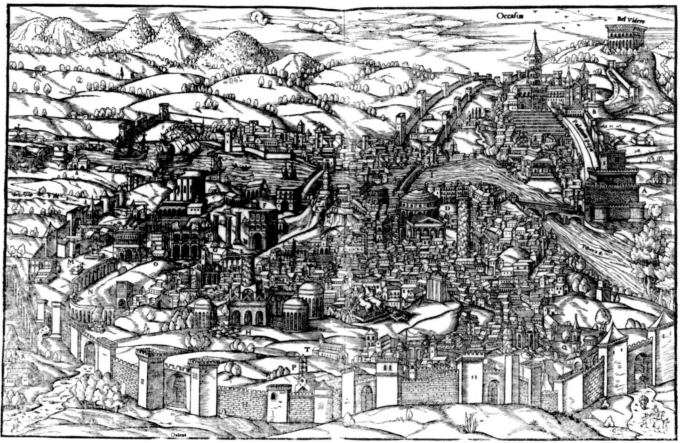

CAT. 37

"I KNOW THAT EVERYONE THERE WANTS TO KNOW ABOUT WHAT OUR LORD IS DOING FOR THOSE WHO ARE IN ROME, THE CITY THAT IS THE HEAD, AND IN ANOTHER RESPECT THE STOMACH OF ALL CHRISTENDOM. FOR THIS SOCIETY IT SEEMS TO BE BOTH THE ONE AND THE OTHER: AND, IF ONE COULD ADD A THIRD ELEMENT, IT IS THE HEART OF THE SOCIETY. IT IS LIKE THE HEAD IN THAT FROM HERE THE SOCIETY IS DIRECTED AND MOVED, AND LIKE THE STOMACH IN THAT FROM HERE ARE DISPENSED AND DISTRIBUTED TO ALL ITS MEMBERS THAT WHICH MAINTAINS THEIR WELL-BEING AND THEIR FRUITFUL PROGRESS. SO TOO ONE CAN CALL IT THE HEART, IN AS MUCH AS IT IS THE [VITAL] PRINCIPLE OF THE OTHER MEMBERS, AND ALSO BECAUSE IT SEEMS TO BE THE SEAT OF LIFE OF THE ENTIRE BODY OF THE SOCIETY. WITHOUT THE CONNECTION TO ROME, NO MATTER HOW MUCH THE SOCIETY WERE TO INCREASE IN NUMBERS, THINGS WOULD SURELY GO BADLY FOR ITS PRESERVATION. FOR THIS REASON, THOSE WHO KNOW THE IMPORTANCE OF THIS HOUSE IN ROME MOST REASONABLY WANT TO KNOW WHAT IS GOING ON HERE IN IT."[2]

—LETTER FROM ST. IGNATIUS' SECRETARY JUAN DE POLANCO TO ANTONIO ARAOZ, OCTOBER 31, 1547

The Saint, the Site, and Sacred Strategy

Ignatius, Rome, and the Jesuit Urban Mission

Thomas M. Lucas S.J.

The perennial temptation when dealing with saints is to sanctify them beyond human recognition. Saints are the stars of the church, figures bigger than life, models of heroic virtue whose closeness to God sets them apart from ordinary human experience. Standard iconography and popular devotion imagines them bathed in celestial light. Only rarely are they seen with feet on the ground, hard at work at the work at hand. In holy pictures St. Joseph the carpenter gazes at his divine foster son, but rarely ever sweats over his tools; Ignatius of Loyola is far more often represented in rapture than writing one of his seven thousand letters in the house he built on Via Ara Coeli in 1544.

It is, however, precisely their humanity that makes the saints attractive. They were normal people whose lives were consistent, focused, charged with and changed by the glory of God. As much as their prayers, their ordinary work serves as a vehicle for the revelation of the power and goodness of the Word made flesh.

Both modern critical theory and common sense teach that in order to understand the past, events and the people involved in them must be read and interpreted within their social, political, religious, and economic contexts. Only by entering into this hermeneutical circle—a return to the sources and contexts—can meaning be appropriated from the past in order to address the pressing issues of the present.

Commemorating the 500th anniversary of the birth of Ignatius of Loyola and the 450th anniversary of papal approval of the Society of Jesus he founded, the present exhibit departs from traditional hagiographic triumphalism in order to study a complex man whose practicality, imagination, and spiritual vision shaped a flexible and powerful model of apostolic religious presence in the urban world of the Renaissance.

In its first section, the exhibit examines Ignatius, a man born between two worlds: the stable cosmos of the Medieval synthesis and the expanding horizons—physical, social, and intellectual—of Renaissance Europe. Born months before Columbus set sail, Ignatius' life was likewise a journey of discovery, an exploration of a world of shifting frontiers, a pilgrimage that led him to the heart of the modern city.

This exhibit argues that the rapid growth and enduring importance of the Society of Jesus are integrally related to Ignatius' flexibility and creativity. Always predicated on the discerning search for God's greater glory and the good of souls, Ignatius' spiritual vision of service was one that adapted itself particularly easily to the practical realities of the changing world in which the Society of Jesus emerged. That search led to the development of new models, "sacred strategies" that enabled the first Jesuits to address the full spectrum of an urban society from popes to prostitutes, leaders to little children learning their first catechism.

The exhibit, finally, seeks to explore the reciprocal relationship between the saint and the city: just as the multiple demands of urban ministry shaped the Institute and the institutions of the Society, so too the Society's explosive growth in the first century and a half of its existence changed the physiognomy of Rome, the Catholic cities of Europe and the mission countries where Jesuits worked.

From Rome and to the remotest missions, the Jesuits brought their own "way of proceeding," a process rather than a fixed program. It sought to make audible through preaching and teaching and visible through buildings and the arts the presence of the person of Christ incarnate in the world. Ignatius' goal was to find God in all things, in the created world as well as in the supernatural, and then to communicate that divine presence in the concrete situations of daily life, using every means of communication available "like the spoils of Egypt."[3] The splendor of architecture and the visual arts, the subtlety of philosophy and the magic of theater no less than the spoken and written word, served as vehicles for the revelation of the divine. The urban scene of the sixteenth and seventeenth centuries provided a particularly well furnished stage for the *Opera Pietatis* that the Companions of Jesus performed.

Between Two Worlds: Expanding the Horizon

In 1491, Iñigo Lopez de Loyola was born between two worlds: between the stable and circumscribed world categorized by the Medieval synthesis and the apparently limitless horizons of expanding knowledge and experience of the Renaissance.

The Medieval world was a place of hierarchically ordered relationships where science served sacred history. Medieval cartography shows this subordination with particular clarity. The medieval map maker did not attempt to make a topographically precise rendering of the world, but showed how the world revealed the orderly plan of the divine Mind that created it and the saving initiative of the divine Son who entered into its history. The map, then, was not so much a guide for getting from one place to another as an icon teaching a moral and spiritual truth to the person who contemplated it. The "T-O" maps,

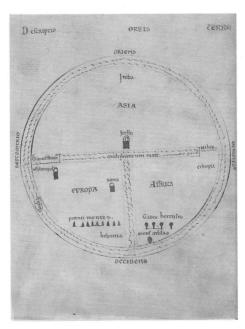

CAT. 4

based on ancient Ionian models from the fifth century B.C.E., are mandalas, sacred circles with Jerusalem at the center.[4] A Tau cross unites the waters and divides the lands, just as the cross of Christ standing at the center of the human world is the font of new life which nevertheless divides believers from non-believers (Cat. 3-6).

The Medieval world never entirely lost touch with the scientific lore of antiquity; in the eighth century the Venerable Bede described the world as "round like a shield, but also in every direction, like a playground ball."[5] Rather, until the translation of Ptolemy into Latin in the early 1400s, cartographers lacked the essential conceptual tools of latitude and longitude for projecting a spherical surface onto a two-dimensional plane. With the Portuguese explorations of the African coast in the fifteenth century, a new era of mathematically and commercially based cartography evolved at the school of Prince Henry the Navigator (Cat. 2, 7- 10).

The Spanish monarchy's desire to undercut Portugal's expanding empire led to the funding of Columbus' westward voyage in 1492. Although it took almost twenty years before the full commercial ramifications of Columbus' discovery were fully appreciated in Spain, the discovery of the New World changed the horizon for all time. The world was no longer circumscribed by divine design but circumnavigable by man. The stable circle gave way to undefined coastlands. A shifting horizon changed how the world was perceived and drawn.

Iñigo Lopez de Loyola was born in northern Spain in 1491. Religiously and socially, the Spain of Ferdinand and Isabella was still a Medieval kingdom. At the urging of their confessor Tomás de Torquemada, "los reyes católicos," their Most Catholic Majesties, instituted the Inquisition throughout their realm, and conducted a long and successful domestic crusade against the Moors who had occupied parts of the Iberian peninsula since the eighth century. In 1492, the same year they routed the Moors, Ferdinand and Isabella exiled from the realm all Jews who would not convert to Christianity. Politically, though, the Spanish monarchs inclined toward the Age of Absolutism, forging various kingdoms together into a united Spain, and successfully taking Naples from the French. Ruthless and unscrupulous in his dealings, Ferdinand served as one of Machiavelli's models for *The Prince*.

Iñigo was the thirteenth and last child of a family of petty nobility in the rugged Basque region of northern Spain. His father was Beltrán Ibáñez de Oñaz, a "pariente mayor," a local clan chief and stalwart crown loyalist. Iñigo's eldest brother Juan Pérez died in the Spanish conquest of Naples, and another brother, Hernando, renounced his inheritance to take part in the colonization of the New World, disappearing in the Americas in 1510.[6] Iñigo himself spent more than ten years as a page to the royal treasurer Juan Velázquez de Cuéllar in the peripatetic court of Ferdinand and his second wife Germaine de Foix.

Ignatius' *Autobiography*, dictated to Luis Gonçalves da Cámara toward the end of his life, evocatively depicts the waning years of

Medieval chivalry. Addicted to the popular romantic novels, well known at the gaming tables and a favorite of the ladies, "given over to the vanities of the world, he took special delight in the exercise of arms, with a great and vain desire of winning fame." His friend and biographer Pedro de Ribadeneira described Iñigo as a lively and trim young man, very fond of court dress and good living.[7] Although he never renounced his Catholic faith, his practice was casual.

In 1521, Iñigo's comfortable existence, a world of Medieval romance and dreams of crusades, was destroyed forever by a French cannonball (Cat. 12). In a battle for control of the border town of Pamplona, the young hidalgo's right leg was shattered. During a long and very painful convalescence at the family manor at Loyola, only two books were available to him to help fill his tedious days: a life of Christ and the *Flos Sanctorum*, the legends of the Saints (Cat. 15, 16). He found that when he contemplated returning to his former life he was satisfied while the thought lasted, but that it brought no lasting contentment. When, however, he thought of following the example of the saints and giving his life in service to Christ, lasting consolation followed.

This conversion experience was contextualized, filtered, and fitted out with his own personal conceptual furnishings. When he read the lives of the great preaching saints Francis and Dominic, he decided that he himself would become a preaching knight-errant. He dreamed of surpassing the holy penitents with the severity of his mortifications. The Medieval quest and the romance of the grand chivalrous gesture underlay his desire to embark on a private crusade to single-handedly reconquer Jerusalem for the faith. Some seventy-five years before Cervantes' Don Quixote appeared, a lame former knight, having given his rich clothes to a beggar, made a vigil-at-arms before the Lady of Montserrat (Cat. 17, 18). There he laid down his sword before her feet, and set off toward Jerusalem.

Iñigo got as far as Manresa, a village not far away on the banks of the river Cardoner, where he spent almost eleven months. Those months mark the beginning of his pilgrimage through time, space, and experience that would end in Rome in 1537.

At Manresa, Iñigo underwent a broad range of experiences, from attacks of conscience to ill health, longings for death, and thoughts of suicide. He went through a kind of psycho-spiritual breakdown, the sort of liminal experience that characterizes all great initiation rituals. At the end of this period he received the greatest mystical graces of his life. From this period date the most important insights and the first writings that developed into the Spiritual Exercises (Cat. 19, 21- 23).

He himself later called this period "my primitive Church." What he did, in fact, was unconsciously to mirror the actions and experiences of the Desert Fathers, the first monks who turned their back on the world. He went back, as it were, in time. Yet he did not remain fixed in that past; rather, he moved ahead toward the next great epoch, the next great passage, the experience of the Crusade.

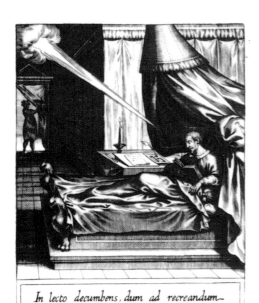

In lecto decumbens, dum ad recreandum animum Chris ti domini vitam et exempla Sanctorum euoluit, diuinarum virtutum imitatione exardescens, ad Deum conuertitur.

4

CAT. 14

Focused by his experience at Manresa, Iñigo set out in deliberate poverty on his journey to the Holy Land, travelling first to Rome to receive a pilgrim's safe-conduct and the customary papal blessing. In his *Autobiography*, Iñigo captured the contemporary Spanish attitude toward Renaissance Rome when he recounted his conversation with a benefactor in Barcelona:

"When he begged from a lady, she asked where he wanted to go. He hesitated [about telling her his destination was Jerusalem] but at last he resolved to say no more than that he was going to Italy and to Rome. Surprised, she said, 'Do you want to go to Rome? Well, I don't know how those who go there come back.' By this she meant that in Rome they profited little from the things of the spirit."[8]

In the summer of 1523, Iñigo travelled to the Holy Land via Venice (where he slept under the colonnades of St. Mark's Square), arriving in Jerusalem on September 4. He fervently made the usual pilgrim rounds of the Christian shrines, and resolved to stay and wage his own *reconquista*. The Franciscan Guardian of Mount Zion Angelo da Ferrara, however, knew trouble when he saw it. Invoking his mandate of governance from the Holy See that included the power of excommunication, he forbade Iñigo to remain, ordering him, for his own safety and because of the volatile political climate of the moment, to return to Europe on the next boat.

Iñigo's romantic vision of an exotic mission collided with the harsh realities of the wider world he encountered in his travels. His desire to serve Christ remained, but he realized that he needed more training and a more credible platform from which to launch his apostolic work. During his return journey to Spain, he made a crucial decision: "After the pilgrim realized that it was not God's will that he remain in Jerusalem, he continually pondered within himself what he ought to do. At last he inclined more to study for some time so he would be able to help souls, and he decided to go to Barcelona."[9] With this decision, Iñigo took a first practical step away from his childhood realm of Medieval romance toward the real and complex world of the Renaissance.

Iñigo's audacious decision at age 33 to return to school "so he would be able to help souls" marks the beginning of his passage into an adult comprehension of a post-Medieval world whose focus was increasingly professional and urban.

From 1524 through 1535, Iñigo's pilgrimage continued as he acquired the educational and professional tools he needed for his upcoming apostolic work. He returned to Barcelona where, for two years, he studied Latin, the indispensable tool for scholarly work in his times. After examination by competent authorities, he was admitted to Cisneros' new University of Alcalá, the center of Spanish humanistic learning, where he studied scholastic philosophy and theology for a year and a half.[10] At Alcalá his private work in spiritual direction caused Iñigo to run afoul of the Inquisition, and he was briefly imprisoned.

Although the charges were dismissed, Iñigo and his companions were ordered "not to speak about matters of faith until they had studied for four more years, because they had no learning. For in truth, the pilgrim was the one who knew the most, though his learning had little foundation."[11]

With his situation at Alcalá untenable, Iñigo moved to the other great Spanish university at Salamanca. Shortly after his arrival Iñigo languished in chains for twenty-two days at the Dominican convent while the Inquisition examined his orthodoxy and, in particular, his Spiritual Exercises.[12]

As at Alcalá "no error was found in his life or teaching," although the requirement of four years of theological studies was again imposed before he could teach about controversial technical matters like the distinction between mortal and venial sin. With Spanish doors slammed behind him, Iñigo "decided to go to Paris to study. When the pilgrim was reflecting at Barcelona, considering whether he should study and how much, his entire concern was whether, after he had studied, he should enter religious life or go about in the world...Now at the time of his imprisonment in Salamanca the same desire to help souls, and for that reason to study first and to gather some others for the same purpose and to keep those he had, did not fail him."[13]

Iñigo's sojourn in Paris lasted seven years, from February 1528 to March 1535. Paris, the largest city in Europe, had a staggering population of 300,000 inhabitants.[14] It was the intellectual capital of Europe with a university numbering fifty colleges and four thousand students (Cat. 25).

During his student years in Paris, Iñigo travelled a number of times to Spanish-dominated Flanders where, in Antwerp and Bruges, he encountered both Spanish benefactors and the followers of Erasmus. Most probably in 1531, he also visited London where he received large gifts from Spanish courtiers for his own and other needy students' expenses. Thus, by the time Ignatius settled definitively in Rome in 1537, he had visited, with the exception of those in Germany, most of the major cities in Western Europe (Cat. 24).

In the records of the University the name "Ignatius of Loyola" appeared for the first time in conjunction with his baccalaureate examination. He received his licentiate in philosophy in 1534, which he followed with courses in scholastic theology at the Dominican Collège de St. Jacques (Cat. 26).

During his Parisian years, Ignatius gathered around him an international group of companions who would form the nucleus of the Society of Jesus. Spaniards Francisco de Xavier, Diego Lainez, Alfonso Salmerón, and Nicholás Bobadilla, Portuguese Simão Rodrigues, and Savoyard Pierre Favre all made the Spiritual Exercises, and frequently joined Ignatius for prayer and companionship (Cat. 27, 28). As their studies drew to a close in 1534, this loose fraternity formalized itself by a vow "to go to Jerusalem to spend their lives in the service of souls; and if they were not given permission to remain in Jerusalem, they would return to Rome and present themselves to the Vicar of Christ, so that he could make use of them wherever he thought it to be to the greater glory of God and the service of souls."[15]

Although the crusade to Jerusalem was still his goal, Ignatius' prior experience, and, it can be argued, his broadening perspective of the needs of the church, caused him to build into the first sketch of the Society of Jesus a particular focus on the person and office of the Vicar of Christ, the pope.

After settling their affairs, the companions gathered in Venice in early 1537. A delegation of these "masters of Paris" travelled to Rome where they received from Paul III a safe-conduct for the pilgrimage, permission for all the companions to be ordained priests (Cat. 29, 30), and a monetary gift. A return to Jerusalem, in fact, was politically impossible. War flared up between the Republic of Venice and the Turks closing the sea lanes to the eastern Mediterranean until 1540.

In Venice, the newly ordained companions engaged in street preaching and formed a plan of focused apostolic work in the major cities of northern Italy. Thus Ignatius' enduring option for urban ministry manifested itself early and vigorously. The cities chosen were either important university towns like Bologna, Padua, and Siena, or strategic centers of population like Venice, Vicenza, and Ferrara. Before dispersing, they decided on a name for their group: "given that they had no other superior except Jesus Christ whom alone they desired to serve, it seemed to them most fitting that they should take the name of him whom they had as their head, by calling themselves the 'company of Jesus'."[16]

Late in 1537, Ignatius himself, accompanied by Lainez and Favre, set out on the last leg of his pilgrim journey. On the outskirts of Rome, in a ruined roadside chapel at La Storta on the Via Cassia, Ignatius had his second great mystical experience, a vision that clarified his mission (Cat. 140). He saw Jesus carrying his cross, and heard the Father ask Jesus to take Ignatius beside him into his service. In the vision Jesus replied, "I want you to serve Us."

Diego Lainez, Ignatius' companion and the second general of the Society, recalled the event in this way: "As we were coming along the road from Siena here to Rome, it happened that our Father [Ignatius] received many spiritual consolations. He told me that it seemed to him as if God the Father had imprinted the following words in his heart: 'Ego ero vobis Romae propitius: I will be propitious to you in Rome.' Since our father did not know what these word might mean, he remarked: 'I do not know what will happen to us: maybe we will be crucified in Rome.' Another time, he said that he seemed to see Christ with the cross on his shoulder, and the Eternal Father said to him ' I will that you take this man for your servant.' And so Jesus took him, and said 'I will that you should serve Us.' Because of this, seized by great devotion to this most holy name, he [Ignatius] wanted the congregation called 'the

Company of Jesus'."[17] This vision, because of its clarity, focus and rich visual elements, became an integral element in early Ignatian iconography (Cat. 31).

The city Ignatius entered in 1537 bore scant resemblance to the Rome of the Caesars. At the height of the Roman Empire, the urban population had numbered somewhere in the neighborhood of 1,000,000 inhabitants. In the centuries following the fall of the Empire in the West, the urban population had plunged. The immense 18 km. circuit of the Aurelian Wall was indefensible, and for security the population huddled into the bend of the Tiber between Campo dei Fiori and Ponte S. Angelo. The collapse of the imperial system of aqueducts, repeated floods, pestilences (including the Black Death of 1348), invasions, and at least three major sacks kept the population small (Cat. 33-36).

Accurate census figures are unavailable, but by most estimates the population between 500 and 1500 averaged between 15,000 and 30,000. Medieval chronicles tell of wolves roaming in the ruins of the imperial palaces on the Palatine. The Capitol, the cultic center of antiquity, was on the very outskirts of the *abitato*, the inhabited part of town; the Romans called it "Monte Caprino," Goat Hill, and the Roman Forum was a cow pasture, "Campo Vaccino."

A good measure of the contraction of the *abitato* is seen in the siting of the large Franciscan and Dominican convents in the mid-thirteenth century (Cat. 32). Although the mendicant orders' preaching ministry focused on towns, as a rule they tended to settle on the fringe of towns. Downtown property was very expensive, and the mendicants wanted to build traditional large church and cloister complexes with large piazzas in front for preaching. In general, they built near or just outside the gates of the Medieval walls, at points equidistant from the town hall or cathedral.[18] Rome had no Medieval walls, so the Dominicans and Franciscans settled on the edge of town. The Franciscans built their large convent S. Maria in Ara Coeli (ca. 1260) on the Campidoglio amid the goats. The Dominicans settled on the rural Aventine Hill in 1219 (S. Sabina), and one block from the Pantheon at S. Maria Sopra Minerva (ca. 1280), which was then open territory at the absolute periphery of the *abitato*.[19]

Late Medieval and Renaissance Rome was a one-industry town: the papal court with its allied service trades, banking, pilgrimage-tourist operations, and building programs absolutely dominated the economic, social, and political life of the city. With the return of the papacy from France at the end of the fourteenth century and the gradual reimposition of papal authority over the Commune, the papacy again began to dominate the shaping of the urban environment.

With the election of Martin V (Colonna) in 1420, a Roman occupied the See of Peter for the first time in more than a century. Although he did no significant building during his pontificate, Martin V reasserted the papacy's concern for the urban fabric by reinstating the powers of the *magistri aedificiorum* (urban building superintendents) bringing their office under the authority of the *Camera Apostolica*. The *magistratura*, originally constituted in the early Duecento and patterned loosely on that of the ancient Roman *aediles*, was composed of two Roman patricians as *magistri*, a secretary-notary, and a staff architect.[20] A statute of 1363 charged them "with opening up, repair, and governance of buildings, streets, and roadways in the city."[21] In 1452, their brief was enlarged to include demolition ("to break down, trim, cut, and demolish whatever might occupy streets, piazzas, alleyways, canals, waterways and other public places"[22]). Under Sixtus IV they were given authority to expropriate or condemn property for the public good, and their title became *magistri stratarum* or *maestri delle strade* ("superintendents of the streets"), a shift in terminology that reflects a growing concern for the reorganization of the street network as Renaissance principles of urban design filtered south from Florence in the late Quattrocento. [23]

The study of Vitruvius was a most influential factor in the shaping of Renaissance urbanism. The ancient author's strong accent on intelligent city planning took into careful account defensive, aesthetic, ceremonial and sanitary considerations. The radial arrangement of streets of the ideally projected city served strategic functions in time of war, linking center to walls, gates, and towers. Proper orientation to winds and cardinal points would create a city at once liveable, beautiful, and healthy. The Renaissance image of the city shifted away from City of the Cross (itself based on the ancient Roman orientation of *cardo* and *decumanus*) to a city whose center is in perfect proportional relationship to all its parts, as the umbilicus of the Vitruvian man forms the center of the circle and square that inscribe him[24] (Cat. 41, 43, 44).

As Rome emerged from Medieval decrepitude to become again briefly the *Caput Mundi*, the popes of the late Quattrocento and early

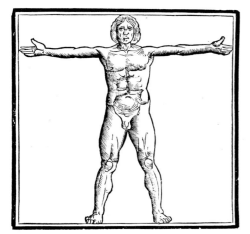

VITRUVIAN MAN, 1511 (SEE CAT. 43)

Cinquecento undertook individual campaigns of urban renewal that opened up the heart of the Medieval city to accommodate the economic, administrative, and ceremonial needs of the reassertive papacy. Topography, sacred history, and economics militated against the redesign of Rome as an ideal Vitruvian city. Nevertheless, architects and popes beginning with Alberti and Paul II began to identify the ancient Capitol rather than the Christian shrines as the center of gravity, the navel of the city (Cat. 42).

Once the papal court returned definitively to Rome in 1443, building recommenced in Rome; the construction of great palaces like the Palazzo d'Estouteville at S. Agostino and the Palazzo S. Marco (modern Palazzo Venezia) signalled the end of a building hiatus that had lasted more than one hundred and fifty years. When Cardinal Pietro Barbo (later Paul II) began his Palazzo S. Marco in 1455, the Via Lata (called the "Via del Corso" for the horse races the Barbos enjoyed during the reinstated *carnevale*) marked the eastern edge of the *abitato*. The new palace at the foot of the Campidoglio was in open countryside, more an immense suburban villa than a princely townhouse (Cat. 39, 40). Next to it stood the tiny Chapel of the Madonna della Strada where Ignatius would preach a century later.

Much of the street work in early Renaissance Rome, initiated to ease the flow of great tides of annual and Jubilee pilgrims, had important commercial overtones. The construction of the Ponte Sisto by Sixtus IV (Della Rovere, 1471-1484) not only gave another river crossing to pilgrims bound to S. Pietro, but also forged a link between the busy commercial neighborhoods of Rione Ponte and Trastevere. Sixtus IV's urban program also included a reorganization of the Campo dei Fiori and the elimination of the open market on the western slopes of the Campidoglio, the widening of the Via Papale from the Banchi to Piazza Pasquino, and the opening and paving of the Via Recta Iuxta Flumen (Via Coronari) from Platea Pontis to the modern Piazza Nicosia. This straight street allowed the pope easier access from the Vatican to S. Maria del Popolo, rebuilt in 1477 as his family church, and set in motion the development of the area of the northern Campo Marzio in the direction of Porta del Popolo. With Sixtus IV, who styled himself the *Restaurator Urbis,* a decided shift began to emerge: Rome at this period began to lose its picturesque Medieval character, as straight and wider streets opened up vistas and eased traffic.[25]

Under Alexander VI (Borgia, 1492-1503), a major reordering of the Borgo took place, with a deliberate focus on the defenses of Castel S. Angelo and its environs. Borgia's repair of the *passetto*, a defensive escape route atop the Leonine wall connecting the Vatican Palace to the papal fortress set into the ruins of Hadrian's tomb, is perhaps more indicative of the mentality of the Borgia pontiff than the processional Via Alessandrina he had built for the jubilee of 1500.[26]

The almost demonic energy of Julius II (Della Rovere, 1503-1513) expressed itself in his Roman building campaigns as well in his military and political exploits. His decision to demolish and totally reconstruct the Constantinian Basilica of S. Pietro often overshadows an even more radical urban policy. The daring slash of the Via Giulia across the heart of the *abitato*, the construction of its parallel in the Via della Lungara on the opposite side of the Tiber (originally planned to connect the Port of the Ripa Grande to the Borgo), and the comprehensive masterplan for the unbuilt "Julian Palace" and a new bridge to connect the two thoroughfares provided Rome with a vision of grandeur and expansiveness unknown since the time of the Caesars. The city fabric became, as it were, an emblematic tapestry of an imperial papacy that Ignatius had first encountered in Rome en route to his abbreviated stay in Jerusalem.[27]

If Julius II styled himself after the *Divus Iulius*, Leo X (Medici, 1513-1521) presided over a brief Augustan age. The Campidoglio became an imperial banqueting hall for a dazzling humanistic court insulated from disharmonious cries for reform from the North. A report to Leo, variously attributed to Raphael or Bramante, described the ancient urban framework as it awaited its Renaissance completion: "the structure exists, without the ornament; the bones without the flesh."[28]

Ever more tangled in the web of Valois-Hapsburg rivalry and intrigue, and lacking a sufficient power base of its own, the papacy floundered during the pontificates of Adrian VI (Florenz, 1522-1523) and Clement VII (Medici, 1523-1534). Clement VII's repeated double-dealings earned him the contempt of French and Imperial factions alike. A half-century long dream of an imperial papacy collapsed in the nightmare of the Hapsburg sack of Rome in 1527.

In May of 1527, unpaid Spanish veterans and German mercenaries of Charles V's imperial army descended on the Holy City for a month of rapine and destruction. The pontiff and his court barely escaped over the *passetto* to Castel S. Angelo. From the battlements they watched impotently as Lutheran troops paraded by in papal vestments and played ball with the heads of Sts. Peter and Paul.[29]

The toll was immense. Perhaps as many as 10,000 Romans died in the month of plundering and looting, while another 10,000 fled the city or died as a result of famine and plague that swept the area in the following summer. A papal census of 1526 had numbered 55,035 persons in the city, already a decrease from the 65,000-70,000 estimated residents at the end of Leo X's reign. By 1530, the population probably hovered around 30,000.[30]

It is tempting but not altogether accurate to look on the extraordinary pontificate of Paul III (Farnese, 1534-1549) as a simple reprise of the Roman Renaissance after the ugly interruption of the Sack. Gone forever, however, was the exuberance and the euphoria which characterized the reigns of Julius II and Leo X. It was replaced by the hard-headed wisdom of the aged Farnese who confronted the geopolitics, religious reform, and urban renewal with cool determination, balance, and resolve.

Paul III's work on Rome's urban fabric demonstrated three major concerns: aggrandizement of the papacy and his family, demonstrated by his continued work on S. Pietro and the construction of his own Palazzo Farnese; the security of the city's defenses; and the opening up and expansion of the street network to provide for contemporary and future growth.

Early in his reign, Paul III initiated a comprehensive program of defensive works including the building of curtain walls and bastions from the Aventine to the river, and the walling of the Janiculum from Porta S. Pancrazio to the Vatican. He also ordered the refortification of the Città Leonina and the Vatican including the construction of a massive bastion on the Belvedere, and designs for a new fortified wall within the Aurelian walls. This last work, designed by Antonio da Sangallo the Younger, would have effectively halved the urban defensive perimeter, leaving the sparsely populated areas around S. Giovanni in Laterano and S. Maria Maggiore outside the circle of walls. This huge new work, which included eighteen bastions with intervening cannon emplacements, was never realized.[31]

On a much smaller scale and closer to home, Paul III continued work on his own Palazzo Farnese and had a tower and enclosed garden constructed for himself on the northern slopes of the Campidoglio overlooking his beloved Palazzo S. Marco and the Corso. Mirroring the relationship between Castel S. Angelo and the Vatican Palace, the Torre Farnese was connected to the papal summer palace by a covered *passetto*. Serving both as retreat and emergency defensive refuge, the tower was, because of its location on the Capitol, a clear signal to the Commune of absolute papal hegemony in the city[32] (Cat. 40, 73, 74).

Paul III's preoccupation with revitalizing the center of the city and extending its commercial core is apparent in the several diverse yet homogeneous works of urban planning he ordered from Latino Giovenale Manetti, the pope's trusted lieutenant, ambassador, and *maestro delle strade*.

Together Manetti and Paul III revised the confusing Medieval grid, opening up clogged arteries in the heart of the Banchi to form the elegant mini-trident linking the Ponte S. Angelo with the fashionable Florentine commercial quarter of Via Giulia. Cutting the Via Paolina Trifaria (modern Via del Babuino) from Trinità dei Monti to Porta del Popolo completed the framework of the great trident, while Via Trinitatis (Via Condotti) linked the new neighborhood to Rione del Ponte and Campo Marzio.

Manetti's and Farnese's work in Rione della Pigna and the approaches to the Campidoglio is of particular interest since it is there that Ignatius settled. Modern Via del Gesù linking Piazza Altieri (Piazza del Gesù) and S. Maria Sopra Minerva was opened to allow carnival processions to pass from the Campidoglio to the Pantheon, whose *piazza* was also paved. The widening and straightening of the Piazza Altieri-Via Aracoeli-Piazza Aracoeli-Cordonata-Piazza Campidoglio axis was carried out between 1538 and 1544. Here was the urbanistic exercise of papal authority at its most visible, in the core, in the center of Rome. Henceforth, papal cavalcades bound from S. Pietro to S. Giovanni in Laterano passed directly over the Capitol, the seat of city government. This re-routing was a clear and unequivocal scenographic statement of papal supremacy (Cat. 72, 74).

At the height of his reign, Paul III very frequently was in residence at the Palazzo S. Marco. In the cruel winter of 1538-1539, when devastating cold and famine paralyzed his city, the pontiff learned of an act of charity taking place practically in the shadow of Palazzo S. Marco. Ignatius and his "Masters of Paris," ten of the best educated priests in Italy, had opened a soup kitchen to feed the hungry in their house, scarcely a three minute walk from the papal residence. Some three hundred people a day endured preaching in bad Italian—there was not a native speaker among the first Jesuits—while they waited for hot, life-saving food.

Arriving in Rome late in 1537 with two companions, Ignatius won quick approval from a pleased pope who gave them faculties to preach and administer the sacraments in the city. The rest of the "Companions of Jesus" arrived in the spring of 1538, and focused their considerable energies on downtown Rome, preaching in churches and the commercial *piazze*. The reforming zeal, thorough training, and apostolic readiness of the companions impressed the pontiff, who had himself begun to steer the church toward reform. After a formal theological debate the Jesuits conducted in his presence, Paul III asked a pointed question. 'Why do you have such a desire to go to Jerusalem? Italy is a good and true Jerusalem if your desire is to bring forth fruit in God's Church."[33] Ignatius' response abandoned his crusader's dream for the more pressing work at hand: assisting the Vicar of Christ in reforming the new "Holy City," Rome.

In the first year the Jesuits moved three times. Their first residence was a vineyard house on the very outskirts of town, near the modern Spanish Steps. They then took rooms on a short term lease somewhere near the Ponte Sisto, and finally, in the fall of 1538, moved to rented rooms in Antonio Frangipane's haunted house in Via dei Delfini 16, on the edge of the Jewish neighborhood and between the Campidoglio and the pope's residence at Palazzo S. Marco.

While they lived at this house, deliberations were conducted that established the Society of Jesus as a religious community bound by a vow of obedience to a superior (1539). In 1541 Ignatius was elected the first superior general (Cat. 58). The new religious community received its first written approval and charter in the papal bull *Regimini Militantis Ecclesiae*, which Paul III signed in Palazzo S. Marco on September 27, 1540 (Cat. 57, 59). The first companions preached throughout the city, worked in the major hospitals (S. Girolamo, S. Spirito, and the Consolazione), and taught in various institutions. A number were sent out to cities in Italy, Germany, and Spain, and Francis Xavier left in 1540 for

India, Japan and the shores of China. From this house a number of apostolic works were organized, including an orphanage and a preaching mission to the Jews of the nearby Ghetto.

The preferred works of the early Society were almost all what we would today call "ministries of the Word:" liturgical preaching, catechetical preaching and teaching, and counselling with a strong emphasis on the Sacrament of Penance, as well as works of charity (Cat. 51). From the very beginning Ignatius was convinced that he needed a central base of operations, and, most especially, a well placed pulpit on a busy corner in the heart of town.

The military theory of the day always located the General's headquarters in the very center of the camp or fortified town so that from a radial center he might oversee all operations and direct all initiatives (Cat. 45, 46). The former hidalgo Ignatius appears to have recalled his earlier training as he reconnoitered the neighborhood for two years, and then set his sights on the territory he wanted. By the time he died in 1556, after 16 years of struggle, he had secured a major objective, a permanent foothold. The Society had a pulpit, a little church, and enough land to build a residence that housed 80 people. The campaign did not end until the large Church of the Gesù was built on that same site in the 1570s and the immense attached residence, the Casa Professa, was added in the early 1600s.

In 1539, even before the Society was approved, Ignatius recruited his first Italian Jesuit. Pietro Codacio, who had been a papal chamberlain at Paul III's court at Palazzo S. Marco, left his lucrative benefices, and was put to work almost immediately by Ignatius as minister of the community and his real estate agent. He started renting, buying, and taking out options on property almost immediately.

More importantly, within two months of the written approval of the Society, Codacio was able to use his influence in the papal court to obtain what Ignatius really wanted: the title to the tiny Church of S.Maria della Strada, Our Lady of the Wayside (perhaps originally S.Maria degli Astalli, named for the Astalli family that had built it as a mortuary chapel) with its annexed buildings[34] (Cat. 48, 51, 56).

A crucial document dating from about 25 years after Ignatius' death relates that Ignatius and the companions had already used the chapel as a center for their ministries, and that Ignatius chose it over others offered to him "because the site was best suited to what the Society intended."[35] Juan de Polanco, Ignatius' secretary, firmly maintained that the church was suited for the Jesuit's purposes "because of its celebrated location, on account of which...it was preferred out of all the city by our Blessed Father, rather than for its comfort or spaciousness."[36]

The buildings were not what made della Strada attractive. From the beginning the church and its outbuildings were far too small. Rather it was the site itself, at the very heart of Rome that suited the Ignatian "proposito." The pope lived on one side of the block, and the

LA MADONNA DELLA STRADA, LATE 15TH CENTURY, IN THE CHURCH OF THE GESU', ROME

prostitutes on the other. The city government was a block away, the large Jewish community two blocks away. In the Rione della Pigna, the papal court, palaces of nobles, comfortable houses of the upper middle class and the hovels of the poor were side by side.

The *piazza* where Ignatius established his headquarters was a traffic breakwater in the flow of streets. It was a place where papal and civic processions slowed, where people gathered to gossip, shop, and to pass the time of day. And perhaps to drop into church—especially if they were offered intelligent preaching or good confessors. The neighborhood was expanding, part of what would be known today as a "redevelopment zone," and Ignatius settled his young society in the very center of it all.

There were, of course, problems: with the bureaucracy, with finances, and especially with the neighbors.

He was given the church in 1540, and early in 1541 the companions moved into rented rooms in the Astalli house next door to S. Maria della Strada. They lived there until 1544, when they moved into the first building the Society ever built. The building was a simple, cheaply built residence with rooms for about 40 men, built on the site of the old della Strada rectory, a lime burning kiln, and another unused chapel that Codacio had secured from the Pope.

During the building of the house, Codacio was delighted to find some finely carved Roman columns in the excavations for the foundations. He planned to sell them to help pay for the construction. Ignatius decided otherwise. He spent the money obtained from the sale to build the Casa S. Marta, a half-way house for reformed prostitutes two blocks away.[37] Shortly thereafter, a house was founded nearby for the "Compagnia delle Vergini Miserabili," a rescue mission to protect the daughters of prostitutes. These institutions joined two orphanages and a house for Jewish catechumens that Ignatius founded. The organizational model of these apostolic works included full involvement of the laity. The Jesuits started the works, administered them in their early stages, and then eventually turned them over to groups of lay people, religious organizations called "confraternities" that controlled and financed them (Cat. 54).

Sacred Strategy

Three traits stand out in Ignatius' personality that help us to understand him: he was practical, he was imaginative, and he was attuned to his changing world.

Ignatius' "pilgrim years" led him from his life as a courtier-knight to become founder of the Society of Jesus and a preeminent supporter of the papacy. That journey through time and space brought him from the primitive hermitic experience of Manresa through the romance of a failed crusade to ten years of hard study in the capitals of Europe. That pilgrimage was a school of experience, experience that he constantly and practically reflected upon and refined as raw material to advance his ministry.

The church needed saints, and at the time of his conversion Ignatius deliberately set out to become one. A short way into that process he realized that the church needed educated leaders who could preach to and evangelize a world that had radically changed from the times of Francis and Dominic. In response, he sought out the kind of specific training such a mission implied.

At Manresa he learned a basic truth of his life that would later be formalized into the "Principle and Foundation" of the *Spiritual Exercises:* "Man is created to praise, reverence, and serve God our Lord, and by this means to save his soul. The other things on the face of the earth are created for him to help him in attaining the end for which he is created. Hence, man is to make use of them in as far as they help him in the attainment of his end, and he must rid himself of them in as far as they prove a hindrance to him"[38] (Cat. 22).

This credo is preeminently practical: use what one needs, do what one needs to do—and, conversely, do not use what one does not need, and do not do what one does not need to do—in order to serve God and save one's soul.

Of course, that means figuring out—"discerning"—what assists the work and what does not: a very subtle and refined process. This process of discerning is more than a mechanical prioritizing of pros and cons. It is, rather, a dialectic between practical experience and spiritual goods: practical experience always measured reflectively and prayerfully against the goal of the greater good and the service of God and neighbor. This discernment, this dialectic, is the key for understanding the actions, movements, and the adventures of Ignatius' life, the structure he designed for his company, and the locations he chose for its many works.

Ignatius, moreover, was an imaginative man attuned to the social and intellectual currents alive in his world, a person who integrated his own vast experience of human nature and the humanistic learning of his age with his own profound spiritual experience.

Most of his ministerial insights were not new ones, just as many of the works performed by his Society were already being done on a more limited scale by other reformed religious groups of his time. What set Ignatius apart from his predecessors and his contemporaries was his ability and willingness to combine new solutions with old problems as well as to apply time-tested procedures to new situations. This dynamic of practical and imaginative attunement to the social and intellectual needs of his age is seen in particular clarity in his relation to the urban phenomena of the mid-Cinquecento.

The first written charter of the Jesuits, the "Formula of the Institute" was submitted to Paul III in 1540 and incorporated into his bull of approbation, *Regimini Militantis Ecclesiae,* and the *Constitutions* that Ignatius would later compose. It specifies the range of ministries in which the Jesuit should engage:

"To strive especially for the defense and propagation of the faith and for the progress of souls in Christian life and doctrine by means of public preaching, lectures, and any other ministrations whatsoever of the Word of God, and further by means of the Spiritual Exercises, the education of children and unlettered persons in Christianity, and the spiritual consolation of Christ's faithful through hearing confessions and administering the other Sacraments. Moreover, he should show himself no less useful in reconciling the estranged, in holily assisting and serving those who are found in prisons or hospitals, and indeed, in performing any other works of charity, according to what will seem expedient for the glory of God and the common good."[39]

The Formula presents as the preferred works of the new Company of Jesus a variety of traditional Christian ministries of preaching and charity, to be adapted to the complex world of the urban Cinquecento.

Such works presuppose a highly trained and flexible corps of ministers who could adapt to the multiple and overlapping needs of a large population. They imply, moreover, a profound, existential knowledge of the social matrix, a readiness to deal with all kinds of people, to cross back and forth over cultural lines usually closed by prejudice, class distinctions, or fear. They also require the financial support of a large urban population, for while the secular clergy of the era lived from benefices, the Jesuits vowed to live entirely on alms, and to have no fixed revenues except to sustain their free schools.

In Chapter VII of the *Constitutions of the Society of Jesus* entitled "The distribution of the incorporated members in Christ's vineyard and their relations there with others," two central issues are developed: the special relationship of the Society of Jesus with the pope as supreme Vicar of Christ, and Ignatius' conception of mission as it relates to place, works, and personnel.

Once the pilgrimage to Jerusalem was out of the question, Ignatius and his companions bound themselves to the person of the pope as he who best understood the needs of the Universal Church. "The vow that the Society has made to obey him as the supreme Vicar of Christ without any excuse meant that the members were to go to any place whatsoever where he judges it expedient to send them for the greater glory of God and the good of souls, whether among the faithful or the infidels."[40] The Pope's direct power to assign Jesuits was and remains today absolute and unqualified.

This intimate hierarchical union with the Roman pontiff expressed in the special vow regarding the missions was Ignatius' personal response to the needs of the institutional church in an age when new continents were being discovered and the once seamless garment of Christendom was being unraveled by the Protestant Reformation.

When dealing with the question of mission, Ignatius proposed a flexible but binding criterion that applies particularly to the general,

CAT. 70

33

who routinely acts on the pope's behalf in assigning Jesuits. "To proceed more successfully in this sending of subjects to one place or another, one should keep the greater service of God and the more universal good before his eyes as the norm to hold oneself on the right course."[41]

For Ignatius, the place means the people who live there: his work was saving souls, not acquiring real estate. The criteria of the greater service of God and the more universal good imply a bias in favor of work in places where the Jesuits can touch the greatest number of people. Moreover, Ignatius sought to influence for the good those who have power and influence over others, so that the effect would be multiplied in the greater population.[42]

This positive option for "places-as-persons" was spelled out in the *Constitutions*: "Preference ought to be shown to the aid that is given to the great nations such as the Indies, or to important cities, or to universities, which are generally attended by numerous persons who, by being aided themselves, can become laborers for the help of others."[43] Only after this unequivocal statement does Ignatius go on to analyze the kinds of work to be done in these settings, and to give criteria for whom to send for these works.

Ignatius' experience as a courtier and soldier provided him with the organizational models that he successfully applied both to his burgeoning order and to his choice for the radial siting of various urban enterprises around central headquarters complexes. Then as now, the superior general received all his authority directly from the pope, and operated as the pope's adjutant sending Jesuit personnel to various works. Chains of responsibility and command are described in the *Constitutions* with precision, and complicated strategies for insuring the unity of the "head" with the "members" are mandated, including the requirement of a constant, detailed, and exhaustive correspondence between the general and the local provincials, superiors, and a variety of internal "consultors."[44] The model of governance is extremely centralized: all important "major" superiors are appointed by the general for limited terms, while the general himself, for the sake of continuity, is elected for life by the only deliberative body in the Society, a "General Congregation" composed of professed delegates from all regions.[45] This "radial" government is, then, more monarchical or military than capitular or collegial.

As general, Ignatius usually reserved to himself important decisions on purchase of property and the ultimate siting of urban works. It is indicative that almost one thousand of the seven thousand surviving letters of Ignatius deal with property transactions, choices of location, strategies for obtaining desired property, details of building and construction and financing his rapidly expanding community. This massive correspondence counsels superiors in the field on the importance of the choice of appropriate property: it must be well located, in a healthful neighborhood with good air,[46] ample and preferably ex-

GARDEN OF THE NOVITIATE OF S. ANDREA AL QUIRINALE-S. VITALE, ROME, IN RICHEOME'S *LA PEINTURE SPIRITUELLE*, 1611

pandable, and reasonably priced (Cat. 67). Gardens were highly prized, and the purchase of a suburban villa for rest, recreation, and the care of the sick very frequently followed the foundation of the downtown center. Indeed, shortly before his death Ignatius himself spent several days at a villa near the baths of Caracalla that the Society had recently purchased for the Collegio Romano. By the mid-17th century the Jesuits in Rome held large tracts of suburban land on the Coelian, Aventine, and Quirinal hills as villas and kitchen gardens for their various institutions.

Ignatius insisted on receiving detailed descriptions of sites, negotiations, and copies of business transactions. In a few cases he left all decision making in the hands of a trusted local superior, but his general tendency was to oversee personally all such matters. In 1568, the Second General Congregation enacted Ignatius' personal practice into law, mandating that the plans and programs of all construction projects be referred to the superior general[47] (Cat. 68).

As his communities grew and spread out over Europe and the mission territories of an expanding world, Ignatius formulated a series of guidelines in his letters to assist his dispersed communities in adapting to their new surroundings (Cat. 67). His guidelines addressed three primary concerns. They first considered how to preserve and foster the religious life of those sent, giving detailed instructions on religious practice and community life. Since for the Jesuits, the place they were sent meant the people to whom they were sent, they were instructed to look to the edification, literally "the building up," of the city to which they were sent. The guidelines strongly emphasized preaching, teaching catechism, hearing confessions, visiting the sick, and the corporal works of mercy. Finally, the documents considered crucial practical questions: how to establish and improve the temporal situation of the new community so it could fulfill the first two goals.

In order to improve the temporal situation the Jesuits were instructed to obtain and maintain the benevolence of the local prince, nobles, bishop and clergy, assisting them in their preferred charities. In order to maintain their appropriate authority in spiritual matters, the Jesuits were instructed to ask well-placed friends to deal with the authorities for them in financial matters, in order to avoid any appearance of greed or avarice. Finally, they were "to have special care to obtain a good site that is spacious, or that can be enlarged in the future, that is sufficiently large for a church and a residence, and if at all possible that is not far removed from the converse of the city, and having bought that, it will be a good beginning for all the rest."[48]

In its first century , the Society of Jesus grew almost by geometrical proportions. Founded in 1540 with ten members in one house, at the time of Ignatius' death in 1556 there were more than 100 Jesuits in Rome and approximately 1,000 Jesuits in almost 100 houses on four continents. In 1579, there were 5,165 members in 200 houses; in 1600, 8,500 in 350 houses. At the time of the Society's first centennial in 1640 the order numbered 15,683 members in 868 houses[49] (Cat. 75-77).

By far the most important factor in this growth was the establishment of Jesuit colleges and universities, which served not only as educational institutions but also ripe fields for recruiting new members. Although it is usually identified with formal education, the Society was not deliberately founded as a teaching order, except in the broadest sense of preaching and teaching Christian doctrine. There is no mention of schools in the Formula of the Institute; their establishment, rather, is another example of the flexibility and imagination of the early Society.

Themselves well educated in Paris, the first companions recognized the need to train their new members with equal rigor, to prepare them thoroughly for whatever apostolic works lay ahead. As early as 1540, novices were sent to Paris for studies, and in 1542, the Jesuits founded their first "colleges," residences for Jesuit students at the Universities of Padua and Coimbra. In 1543, a Jesuit faculty began teaching in Goa. In 1546, in response to the insistence of its founder Francis Borgia , the Jesuit college in Gandía was opened to lay students as well as Jesuit seminarians. The first school principally for lay students was opened in Messina in 1548.[50]

For bright sons of all classes, but particularly the burgeoning middle class, Jesuit schools provided access to humanistic training that before had been reserved to the nobility or clerics. Basing their curriculum on the classics and the liberal arts and their pedagogy on the style of the University of Paris, the colleges filled a vast educational vacuum in Catholic Europe, serving as a major reinforcement in the church's struggle against the spread of Protestantism. In the 1590s, after half a century's experience, a long series of academic and curricular guidelines was systematized into the *Ratio Studiorum*, the classic Jesuit program for education (Cat. 66).

When Ignatius died there were already about forty colleges; in 1640, there were 540 in major cities and towns circling the globe from Rome to Mexico, Peru, the Philippines, Macao, India, and the Baltic States. In cities where the colleges were not founded as the primary work, they tended to "spin off" the central residence as they had in Rome. As time went on, however, the establishment of a college was usually the first and most important Jesuit foundation.

Even during Ignatius' lifetime, such expansion demanded careful regulation as well as experimentation. After a number of financially disastrous foundations, Ignatius began to insist upon a foundation to support at least 14 Jesuits.[51] Each college was to have a church in which its faculty could preach and teach. Papal exemptions were granted allowing the establishment of Jesuit colleges and their chapels near mendicant and parochial churches that feared the encroachment of their Jesuit neighbors. Often older churches suffered major defections

CAT. 85, MEDAL OF 1568 REVERSE:
VIGNOLA PROJECT FOR THE FAÇADE OF THE
CHURCH OF THE GESU'

CAT. 85, MEDAL OF 1568, OBVERSE:
CARDINAL ALESSANDRO FARNESE

CAT. 86, MEDAL OF 1575 REVERSE:
DELLA PORTA FAÇADE OF THE
CHURCH OF THE GESU'

in their congregations when the Jesuit preachers moved in next door (Cat. 69).

The Strategy, the Site, and the Saint

The strategy of the Society's diffusion in Rome became more or less paradigmatic for other installations. Beginning with a small church and a piece of property for a residence in the center of town, a base of operations was founded at S. Maria della Strada, the site of the present Church of the Gesù. As ministries multiplied and numbers in the community increased, both church and residence were enlarged and ultimately replaced by larger, more noble structures erected for the Society by important patrons.

Although the building of a large downtown church was Ignatius' first priority, his dream was not realized until after his death. Three times he tried to build a new church, and had plans drawn, twice by Nanni di Baccio Bigio (perhaps assisted by Vignola, Cat. 82), and a third by the aged Michelangelo in 1554.[52] These attempts were thwarted by insufficient funds and neighborhood opposition. In the 1560s Vignola reworked the plan of Nanni di Baccio Bigio, and his plan for the Gesù— a large single nave that served as an aula for preaching and a shallow sanctuary that stressed the visibility of sacramental activity—admirably suited the order's needs (Cat. 85, 87- 89).

Work on the new church did not actually begin until 1568. Some twelve years after Ignatius' death, Francis Borgia, elected third superior general of the order in 1565, was able to combine diplomacy, political pressure, and enough ready cash to buy out the Altieri, Astalli, and Muti families that had stubbornly blocked the project. He had secured as his major benefactor Cardinal Alessandro Farnese, grandson of Paul III. Farnese took an active role in the design of the church, insisting that the nave have a vault rather than a flat ceiling, and that the facade be oriented squarely onto the *piazza* that fronted the Via Papale. After the laying of the cornerstone, Farnese considered various designs for the facade prepared by Vignola, Galeazzo Alessi, and Giacomo Della Porta. He chose Della Porta's plan, which was nearly completed for the Holy Year 1575 (Cat. 86, 90). Thus, after the laying of three cornerstones and the approval of five separate building permits, the Chiesa del Gesù, oriented to face the processional flow of the Via Papale, finally arose on the site chosen by Ignatius almost thirty years before.[53]

The majestic new church adjoined the first Casa Professa, a simple residence that was erected in 1544.[54] Property acquisition proceeded fairly smoothly until the death of the much respected Codacio in 1549.

About that same time, Ignatius' neighbors Muzio and Lucrezia Muti attempted to expropriate an abandoned cemetery belonging to the Jesuits in order to use it as a chicken yard. The Muti began a war of nerves against the Jesuits: Signora Muti placed screaming peacocks under the Jesuits' windows to annoy her neighbors. The Muti also denied the Jesuits permission to open blind windows facing their property so that the fathers were required to light candles at their midday meal.[55] This war of nerves quickly escalated into all-out hostilities, as the Muti used all legal means available and a variety of illegal tactics, including the opening of gateways to prevent the closing of alleys, and attacks against Ignatius' bricklayers, to prevent the expansion of Jesuit building projects. The Muti organized a concentrated neighborhood action against Ignatius, who entirely gave up his attempts to build the church and new Casa Professa complex in the face of his neighbors' hostility (Cat. 83).

Neighborhood opposition continued throughout the last years of the Cinquecento, always led by an increasingly cantankerous Muti and his heirs.[56] Because of serious structural damage caused by the flood of December 24, 1598, Claudio Aquaviva, the fifth general, appealed again to the Farnese family, and Cardinal Odoardo, the nephew of Cardinal Alessandro, paid for the replacement of the original residence. The new Casa Professa, designed by Jesuit Giovanni de Rosis, encompassed the entire block bounded by the church, Via degli Astalli, Via S. Marco, and Via d'Aracoeli, a perimeter of more than 300 meters. Built with rooms for one hundred forty-five residents, it served as the Jesuits' General Curia or headquarters from the time of its construction until the suppression of the Society in 1773, and again from the restoration of the Society in 1814 until the Risorgimento (1873).[57]

Incorporated into the fabric of the new construction were the rooms where Ignatius had lived the last twelve years of his life and in which he died in 1556. A simple apartment with low beam ceilings and roughcast walls, Ignatius' four rooms were underpinned with complicated vaults in 1602, encapsulated into the *piano nobile* of the Casa Professa, and transformed into a shrine by General Claudio Aquaviva in 1605, four years before the beatification of Ignatius.[58] The painted decoration of the corridor next to the rooms is the work of Jesuit artists Giacomo Cortese, "il Borgognone" (1667) and Andrea Pozzo (1680s).

The last piece of property for the Casa Professa, located on the southeast corner where Via degli Astalli meets Via S. Marco, was not obtained until 1618. As late as 1612 General Aquaviva had to deal with complaints from the Venetian ambassador (in residence at Palazzo S. Marco) who complained that the Casa Professa was "squeezing the street."[59]

Both in terms of historical importance and sheer volume, the Collegio Romano-S. Ignazio complex rivals its nearby neighbor the Casa Professa-il Gesù. Ignatius himself founded the college, a seminary for Jesuit students of all nations. In early 1551, a "free school of grammar, humanities, and Christian Doctrine" opened in rented rooms at the Campidoglio end of Via Aracoeli. Quickly outgrowing these limited quarters, the college was soon relocated on Via del Gesù near the apse of the Church of S. Stefano del Cacco, and in 1552, students from the Jesuits' newly founded Collegio Germanico began to take

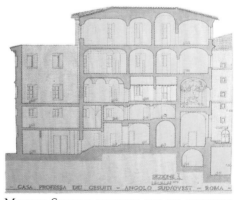

MODERN SECTION SHOWING THE RELATIONSHIP OF THE ROOMS OF ST. IGNATIUS TO THE CASA PROFESSA, STUDIO OF ING. FRANCESCO NOVELLI, ROME, 1990

their lessons there as well. The course of study included Latin, Greek, Hebrew, and the liberal arts, and the college's public "disputations," demonstrations of the academic and linguistic prowess of faculty and students held in local churches, became a sort of popular entertainment for the Roman intelligentsia. Philosophy and theology were soon added to the curriculum, and in 1556 Paul IV (Medici, 1559-1565)gave the college the authority to confer academic degrees.

In 1557, the college was again moved to larger quarters, this time in Palazzo Salviati, near the site of the present Piazza Collegio Romano. In 1560, Pius IV convinced the Marchesa della Valle, widow of Principe Camillo Orsini and herself sister of the late Paul IV (Caraffa,1555-1559), to donate her *palazzo* and adjoining property to the Society of Jesus. Standing on the site of the present Church of S. Ignazio, it is described in a contemporary document as "very lovely, and located in a very convenient part of Rome: nearby to the east is Monte Quirinale, to the west the Pantheon, to the south the Arch of Camillus and to the north, the Portico of Antonino Pio where there is the orphanage [directed by the Jesuits]. The site is ample, although not yet organized in the most desirable form."[60]

The organization of that conveniently located site would occupy Jesuit architects, builders and patrons of the Society for the next century. Brother Giovanni Tristano, the Society's first important architect, designed and oversaw the construction of the Church of SS. Annunziata on the site between the years 1561 and 1567. The skeptical Romans were impressed not only by the grace of the small church, but by the fact that it was constructed entirely by the labor of Jesuit lay brothers and students.[61]

The admission of lay students and non Jesuit seminarians strained the facilities of the Collegio to the breaking point.[62] Jesuit Giuseppe Valeriano designed a new facility, whose immense facade and large classrooms more than doubled the space of the college. In 1581 Pope Gregory XIII (Boncompagni, 1572-1585) expropriated the neighboring houses, and then paid for the construction of the edifice, actions for which the grateful Jesuits named him "founder" of the College. Gregory's lavishness in building matched the faith he had in the Society, to which he also entrusted the English College, the Church of S. Stefano Rotondo, and S. Apollinare near Piazza Navona as a seat for the German College. During the early stages of construction of the Collegio Romano, he ordered that fired brick walls replace simple rubble walls that were rising on the site, a construction detail that Cardinal Odoardo Farnese would later insist upon in the building of the Casa Professa (Cat. 94). The quality and expense of this "Jesuit" brickwork was commented on by architect Vincenzo Giustiani in his *Discourse on Architecture:* "this way is not generally used because it is of more than middling expense, even though it turns out to be beautiful and long lasting, since it resists the influence of both air and fire, and for that reason, the Jesuit fathers are accustomed to using it more than others, as men who exquisitely

La Chiefa dell'Annonciata del GIESV.

CHURCH OF SS. ANNUNZIATA, DESIGNED BY GIOVANNI TRISTANO, IN GIROLAMO FRANCINO'S *LE COSE MERAVIGLIOSE DELL'ALMA CITTÀ DI ROMA*, 1590

observe the beginnings, the progress, and the end of all their actions."[63] Gregory XIII inaugurated the complex in 1584, amid loud applause for the dawning of a golden age (Cat. 98, 100-103).

Tristano's small Church of SS. Annunziata was quickly outgrown. By the beginning of the seventeenth century the Collegio had more than 2,000 students, and it lacked a space adequate for its liturgical and ceremonial functions. Encouraged by the canonizations of Ignatius and Francis Xavier in 1622, the Jesuits appealed to Gregory XV (Ludovisi, 1621-1623) to help them with the construction of an ample and decorous church on the site of the oldest residence buildings donated to the Collegio by the Marchesa della Valle. The Pope's nephew Cardinal Ludovico Ludovisi and other members of the Ludovisi family endowed the construction, and in 1626 the cornerstone of the new church was laid (Cat. 103). Orazio Grassi, professor of mathematics at the Collegio Romano and opponent of Galileo, designed the church and the last portion of the residence complex. When Grassi was transferred to Savona, the direction of the works was passed to Jesuit Antonio Sassi, whose alteration of Grassi's design was to cause a lengthy, acrimonious, and ultimately futile dispute that blocked the construction of the cupola. The Dominicans of S. Maria sopra Minerva complained because the cupola would rob light from their library; Grassi lamented because Sassi's heightening of the facade destroyed the proportions of the structure. Bernini, Borromini, Algardi, and Girolamo Rainaldi all gave written opinions, and Grassi proposed a number of alternatives. In the end, lack of funds for further construction resolved the question, and in 1685 Andrea Pozzo's masterful false cupola, a canvas some 17 meters in diameter, was installed[64](Cat. 135). Construction of the church continued fitfully for almost a century, and the structure was finally consecrated in 1722.

Jesuit Benedetto Molli's work at the Collegio Germanico, Bernini's jewel-like S. Andrea in Quirinale built as the chapel for the Jesuit novitiate, and Alexander VII's grandiose design for Piazza Collegio Romano and widening of the corridor from Piazza del Gesù to Piazza Venezia (a work unfortunately undone by Clement X's construction of the long wing of his family's Palazzo Altieri), marked the culmination of a century of Jesuit urban construction and impact.

The second half of the Seicento would be a period of intense activity devoted largely to the decoration of the structures already built. Ignatius had insisted on the importance of the urban church as a magnet. Although he insisted that the churches have no fixed revenues and that the liturgical celebrations of the Society be marked by simplicity and decorum rather than pomp, he himself had worked almost continuously to expand and make suitable the della Strada Chapel at the Casa Professa. The earliest Jesuit "building code," canon 11 of the first General Congregation 1558, insisted on spartan utility, strength, and simplicity for Jesuit houses and colleges, yet churches were deliberately and explicitly exempted from the regulation[65] (Cat. 68).

Jesuit spirituality and the practices of the Spiritual Exercises insist on finding God in all things, and using the senses and the imagination as trained instruments for discerning that Divine presence. The great Jesuit decorative enterprises of the seventeenth century need to be read, then, in this context: following the insight of their founder, successive generations of Jesuits were not afraid to use created beauty to reflect the Uncreated Beauty of God. The works of great secular and Jesuit artists Bernini, Ciro Ferri, Algardi, Gaulli, Valeriano, Cortese, and Pozzo were put to this use in a spectacular way, just as the Jesuits did not hesitate to use spectacle on the urban stage, dramas, processions, music and even fireworks, to attract the populace to hear a message "packaged" within the event itself.

In the second half of the Cinquecento, the papacy in effect ceded the center of Rome to the Jesuits and the other reformed religious congregations, the Theatines (S. Andrea della Valle), the Oratorians (Chiesa Nuova) and the Barnabites (S. Carlo ai Catinari), creating a "third pole" of religious impact between the papal residence at S. Pietro and the Roman cathedral at S. Giovanni Laterano and the suburban pilgrimage Basilicas.[66] As the frescoes in the Salone Sistino of the Biblioteca Apostolica Vaticana (see p. 42) and a 1610 map called the "Roma Ignaziana" (Cat. 71) testify, at the very center of this pole stood the Church of the Gesù.

In both the Salone Sistino frescoes and the "Roma Ignaziana" one sees the Gesù complex, imagined during Ignatius' lifetime and expanded over the next 50 years, which stood at the center of a corona of social, educational, and pastoral works. The church stood as the radiating and radiant center of a multiform urban ministry. The other great Roman building programs of the Jesuits (the Collegio Romano, the Collegio Germanico, and S. Andrea) served to underscore the Society's profound commitment to serving the Universal Church by preparing young ministers in the heart of the City of the Popes.

With discerning care, four hundred and fifty years ago Ignatius of Loyola chose the site of the Gesù complex for his headquarters in the middle of Rome. That choice was based on the criterion, the "sacred strategy," of the greater service of God and neighbor, which identified the place with the people ministered to in it. Ignatius'choice of the Rione della Pigna in 1540 was the option of a man who clearly understood his mission. He preached and embodied in service the Gospel of Christ in his crowded neighborhood, to beggars and prostitutes in the *piazza* no less than to the papal court next door, to the casual passerby as well as to the devout. From this vibrant center, his social ministries touched the most emarginated members of the community, while his ministries of education and his active support of the papacy prepared and assisted those who would diffuse the Good News.

Four hundred and fifty years later, Piazza del Gesù is still the heart of Rome. The museums of the Campidoglio and the Palazzo Venezia, the City Hall, important banks and businesses are nearby. The homeless

ANONYMOUS FRESCOES IN THE SALONE SISTINO OF THE BIBLIOTECA APOSTOLICA VATICANO, CA. 1590
THE UPPER FRESCO (OVER THE ENTRANCE) SHOWS THE RELATIONSHIP OF THE GESÙ' TO THE STREET WORK OF
SIXTUS V. THE LOWER (ON THE NORTHERN WALL) INDICATES HOW THE COLLEGIO ROMANO (SEEN FROM
BEHIND, FROM PIAZZA COLONNA) AND THE GESÙ' TOWERED OVER THE DOWNTOWN LANDSCAPE.

still sleep on the steps of the church. Across the *piazza* are the headquarters of the Christian Democratic party and the Italian Masons. The windows of the recently restored rooms of St. Ignatius overlook Via delle Botteghe Oscure, the headquarters of the Italian Communist Party.

The Church of the Gesù remains an important apostolic center in the life of the Rome, the goal of pilgrims who come from around the world to pray at the tomb of Ignatius and a much-frequented center of sacramental ministry. The adjoining Casa Professa is the residence of the Italian Jesuit Provincial, of the staff of the Church of the Gesù, and of Jesuits who teach and work in social and pastoral ministries throughout the city. It also houses an international community of more than fifty Jesuit students who study at the nearby Gregorian University, which continues the work of the Collegio Romano Ignatius founded in 1551. In the basement, the Jesuit Refugee Service working with lay volunteers feeds and assists Ethiopian refugees. The Gesù complex still testifies to the vision and genius of the man who chose the site as his headquarters four and a half centuries ago.

Figuratively speaking, the Jesuit church stands as a great opening in the urban fabric, a portal through which the faithful enter to encounter God in Word and Sacrament, and from which Jesuits stream into the streets, schools, and social centers of the city.

Where that portal is placed, where it opens onto the world, makes all the difference.

Notes

1. "'Bernard loved the valleys, Benedict the mountains, Francis the towns, but Ignatius the great cities.' There are several variant readings of these two lines. In one of them Ignatius loved 'the famous crowded cities,' (*celebres Ignatius urbes*) rather than the great cities; in another Dominic replaced Ignatius as the subject (*celebres Dominicus urbes*) in another Dominic replaced Francis in loving the towns (*Oppida Dominicus*) and Ignatius still had the great cities as an object of affection. History, scansion of verse, and only four places for five great personalities in religious life make for some uncertainty...These lines recur through the centuries; the circumstances on which they were based seem to have been true through most of the history of the Society [of Jesus]." Padberg, 1988, p. 29.

2. *EppIg.* I, 208.

3. *Const.* IV, 5, [359].

4. Campbell, 1987, p. 2.

5. Venerable Bede, *De temporum ratione*, in Woodward, 1985, pp. 514-515.

6. *FD*, p. 786.

7. *Autobiography,* no. 1; Ribadeneira, *Vita* I, ii, in *FN* IV, p. 85 ("mozo lozano y polido y muy amigo de galas y de traerse bien").

8. *Autobiography,* no. 36.

9. *Autobiography,* no. 50.

10. Tellechea-Idígoras, 1986, p. 171.

11. *Autobiography,* no. 62.

12. *Autobiography,* no. 64, 70.

13. *Autobiography,* no. 70, 71.

14. Schurhammer, 1973, pp. 79, 85.

15. *Autobiography,* no. 85.

16. *FN* I, p. 204.

17. *FN* II, p. 133.

18. Guidoni, 1977, pp. 76, 79, 82.

19. Krautheimer, 1983, p. 275.

20. Pecchiai, 1948, p. 258.

21. Sciaparelli, 1902, p. 16.

22. Re, 1920, p. 88.

23. Ceen, 1986, p. 95.

24. Guidoni, 1972, pp. 10-12; Vitruvius, III, i.

25. Castagnoli, 1958, pp. 356-357.

26. Stinger, 1985, p. 78.

27. Partner, 1979, p. 22.

28. Argan, 1969, p. 32.

29. Stinger, 1985, p. 322.

30. Pecchiai, 1948, pp. 445-447; Stinger, 1985, p. 323. For details and analysis of the 1526 Census, cf. Gnoli, 1894, pp. 375-493.

31. Partner, 1979, p. 174.

32. Coffin, 1979, pp. 31-32; Stinger, 1985, p. 257. The "Torre Farnese" stood until 1886, when it was demolished to make way for the monument to Victor Emmanuel II.

33. *FN* III, p. 327.

34. "Sacrosanctum Romanum Ecclesiam," Archivio Segreto Vaticano, Paul III, Bull. Secret., Arm. XXIV, 1695, fol. 73.

35. *FN* III, p. 178.

36. Orlandini, 1615, I, iii, p. 76.

37. *FN* IV, p. 411.

38. *SpEx*, 23. A *caveat*. Rather than doing violence to the very delicate balance of

these key sentences by forcing an inclusive translation (i.e. "created for him or her to help him or her in attaining the end for which he or she is created"), a literal translation of the text is provided. Late Medieval Spanish was not an inclusive language. From the sense of the text, Ignatius' use of the word "man" in the text of the *Spiritual Exercises* must be understood generically, as "the human person" rather than as gender specific, "a male."

39. "Formula Instituti" of 1550, in *Const.* [3].

40. *Const.* VII, 1, [603].

41. *Const.* VII, 2, [622 A].

42. Conwell, 1979, p. 33.

43. *Const.* VII, 2, [622 E].

44. *Const.* VIII, 1, [655-681], "Helps towards uniting the distant members with their head and among themselves, aids toward the union of hearts."

45. *Const.* VIII, ch. 2-7, and IX, "The Society's Head and the government descending from him," esp. ch. 1.

46. *Const.* X, 1, [827].

47. *Canones Congregationum*, 1581, p. 9.

48. *EppIg.* IV, 2861, cf. III, 1899.

49. *Synopsis*, 1950, pp. 34, 82, 122; *Imago*, 1640, p. 248. In 1990 there are approximately 24,500 Jesuits in approximately 2,500 houses: cf. *Inscriptiones Epistolarum S.I.*, 1988.

50. Bangert, 1972, pp. 26-27.

51. *Const.* IV, 2, [331].

52. Tacchi Venturi, 1899, p. 60; *EppIg.* VII, 4529, 4531.

53. Pirri, 1955, pp. 138, 154.

54. *Chron* I, 1, pp. 128, 148.

55. Pirri, 1941, p. 190; Tacchi Venturi, 1899, p. 47.

56. Tacchi Venturi, 1899, p. 52.

57. Pirri-Di Rosa, 1975, pp. 28-30.

58. Pecchiai, 1952, pp. 302-303; Lucas, 1990, p.13.

59. Pirri, 1955, p. 266.

60 "De Collegio Romano, 1551-61," in Rinaldi, 1914, p. 67.

61. Pirri, 1955, p. 29.

62. When Pius IV entrusted the newly founded Seminario Romano to the Jesuits in 1563 and ordered its students to attend classes at the Collegio Romano, one auxilliary bishop complained "ch'era cosa intollerabile che si affidasse l'educazione della gioventù romana a Tedeschi e Spagnuoli, cioè, ad eretici e Marrani." Sacchini, 1620, II, p. 303.

63. Connors, 1980, p. 146, n. 46.

64. Montalto, 1957, p. 33.

65. *Canones Congregationum*, 1581, p. 3.

66. Guidoni, 1982, p. 614.

THE CHAPEL OF S. IGNAZIO (1695-1699) AFTER RESTORATION, CHURCH OF THE GESU', ROME

"A Noble Medley and Concert of Materials and Artifice"

Jesuit Church Interiors in Rome, 1567-1700

EVONNE LEVY

The last section of this exhibition is devoted to the interior decorations of the Jesuit churches in Rome, from the Gesù and the renovated Early Christian college churches of the sixteenth century to the seventeenth-century churches created *ex novo* for the Society: S. Ignazio, and S. Andrea al Quirinale. The objects have been chosen to illustrate the two major phases of permanent decoration of these churches that occurred between the years 1567 and 1700 as well as those ephemeral decorations that attracted a large public to the churches for funeral exequies and Forty Hours devotions.

Throughout this discussion it should be borne in mind that over the last century scholars have debated whether or not there existed a Jesuit style.[1] This question, equally important for architecture and the figurative arts, was provoked by the impressive opulence of the Jesuit churches, and the central place occupied by works of art in Jesuit churches in the history of art. Moreover, historians studying the question have attempted to come to terms with the control exercised by the Society's leaders in Rome over the architectural design of churches and colleges both locally and abroad. More recently the question of a Jesuit style has been less discussed.[2] Rather, scholars have turned their attention to identifying the attitudes that characterized different phases of decoration, and to placing Jesuit art patronage within an historical context.

Two fundamental issues are involved here. The first concerns the Jesuits' seemingly divided attitude toward the decoration of churches, oscillating between, on the one hand, an economically conservative position favoring austerity, and, on the other, those for whom the place of worship could never be too richly decorated. The second issue concerns the development of a Jesuit imagery. The decoration of Jesuit churches in the seventeenth century emphasized the Society's saints. But it is often asked whether, before the canonization of the first Jesuits in 1622, the form or subjects of the early decorations in Jesuit churches reflected a specifically Jesuit way of thinking.

During the first phase of decoration of Jesuit churches in Rome between 1567 and 1600, seven new college churches and the Gesù were decorated or renovated. The first churches to be built and decorated by the Society do not survive: the small Church of the Annunziata (see fig. on p. 39) at the Collegio Romano was later replaced by S. Ignazio, and the earlier church of S. Andrea al Quirinale was replaced by Bernini's church.[3] In both of these modest churches, which had altars positioned along the nave, the decorations seem to have been limited to side-chapel altarpieces with more elaborate embellishment reserved for the high altar. The focus on the high altar was further reinforced by the manufacture of elaborate wooden tabernacles for the eucharist on the altar itself, this in accordance with a growing emphasis on the central mystery of the faith.[4]

From what we know of them, the Annunziata and S. Andrea seem to have been similar to other longitudinal churches built in these decades. This type developed in response to new functions in churches established by reform leaders such as Saint Ignatius.[5] However, because the Annunziata and S. Andrea, the first two churches built by the Society in Rome, were rather unambitious, they have been largely ignored in the scholarly literature.

The basic principle behind the interiors of these early churches repeats itself, however with significant change in scale and variation, in the Gesù, the Mother church of the Society.[6] The interior of the sixteenth-century Gesù (recorded in Sacchi's painting, Cat. 109) was vastly different than that which we see today. The nave and barrel vault favored by the patron, Alessandro Farnese, and to which the Jesuits were opposed (preferring the acoustics of the flat roof),[7] were white-washed. The disagreement between the Society and their wealthy patron provides fundamental evidence for those historians who argue that in the late sixteenth century Jesuits espoused austerity in their churches. However, the argument is contradicted by Canon 11 of the First General Congregation (1558), which, in addressing the subject of the Society's buildings, specified that the Jesuit houses were to be neither "sumptuous nor novel," but pointedly decreed "nothing about churches" (Cat. 68). Furthermore, there is little physical evidence to support the conclusion that the Jesuits wanted the interior of the Gesù to remain unadorned.[8] The cupola and pendentives were decorated, as were the arches above the side chapels in the nave. The wood ceiling, which they preferred for its superior acoustics, would probably have been decorated in the current mode with painted and gilded coffers.[9] And although the transept chapels remained rather simply adorned well into the seventeenth century, rich decorations comparable to the most modern chapels in S. Maria Maggiore or S. Pietro had been planned for them in the 1580s and 1590s, but were unexecuted.[10] The side chapels were richly decorated at the discretion of private patrons and there is no evidence that the types of decoration were either imposed upon them or opposed by the Jesuits.

The iconography of the chapels, however, seems to have been more closely supervised. The original dedications of the ten minor altars initially reflected a spiritual program that has, with some diffi-

INTERIOR OF S. STEFANO RODONDO, ROME

culty, been found to correspond to the devotional practices of the Society.[11] The difficulty we have in recognizing patterns in the imagery is significant. Only a highly educated worshipper, well-versed in the dogmatic debates of the time, would have realized that certain themes could only appear in a Jesuit church. However, the ordinary person entering a Jesuit church built and decorated in the 1570s, probably would not have known it from the subject or appearance of the decorations.

A first move towards the development of what we recognize as a specifically Jesuit imagery begins in the early 1570s in the private quarters of the novices at S. Andrea.[12] According to Richeome (Cat. 118), the refectory and recreation room of the house were decorated with scenes of the recent martyrdoms of Jesuit missionaries. This imagery would soon appear in the college churches as well.

By the early 1580s, Gregory XIII had entrusted the Jesuits with the direction of two national colleges and their associated churches: the Collegio Germanico with S. Apollinare (Cat. 117) and the suburban church of S. Stefano Rotondo, and the English College with its church of St. Thomas of Canterbury (Cat. 116).[13] Within perhaps as little as three years (1582-1584), Nicolò Circignani frescoed the interiors of all three churches with extensive martyrdom cycles that spared the viewer none of the brutality of the martyrs' deaths. In the case of the first two, the frescoes concerned Early Christian martyrs and the suffering of the Early Christian saint to whom the church was dedicated. However, in the case of the Church of St. Thomas, the cycle represented the history of martyrdoms in England to the present day. Circignani's frescoes had an unusual format, with letters within the images identifying events explained in a text below.

The final project of the first phase of Jesuit patronage was the restoration of S. Vitale (Cat. 118), a fifth-century church given to the novices of S. Andrea by Clement VIII in 1595. The decoration of this Early Christian church involved a complete cycle of frescoes of martyrdom scenes and figures of Old Testament prophets all set in a fictive architectural framework of monumental proportions. S. Vitale is the first Jesuit church in Rome that we know for certain had a visually unified interior.

By the turn of the seventeenth century, with all of these new colleges and their churches recently renovated, the Society had acquired a reputation for its church interiors. In a guidebook of 1600 it was noted of the St. Thomas renovation that the Jesuit fathers "secondo il solito loro nelle altre Chiese" had the church "molto bene affetata" with a beautiful ceiling and clean altars.[14] Although this remark indicates that it was the general appearance of these interiors that was considered to be characteristic of the Society, there is much evidence to suppose that it was equally the content of the decorations, martyrdoms, that was strongly associated with the Jesuits by the mid-1580s.

Recent studies of the art of the Counter Reformation have emphasized that the Jesuits' renovation of Early Christian churches in the 1580s and 1590s was part and parcel of a larger program of urban renewal and Early Christian revival. One of the first studies to address this subject was an article by Buser on Jerome Nadal's *Evangelicae historiae imagines* (Cat. 119) in which the Society's art of the late sixteenth century was considered as part of a "conscious aesthetic program" used "in a propaganda battle with the Protestants over the significance of martyrs."[15] Buser concluded that Ignatius' *Spiritual Exercises* with their emphasis on visualization, did have an impact on the decoration of Jesuit churches and that Nadal's illustrated meditations provided the impetus and the most important model for the annotated frescoes in the college churches. Monssen interprets the frescoes at S. Stefano Rotondo not merely as an exhortation to imitate the martyrs, but as a cohesive cycle revolving around Christ's Crucifixion, and the "profound sacrificial emphasis in the Society's Apostolate."[16] For Monssen, this cycle (and by extension, those of the other Jesuit churches of this period) does not make for a Jesuit style, but for a Jesuit message. Herz, following Monssen, tends to make less of the martyrdom scenes as models for the novices, and sees them, rather, as an example of one path that can be pursued towards a larger goal of salvation.[17]

It is, however, particularly important to note that the Jesuits were not alone in creating such imagery in the late sixteenth century, and that the Oratorians, the Jesuits' rival order, made an enormous contribution to the "Early Christian revival."[18] Starting in 1580, both the Jesuit Roberto Bellarmino and the Oratorian Cesare Baronio worked on a revision of the *Roman Martyrology*, a project initiated by Gregory XIII. This is part of the context shared by the powerful Counter Reformation orders. However, as Zuccari's excellent studies have demonstrated, there existed profound differences between the Jesuits and the

Oratorians.[19] Whereas the Oratorian Baronio *restored* several Early Christian churches, the Jesuits *renovated* their college churches. There can be no doubt that the danger posed to Jesuit missionaries in Reform and non-Catholic lands was real. The Oratorians shared no such missionary goals with their rivals, had no such colleges; no such reality faced their seminarians. Baronio's restorations of Early Christian churches in the city were not undertaken with a specific audience in mind as were the Jesuit churches. Baronio's approach, which was very much in line with Neri's reform goals for the Oratorio, reflects his work as church historian; the restorations he effected tended towards the imitation or evocation in form and subject of a more devout period in the Church's history.[20] On the other hand, the Jesuits, the first to represent martyrdoms on their walls in this period, were reacting to a new wave of brutal persecutions to which their own members were subjected. The Society's particular claim to this type of imagery should not be diminished.

With all of the new churches decorated by the turn of the seventeenth century, there was a long hiatus in the decoration of Jesuit churches in Rome. In 1622 there was a momentary flurry of activity surrounding the canonization of Sts. Ignatius and Francis Xavier. But this event produced more ephemeral decorations than permanent ones, and about the permanent ones there is no shortage of confusion (Cat. 134, 141).[21] More important perhaps in the first decades of the century is the print medium, widely used in promoting the cults of new saints.[22]

Although 1622 may not have generated important permanent changes in the Jesuit churches, it marked a turning point for the imagery of the Society. Whereas the first phase of decoration was based on dogmatic beliefs and the implicit comparison (directed at a specific audience) of Jesuit martyrs with the Early Christian martyrs, from this time on, with their founder and Xavier canonized, the Jesuits could commemorate the Society itself. Churches and altars were rededicated to reflect the new status of the founder and first missionary; the Society's own history began to occupy a position of eminence in their public churches.

The second important phase of decoration of Jesuit churches begins in the 1660s with the construction of the new S. Andrea al Quirinale, and the decoration of the nave and transept chapels in the Gesù and in the new Church of S. Ignazio. Haskell has shown that the determining personality behind at least two of these projects was Gian Paolo Oliva, general of the Society between 1664 and 1681.[23] A renowned preacher and personal friend of Bernini, Oliva believed in the appropriateness and the necessity of magnificence in the church. Even before he was elected general, he may have had a hand in Bernini's involvement with S. Andrea and under his direction of the Society the interior decoration was radically revised and enriched in the 1660s.[24]

It is first with Bernini at S. Andrea that the interior decoration of a Jesuit church becomes an indivisible element of design, not a skin

GIOVANNI BATTISTA GAULLI, *ADORATION OF THE NAME OF JESUS* (1676-1679), CHURCH OF THE GESU', ROME

applied by later generations of artists. Bernini's S. Andrea unified the high altar and vault through a narrative sequence. As Wittkower noted, the Jesuits were so aware of the immutability of Bernini's idea for the church, that, in the first years of the eighteenth century, over twenty years after the death of Bernini, they rejected a plan by Pierre Legros to substitute his polychrome sculpture of Stanislas Kostka for a painted altar in the church for the reason that it would alter the unity of Bernini's design.[25] It is obvious that Bernini's conception of the church also extended to the painted altars and the *Death of St. Francis Xavier* by Giovanni Battista Gaulli (Cat. 124)—the painter with whom Bernini preferred to collaborate in the 1670s—is particularly responsive to the colored marbles used for the altars, frames and enframing arches.

The radical renovation of the Gesù was the most important decorative project undertaken by Oliva. Between 1672 and 1685 Gaulli, whose work on this project was guaranteed by Bernini, frescoed all of the surfaces above the cornice: the nave (1676-1679), cupola (1672-1675), pendentives (1675-1676), apse (1680-1683), and left transept (1685) with only the right transept being decorated by Gianandrea Carlone (c.1672-1674). Antonio Raggi and others executed the stucco figures that activate the vault at the level of the windows.

Although, broadly speaking, Gaulli's scheme for the whole church resembles Pietro da Cortona's decorations in the Chiesa Nuova, there is a spectacular degree of illusionism that differs fundamentally from Cortona's design.[26] Frescoed surfaces creep over the architecture and in the nave vault groups of figures on clouds cast deep shadows painted onto the gilded vault, creating the illusion that the painted figures occupy a space that is coextensive with our own.[27] In the large space of the Gesù, unified by Gaulli's decorations, the spectator in the nave was wrapped up in a singular spiritual experience.

The Gesù nave also marks the first major public appearance in Rome of a type of triumphal imagery that specifically exalts the Society. The nave fresco (Cat. 122), representing the *Adoration of the Name of Jesus*, celebrates the dedication of the church and the name of the Society. The blessed ascend to the golden light of the name and the Vices are cast out of heaven. The stucco figures lining the nave make clear the geographic domain of the Society, with different parts of the world reaching out to the name.

Although rooted in the late sixteenth-century church decorations, the pointed interest in a visually and iconographically unified interior, expressed in rich materials, emerged during Oliva's tenure as general, and endured long after his death. Of course the usual pockets of resistence to the spending of money on art in the churches still existed, but they never posed a serious threat to the overwhelming support of magnificence by the Society's leadership. This is apparent as the Jesuits continued to complete the chapels in S. Andrea after Bernini's designs and in their deliberations over the Chapel of S. Ignazio in the Gesù.

In the Oliva decades the Jesuits became both highly visible patrons and extremely conscious of the relationship of their church decorations to those of other churches in Rome. Whereas Jesuit artists seem to have been used freely in the late sixteenth-century churches, by the late seventeenth century the Society was no longer free to choose a Jesuit artist without answering to the public. Gaulli's work, perpetually under attack, had to be guaranteed by Bernini, and a long statement justifying the appointment of Andrea Pozzo to paint the vault of the Church of S. Ignazio, stating all of his qualifications and listing his supporters, had to be made to members of the Society itself. Pozzo had to compete with other painters to carry out what was probably his own idea for the fictive cupola in S. Ignazio (Cat. 135), and it was also at both the request of Jesuit "periti" and because of public clamoring that an architectural competition took place for the Chapel of S. Ignazio in the Gesù (Cat. 133). Surely times had changed.

There still remained the private quarters of the Society that could be decorated freely. Oliva was particularly fond of the Jesuit Giacomo Cortese, a sought-after specialist in battle painting who was often employed by the Jesuits providing paintings as gifts, but who only did significant work for the Society, in more private settings, on two occasions:[28] for the chapel of the Prima Primaria at the Collegio Romano he executed a cycle of Christian battles (1658-1661) and in the corridor outside of the rooms of St. Ignatius in the Casa Professa (1667) he began an Ignatian cycle.

In the 1680s, the corridor begun by Cortese was transformed by Andrea Pozzo. A brother of the Society from Trento, Pozzo was summoned to Rome by Oliva,[29] who died (1681) before the artist arrived. Between 1682 and 1688, Pozzo continued the corridor project.[30] It is doubtful that he destroyed any of Cortese's work, but rather than limit the cycle to the window surrounds already painted, he frescoed the entire space, uniting the two corridor walls and the ceiling, and "correcting" the angled terminal wall through a fictive perspective. Recent restoration of the frescoes has uncovered new bays of Pozzo's scheme that had been painted over in the nineteenth century. This project, about which little is known, makes a more sophisticated use of perspective and anamorphoses than was previously visible and further study of the corridor in the context of the Minims' visual experiments at Trinità dei Monti may shed further light on Pozzo's development as painter and perspectivist.[31] The corridor project also filled an enormous iconographic lacuna in Rome. For though painted in the 1680s, more than 120 years after Ignatius' death and 60 years after his canonization, this was the first extensive cycle of Ignatius' life to be made in Rome. Within the next fifteen years Pozzo would apotheosize the saint in the vault of the Church of S. Ignazio and recount his miracles and visions in both the latter church and in his tomb at the Gesù.

Neither the decoration of the Gesù by Gaulli nor the next large decorative project, the frescoes adorning the vault (Cat. 136), crossing (Cat. 135), and apse (Cat. 137) in the Church of S. Ignazio, taxed the general financial resources of the Society. The funds for the Gesù came from the Jesuit Father Durazzo and those for S. Ignazio were provided by the sale of the first volume of Pozzo's *Perspectiva pictorum et architectorum.*[32] As such, the question of austerity versus wealth hardly pertains to these projects in the way that it had when wealthy patrons were funding construction or decorative projects.

Rather, the question to be asked of the S. Ignazio campaign is to what extent the Society approved of and wished to perpetuate the narrative and pictorial unities in S. Andrea and the Gesù. With the nave of S. Ignazio completed since 1650 and construction of the crossing and tribune dragging on into the 1680s, the main body of the church had remained simply adorned with six rather mediocre altarpieces executed by the Jesuit painter, Pierre de Lattre, Algardi's elegant frieze below the cornice, and the vault "armoniosamente ornata di stucchi."[33] Within the Society itself objections to painting the vault were raised.[34] Surely this was partly the expression of an austerity party. But this view may also have been shared by a sophisticated group that had in mind, for example, a Borrominian type of interior that was complex and powerful without using color. Pozzo's cycle (1685-1702), like Gaulli's in the Gesù, covered all of the vault surfaces united by the cornice. Like Gaulli's frescoes, they are based on the illusion—this time achieved by means of *quadratura*—of a vault opened to the heavens. Those who supported the decoration of the nave must also have endorsed the appearance, finally, in a public church of an important cycle of Ignatian imagery. Pozzo's frescoes celebrate Ignatius as the heavenly illuminated point of origin of a vast organization of missionaries who converted the heathen and heretics worldwide. Ignazio appears here as saint, as miracle worker, and as one who had visions.

With the nave decorations of its two principle churches completed, the Society committed its attention, and vast financial resources, to the construction of transept chapels containing the tombs of two of its saints: Ignatius and Luigi Gonzaga.[35] The latter, located in the right transept of the Church of S. Ignazio, was built between 1697 and 1700 (Cat. 138, 139), simultaneously with its complement in the Gesù, the Chapel of S. Ignazio (Cat. 131-133). Both chapels were designed by Andrea Pozzo, the young French sculptor Pierre Legros executed the sculptural centerpieces (and other elements), they shared the same administrator, and materials and workmen moved back and forth between the two projects.

In designing the transepts of both churches, the Jesuits were interested in maintaining the newly attained unity of the public spaces. In the Church of S. Ignazio this was eventually accomplished by mirroring the Luigi Gonzaga altar in the left transept Chapel of the Annunciation (1749). But in the Church of the Gesù the Jesuits found themselves in a quandray. In order to unify the transepts, there would at least have to be a painting on the altar and ideally the architecture would be harmonized with the Negroni Chapel of St. Francis Xavier designed by

TEODORO VERCRUYS AFTER ANDREA POZZO, APSE OF THE CHURCH OF S. IGNAZIO, IN *PROSPETTIVA DE' PITTORI E ARCHITETTI,* II, ROME, 1717

Pietro da Cortona and Luca Berrettini (c. 1669-1676) in the right transept.[36] But already at that time the Jesuits were extremely dissatisfied with the Negroni altar. Not only did the vault decorations differ from Gaulli's in the rest of the church, but the design was disrespectful of Vignola's church because it excavated the wall and broke through the cornice. In spite of the rich materials employed, the Jesuits found the chapel so undistinguished that it was considered "una spesa quasi gettata."[37] The idea of moving Ignatius' tomb to the high altar so as to be able to build him a truly magnificent chapel without compromising the unity of the church had been crushed by the Farnese heirs' refusal to spend any money on the church. Ultimately, the desire to exalt the Society's founding saint with a sumptuous tomb won out over maintaining a unified interior.

The Chapel of S. Ignazio in the Gesù also marks a climax to Pozzo's previous development of Ignatian imagery in the Roman churches and houses. The miracles painted in the corridor, having shed the anecdotal intimacy of that setting, provided the designs for five of the seven gilded bronze reliefs.[38] In the episode of *St. Ignatius Exorcises a Man Possessed* Pozzo's depiction of himself telling a child to be quiet, a reference reported by Pascoli to all of the brothers who disturbed him as he worked,[39] was eliminated and the attention focused on the two central figures. Pozzo's Forty Hours *apparati* and proposals for permanent altars (Cat. 130) influenced the employment of a moveable painting which slid down on tracks to reveal an over life-sized silver statue of the saint in an ornate niche. Recently restored, the chapel can once again elicit the kind of wonder it aroused in the viewers present at its unveiling: "No words can describe how astonished the visitors on that occasion were at a work of such enchantment. The silence was such that you couldn't even hear a sigh amongst such a large crowd... Amongst them the Pope, all suspended in looking and admiring such a noble medley and concert of materials, and artifice, and to bring even greater admiration was the painting which silently disappeared to reveal the niche in which the splendor of metals and of the most prized stones made such an impression on the eye and on the minds of the viewers that they didn't know how to draw themselves away and there were those who stayed there for hours and hours immobile, like statues."[40]

From documents reporting deliberations about the design of the chapel a primary concern that the chapel convey magnificence clearly emerges. In no other project developed previously by the Society was this intention so emphatically stated and without apology. Much of the early design discussions focused on the materials to be employed: "Marbles, although beautiful, and precious, today however in the chapels are beginning to become base, and like a common material. So that making this chapel of marble it would not be distinguished from common things; and after fifty years the Society would regret not having foreseen the error and not having exceeded rather than undershot in the richness of the material, demonstrating the practice which

ANDREA POZZO, *ST. IGNATIUS EXORCISES A MAN POSSESSED* (CA. 1682-1688), CORRIDOR OF THE ROOMS OF ST. IGNATIUS, CASA PROFESSA, ROME

ANGELO DE'ROSSI, *ST. IGNATIUS EXORCISES A MAN POSSESSED* (1695-1696), CHAPEL OF S. IGNAZIO, CHURCH OF THE GESU', ROME

GIROLAMO FREZZA AFTER ANDREA POZZO, *THE CHAPEL OF S. IGNAZIO*, IN *PERSPECTIVA PICTORUM ET ARCHITECTORUM*, II, ROME, 1700

is always growing, as it should, of pomp in the churches ... so that the beautiful, the rich, the grand and the precious of the same should stand out."[41]

Although the Jesuits' pursuit of material splendor is a well-founded cliché, the use of these materials was expressive not only of the Society's mundane, but also of their spiritual aspirations. As we have already seen, the Jesuits seem to have sought for the status of venerability for the Gesù at its inception, in their debate with the Farnese over the ceiling. A century later, in the Chapel of S. Ignazio, materials like lapis, bronze, and silver were employed with implicit comparisons to chapels in the Roman basilicas in mind.[42] The late seventeenth-century transept chapels redressed unexplainable lacunae in the imagery of the Society's saints in their Roman churches. But with enormous funds now at their disposition for these projects, the Jesuits attempted materially to manifest the hagiographic and pictorial traditions surrounding their saints. For instance, above Ignatius' tomb, the saint is represented in silver, the material that is most like light. On the vault of the Church of S. Ignazio the saint had appeared, like a mirror, as the reflector of divine light. As a silver statue, he emits his own divine radiance, that quality most central to his saintliness. To say, as Picinelli had in his *Mundus symbolicus*, that Ignatius was like silver, cold on the outside and "burning with the very bright flame of charity on the inside," may be too literal an interpretation of the statue.[43] But to dismiss the Chapel of S. Ignazio, and the other "magnificent" late seventeenth-century projects as simply material profusions, would be to miss out on both the meaning of these monuments and the specific concerns for cult and imagery expressed in their creation. As we have seen, the deliberations over the late seventeenth-century saints' tombs brought out a conflict between an aesthetic drive for a unified interior and a spiritually motivated desire to create an exceedingly special space for a saint's cult. In the context of late seventeenth-century Rome, the Jesuits were sophisticated patrons and promoters of their own saints yet the specific issues behind the imagery and types of decoration have yet to be explored by historians.

The last decorative project undertaken by the Jesuits at the close of the seventeenth century was a modest remodelling of a roadside chapel at La Storta (Cat. 140). This small chapel is where Ignatius, about to enter Rome in 1537 to establish the society permanently, had his famous vision of Christ carrying the Cross (Cat. 31). Christ's words to the saint, "Ego vobis Romae propitius ero," became a symbol for the Society's missionary work in Rome and the basis for Ignatius' choice of Jesus' name for the Society. Partly owing to its location on the Via Cassia near the crossroads of heavily travelled routes that brought travellers into Rome from the north, the chapel became an important devotional locus.[44]

Upon the request of the general of the Society, Thrysio Gonzalez, the chapel was completely renovated between November 1699 and

August 1700. It is likely that the restoration was initiated as an effort to promote the Society and the cult of the saint for the Jubilee Year. With the tomb of Ignatius just completed, the Jesuits called attention to one of his most important visions, one that occurred as the saint himself, like the pilgrims, approached the city.

Although the engraving representing the chapel at La Storta is but a modest image, it is a highly significant one. The urban expansion of the Society and the embellishment of its churches had reached its peak and the Jesuits had begun to embellish even the small roadside shrine. The redecoration of the chapel at La Storta, like the Gesù vault, celebrated the choice of the name Jesus for the Society, and like the corridor outside the rooms and the tomb of the saint it celebrated the visions that distinguished him from ordinary men. In the year 1700 the map of Rome was dotted with sites sacred to the Jesuits and this chapel outside the walls of Rome marked the first stop on the pilgrim's experience of Roma Ignaziana.

Notes

I would like to thank Jack Freiberg, Thomas DaCosta Kaufmann, Margaret Kuntz, Irving Lavin, and especially Steven F. Ostrow for their careful reading of earlier drafts of this essay. Their suggestions, many of which have been incorporated into the final version, are acknowledged with gratitude. My thanks also to P. Wiktor Gramatowski S.J., for invaluable assistance in the Archive (ARSI), to Priscilla Grazioli Medici, Director of the restoration of the Chapel of S. Ignazio, for graciously allowing me access to the chapel during the restoration, and to Thomas Lucas S.J. for opening innumerable doors to *Roma Ignaziana*.

1. The classic study is Galassi Paluzzi, 1951.

2. The notion of a Jesuit style was largely rejected by contributors to the volume, edited by R. Wittkower and I. Jaffe, *Baroque Art: The Jesuit Contribution*. New York, 1972. The problem has been recently reassessed by Bösel, 1989.

3. For an elevation of Tristano's Annunziata see Bösel, 1986, II, fig. 123; for a seventeenth-century plan of the earlier church of S. Andrea designed by G. Tristano, 1567-1568, see Pirri, 1955, tav. XVI.

4. The Annunziata, like numerous other Jesuit churches being built in this period received an impressive tabernacle made by Bartolomeo Tronchi, a Jesuit woodcarver. Pirri, 1952, pp. 4-10.

5. Lewine, 1967, pp. 24-26.

6. Ackerman, 1971, pp. 16, 18-19; Lewine, 1964.

7. Ackerman, 1971, pp. 17, 19-20, 23; Pirri, 1955, pp. 147, 228-229.

8. For a detailled analysis of the sixteenth-century interior of the Gesù see Kummer, 1986, pp. 185-227.

9. For example, the polychrome and gilded wooden ceiling in S. Giovanni in Laterano, attributed to Pirro Ligo-

rio (1562-1567). According to Lewine, richly decorated ceilings were traditional replacement ceilings in venerable churches in Rome and whether coffered or not their association with venerability was so strong that it determined their use in more than one new church of the late sixteenth century. Lewine, 1960, p. 61. Compelling evidence that the Jesuits viewed ceiling decorations in this way is provided by two slightly later examples: the "painted and gilded" ceiling in S. Apollinare (1588, see Cat. 117) and the decorations of the ceiling in S. Vitale (1597), "which, although not costly, render the church very beautiful *and worthy of respect*" (Cat. 118).

10. For Della Porta's design for the left transept see Ackerman, 1965 and for Maderno's design for the Rusticucci chapel in the right transept, characterized by Hibbard as the architect's "most highly ornamented" of a group of chapel designs from this period, see Hibbard, 1971, pp. 39, 61, fig. 3.

11. Specifically, to the week by week progression of devotional subjects built into the *Spiritual Exercises*. Hibbard, 1972; Herz, 1988a, pp. 65-67; New York, 1985, p. 172.

12. Herz, 1988a, p. 59, for dating of work on the house.

13. The Collegio Greco also founded by Gregory XIII in 1577 did not come under the exclusive control of the Jesuits until 1591.

14. Panciroli, 1600, p. 795.

15. Buser, 1976, p. 424.

16. Monssen, 1981, p. 134.

17. Herz, 1988a and 1988b.

18. Herz, 1988a, emphasized this point.

19. Zuccari, 1981a and 1981b.

20. Zuccari, 1981a and 1981b; Herz, 1988a.

21. On the transept chapels in the Gesù see Basile, 1922; for altarpieces in the Gesù see König-Nordhoff, 1982, pp. 76-91; for the private chapel of Odoardo Farnese in the Casa Professa, see Papi, 1988.

22. König-Nordhoff, 1982.

23. Haskell, 1972.

24. Connors, 1982, pp. 18-20. For a new analysis of the facade of S. Andrea al Quirinale, see Marder, forthcoming. I would like to thank the author for allowing me to read the manuscript of the article and for his advice and assistance on other problems in connection with this exhibition.

25. Wittkower, 1972, pp. 11-12 and Haskell, 1955.

26. There is a long tradition of attributing the invention of the frescoes to Bernini. See Enggass, 1964, pp. 52-53.

27. For a discussion of this particular illusionistic technique with reference to precedents in chapels designed by Bernini, see Lavin, 1980, pp. 43-44, 127-129.

28. Cortese's work for the Jesuit churches may have been limited by his lack of ability or desire to paint in fresco. In the Corridor next to Ignatius' rooms in the Casa Professa he painted in tempera directly on the wall and in the Cappella della Prima Primaria in oil, also directly on the wall. For Cortese's work in general

see Salvagnini, 1937; Rudolph, 1972; Holt, 1966 and 1969.

29. Baldinucci, 1975, p. 321.

30. Kerber, 1965, p. 500; Baldinucci, 1975, p. 323; Pascoli (1730), 1933, pp. 252-253.

31. The restoration of both Pozzo's corridor and the rooms of St. Ignatius in the Casa Professa will be discussed in a future publication by Thomas Lucas, S.J.

32. For Durazzo's contribution to the decoration see Banfi, 1959, p. 10. Antonio Baldinucci, son of the Florentine biographer and a novice at Sant'Andrea al Quirinale wrote to his father in April of 1693: "Since this father [Andrea Pozzo] is setting out to paint our church, we need much money and hope to raise it from this first volume. The second volume will be printed when there is money and when the church is painted." Goldberg, 1988, p. 179.

33. Pascoli (1730), 1933, p. 261. For the Algardi frieze see Montagu, 1986, II, pp. 456-457, fig. 109-111. There are regular payments to de Lattre for altarpieces in the six side chapels from November 1649 to July 1650. ARSI, F.G. 1343. The first two altars on the left still have the original paintings by de Lattre, who also executed the much more impressive cycle of visions and miracles of Ignatius in the sacristy around the same time. Galassi Paluzzi, 1926.

34. Wilberg Vignau, 1970, pp. 33-35, n. 5.

35. The Chapel of S. Ignazio is the subject of my doctoral dissertation, in preparation at Princeton University.

36. Trevisani, 1980.

37. ARSI, Rom 140, fol. 117v. For Pozzo's implicit criticism of the right transept chapel see the document quoted in Kerber, 1971, p. 142.

38. Kerber, 1965a; Enggass, 1976, I, p. 169.

39. The self-portrait was first noticed by Thomas Lucas, S.J. (oral communication).

40. ARSI, Rom 140, fol. 24r.

41. ARSI, Rom 140, fol. 116r-v. For a discussion of the significance of the marble encrusted chapel, revived in the late sixteenth century in Rome, see Ostrow, 1990.

42. For example, the model for the lapis columns in the Chapel of S. Ignazio was Bernini's sacrament tabernacle in S. Pietro in Vaticano.

43. Picinelli (1694), 1976, Liber 13, ch. 2, 8.

44. For the importance of the location see I. B. Barsali, "Le strade dei pellegrini," pp. 221-222, in Fagiolo and Madonna, eds., 1985b.

1. Anonymous, *St. Ignatius of Loyola*, Painted terracotta, 82 cm., mid-17th century
Rome, Church of the Gesù, Sacristy

This portrait bust of St. Ignatius is part of the rich decoration of the sacristy built for the Church of the Gesù by Cardinal Odoardo Farnese in the early seventeenth century. The bust has as its most important antecedents the various reworkings of the death mask of the saint which was cast on July 31, 1556, perhaps by Jacopino del Conte who made sketches at the deathbed. Ignatius himself never allowed his portrait to be painted during his years in Rome as General of the Society, so del Conte's 1556 portrait (in the collection of the General Curia of the Society of Jesus, Rome) and the death masks are of great importance for establishing his facial characteristics.

At least one of these masks has always been conserved in the Archives of the Society of Jesus which, at the time of the construction of the Sacristy, was located in the Casa Professa immediately adjoining the Church.

TL sj

FN III, pp. 240-241

2. Gerolamo da Verrazano, *World Map*, Illuminated parchment, 130 x 260 cm., Rome, 1529

Vatican City, Biblioteca Apostolica Vaticana, Borgiano I

The name of the author of this immense world map is written in the upper left: "Hyeronimus de Verrazano faciebat." Another inscription, placed in North America (*Verrazana* or New France which Giovanni da Verrazano, a Florentine, discovered five years ago by the order and command of the Most Christian King of France") allows a secure dating of 1529. Commissioned by Francis I the famous navigator Giovanni da Verrazano, brother of Gerolamo, set sail on January 17, 1524 from the island of Madeira and first sighted the New World on March 7, 1524, a year after Ignatius of Loyola had returned to his homeland from his pilgrimage in the Holy Land.

After having participated in his brother's second expedition to the New World in 1528, Gerolamo da Verrazano settled in Rome where he lived until 1537 and where he probably executed this map. Painted rather carelessly on parchment, this typical chart shows all the known world in 1529. In the upper center, a graphic scale is divided in 6 parts each equivalent to 200 miles. A large rose of 32 winds is found in Western Africa, and two other roses of 25 and 16 winds are scattered about the map; all show lines of direction.

The equator and the tropics are delineated in red and on the initial meridian of the "Isole Fortunate" or Canaries are indicated, degree by degree, the latitudes from 0° to 90° north and from 0° to 60 ° south. The indications for internal regions are few, but the coastal zones have abundant legends. Of particular interest is the rich toponymy of the Atlantic coast of the Americas, similar to other contemporary maps for the tract from the Strait of Magellan to Florida, but significantly different from Florida to Cape Breton. In this northern section, Gerolamo inserted all the locales discovered and christened by his brother Giovanni in the voyages of 1524 and 1528. The seas are decorated with drawings of ships.

This chart, like many others, is derived from an official Spanish marine chart or *Padrón Real* which was continually revised and updated by the cartographers of the "Casa de Contratación" in Seville, and used by pilots and navigators on oceanic voyages.

AD

ALMAGIÀ, 1944, pp. 53-55

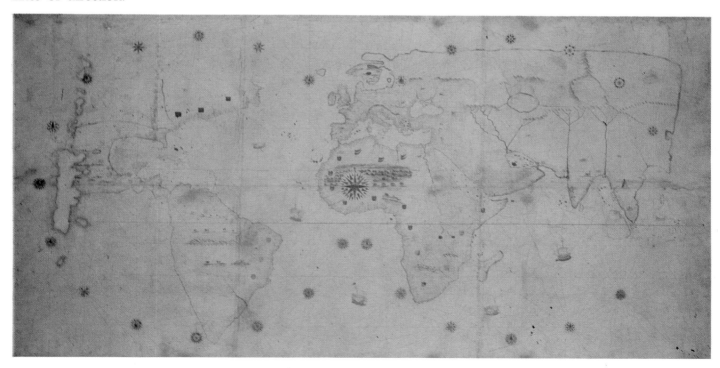

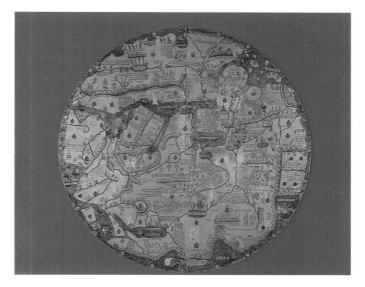

3. *Planisfero Borgiano*, Copper, diameter 63 cm., first half of the 15th century

Vatican City, Biblioteca Apostolica Vaticana, Borgiano XVI

In 1794, Cardinal Stefano Borgia acquired this important cartographic document for his museum in Velletri, a village in the hills of Lazio. This circular world map is engraved on two sheets of copper fastened together with small nails, and weighs about 10 kilograms. The engravings were filled with a black substance called *nigellum* or niello, a technique common in the repertory of Medieval goldsmithing. At some later time holes were drilled in the copper plates, probably in order to attach figures of kings or other decorative elements as was done on many Portuguese maps.

The map, duplicated in several copies by the Cardinal's nephew Camillo Borgia in 1797, is called the *Mappamondo Borgiano* or the *Tavola di Velletri*, and came to the Biblioteca Apostolica in 1902 from the *palazzo* of the Propaganda Fide together with the manuscripts of the Fondo Borgiano. Oriented with the south uppermost, it shows the world upside down, and is covered with legends engraved in gothic script.

The legends placed vertically in Asia Minor (modern day Turkey) allude to the so-called Battle of Angora in which Tamerlane defeated Bayazid I on July 20, 1402. This permits a secure dating after that event, while the interpretation of other inscriptions suggests that the work was executed around 1430.

As was common in Medieval cartography, the known world (Europe, Asia, and Africa) was shown surrounded by Ocean, which, together with the seas issuing from it and the lakes, are represented by wavy lines. Many and diverse types of boats plow the waters. The few rivers on the plan are delineated with thick lines, the mountain ranges with saw-toothed stripes, and inhabited areas with houses and towers.

The map is, moreover, richly decorated with animals, fantastic monsters, and vegetation. Expressive scenes of human life include the Moslem faithful praying at Mecca, an encampment with tents and wagons arrayed in a circle, and a battle between infantry and cavalry armed with bows and scimitars against cavalry armed with shields and lances.

Worked with great technical precision, this work nevertheless lacks refinement in the depiction of geographical forms. The rendering of the peninsulas of Europe, for example, is shapeless and haphazard. The sources of the map are multiple. Several elements suggest Isidore of Seville (Cat. 5), while others call to mind classical cosmology (Cat. 4), the Medieval belief in the legends of Gog and Magog, and contemporary or slightly antecedent historical events which predate only by a few decades the revolutionary geographical discoveries of the Renaissance. The work appears to be a copy with some annotations and amendments of some previous map rather than a creation of great originality.

AD

ALMAGIÀ, 1944, pp. 27-29

4. *Prospetto dell'Orbe Terracqueo*, Illuminated parchment in: Paulus Orosius, *Historia*, fol. 3v, 13th century
Vatican City, Biblioteca Apostolica Vaticana, Vat. Lat. 7318

5. *Orbis Terrae*, Illuminated parchment in: Isidore of Seville, *De Natura Rerum*, fol. 64v-65r, 8th-9th century
Vatican City, Biblioteca Apostolica Vaticana, Vat. Lat. 6018

6. *World maps*, in: Jacopo Filippo Foresti, *Supplementum Chronicarum*, pp. 3v-4r, Venice, 1503
Vatican City, Biblioteca Apostolica Vaticana, Stamp. Ross. 3030

The chart entitled *Prospetto dell'Orbe Terracqueo* found in a thirteenth-century manuscript of Paulus Orosius' *Historia* is a typical example of the family of so-called "T-O" maps that often appear in Medieval manuscripts (see p. 19). The cosmological chart is an extreme schematization, a reduction of the world into the highly charged symbolic forms of circle and cross. The plan is theological rather than geographical: its goal is the transmission of spiritual truths rather than the precise pinpointing of exact locations.

Jerusalem stands at the center of the map, at the very center of the world. For the Medieval crusader, as for Ignatius, Jerusalem was the goal of the pilgrim, the Holy City sanctified by the passion, death and resurrection of Christ. It is located at the intersection of the waters (the River Don, Black Sea, the River Nile and the Mediterranean) at the head of the *crux commissa* or Tau cross of the crucifixion. Thus, the cosmos, imprinted with the sign of salvation, was figured as the ordered reflection of the divine design, and terrestrial reality was understood as mirroring the supernatural reality of divine action in human history.

Early in the seventh century, Isidore of Seville's encyclopedic *De Natura Rerum* appeared in Visigothic Spain. An important figure that appeared in many of the early editions of the work is the *rota terrarum* or *orbis terrae*, a map that derives from the T-O models of antiquity.

The 8th-9th century world map found in Vat. Lat. 6018, is a particularly well-developed example of early Medieval cosmology. Jerusalem occupies the center of the field of vision, while Africa, Asia, and Europe surround a triangular Mediterranean dotted with islands. Lack of precise definition of coasts and land masses suggests that this map proposes historical and confessional arguments rather than attempting accurate geographical description. Ocean, the mysterious circle of waters surrounding the lands, is also sprinkled with distant islands—among them the Azores, the Canaries, and Ceylon—whose foreshortening suggests the spherical globe rather than a flat earth.

Fra Jacopo Filippo Foresti's 1503 encyclopedia, published seven Ignatius' brother Hernando disappeared in the Americas, shows the time lag between the discovery of the New World and the diffusion of the knowledge of that discovery. Indeed, the first printed map that indicated the New World was published only in 1508.

Bergomate presents two images that summarize two traditions of Medieval cartography: the T-O map and the zonal map, which was based on pythagorian principles of the division of the world into five *climata* or meteorological zones.

TL sj

Campbell, 1987, p. 2; Destombes, 1964, pp. 17, 30; Stevens, 1980, pp. 271-272; Woodward, 1985, p. 515

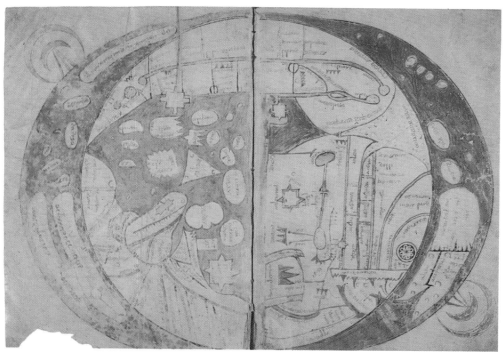

CAT. 5

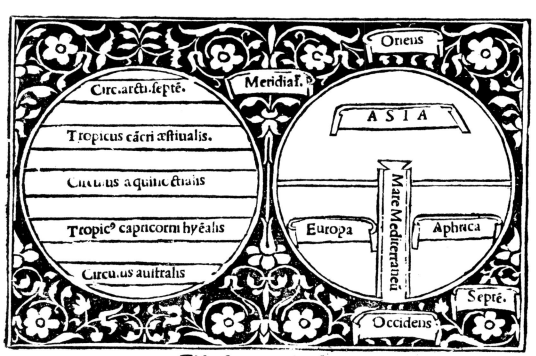

CAT. 6

7. Studio of Battista Agnese, *The Atlantic, Europe, Africa and the Americas,*
   Illuminated parchment, ca. 1542
Vatican City, Biblioteca Apostolica Vaticana, Barb. Lat. 4313, fol. 5

This map, contained in a codex whose front page reads "Tabulae nautice maris interni, et Oceani," shows a number of characteristics of the nautical maps of Agnese: the accuracy and the delicacy of the design (here of slightly inferior quality than in Cat. 9), the abundance of topographical nomenclature along the coasts and an almost total absence of the same in the interior sections, and the lack of decorative elements such as coats of arms, flags, animals, etc.

At the center of the map (which measures 19.5 x 29.5 cm.) at the point where the Ptolemaic meridian meets the equator, there is a rose of the 32 winds with direction lines in black, red, and light green. The meridian, along which the latitudes are marked in increments of 10°, extends beyond 60° north and south, while the equator, measuring longitude in gold lines, covers more than 90° east and west. At the lower right-hand corner is the scale: 100 miles from point to point ("mia 100 da punto a punto"). The coasts are shown in blue, the islands in gold or green, green being used as well for the coast of the Caspian Sea. The coasts of the New World are left incomplete. On the Pacific Ocean, we see only the outline of the coast of California down to the "prouincia de siera," while on the Atlantic side there is practically nothing from 60° north latitude to the Strait of Magellan in South America, with a strip of land to the south. The coasts of Europe are designed in summary fashion (note especially that Scotland is totally separate from England), whereas the Red Sea (in red) and Africa are shown in great detail, as is Arabia. The numerous coastal names are written in red or black. Finally, there is a striking forest in green, gold and brown in Brazil, the Andes in gold and brown, and the city of Timititan (Mexico City) amid a large blue lake located on this map north of the California peninsula.

AD

8. Studio of Battista Agnese, *Compass with Illuminated Rose of the Winds,* ca. 1542
Vatican City, Biblioteca Apostolica Vaticana, Barb. Lat. 4357, inside cover

At the center of a large rose of 32 winds, drawn on a sheet of parchment which covers the entire inside back cover of the binding of this book of charts is a small compass (see fig. p. 2).

This simple device, which relies on the north-seeking property of a magnetized needle, was known from ancient times. Understood by the Chinese from the fourth century A.D., it was perfected and disseminated by Amalfian sailors in the thirteenth and fourteenth centuries.

The magnetized needle, which in primitive compasses was placed on a small piece of wood floating in water, is in this case mounted on a pin inserted in the center of a cylindrical cavity hollowed in the thin wooden boards that support the binding of this nautical atlas. It is protected by a glass cover.

Although it is not signed, the volume can be attributed to the studio of Battista Agnese and dated ca. 1541-1542.

This collection of nautical charts, given by the Scottish ecclesiastic George Conn to Cardinal Francesco Barberini in the mid-seventeenth century, originally belonged to Henry VIII. Thus, it is natural that the names of the winds were written in English. It is however curious that a practical navigational device should appear in this, as in other volumes of the same atelier, destined for scholars, famous personages, and desk-bound students.

AD

ALMAGIÀ, pp. 68-69

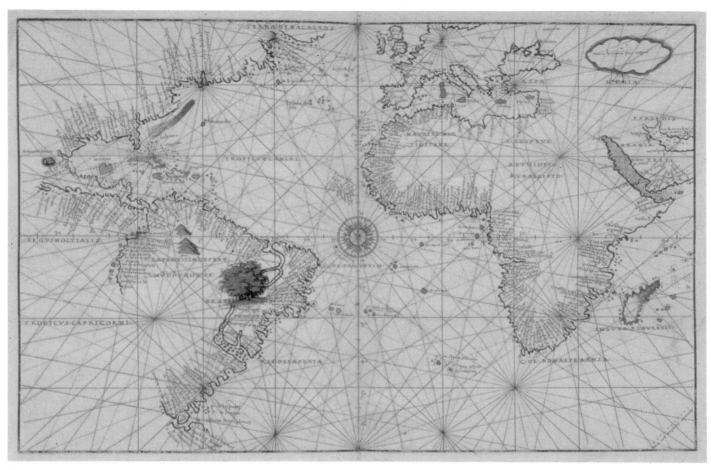

CAT. 7

9. Battista Agnese, *Oval World Map*, Illuminated parchment, 1542

Vatican City, Biblioteca Apostolica Vaticana, Pal. Lat. 1886, fol. 13

This world map is one of eleven colored plates which make up a nautical atlas made in Venice in 1542 by Battista Agnese. The work is identified by the inscription on a map of the Black Sea and the Sea of Marmara (fol. 11v-12r, upper left) which reads "baptista agnese Januesis fecit uenetiis 1542 die 28 Jun."

In Agnese's atlases, there is almost always an oval world map, one of the cartographer's most characteristic products. In this map, the oval is framed in a rectangle (19.5 x 29.3 cm.), traced with a thick black line. The refined color work typical of Agnese's maps is quite evident. The design is rendered in black ink, as are all the inscriptions; the equator, the Tropics, and the polar circles, however, are drawn in gold. Within the green continents, mountain ranges are rendered in brown and white or gold, a few watercourses in blue, and some inhabited locales are indicated by small red and gold houses. As can be noted from the drawing and from the very few legends, the author placed together Ptolemaic elements and data from new discoveries. In fact, while he was constrained by the older conventions for the areas around the Mediterranean (Black Sea and Sea of Azov), the African coasts and the southern parts of Asia ("Taprobana," Sumatra), he attempted to construct the still unknown areas of Asia and the Americas where, for example, he represented the peninsula of California with the "mar uermeio" highlighted with red lines like the Red Sea. Another noteworthy detail is the long and narrow peninsula "Terra Noua" which extends from Norway to the North Pole. The route of Magellan's circumnavigation, indicated in black with the inscription "per andar ale maluche" and "el tornar dale maluche" was a kind of trademark of the works of Agnese's studio; also indicated in gold is the route from Cadiz to Peru, "el uiazo de peru."

Twelve small multi-colored cherub heads accompany the names of the winds they represent.

AD

ALMAGIÀ, 1944, pp. 64-67

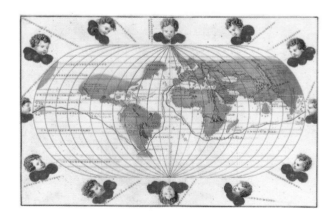

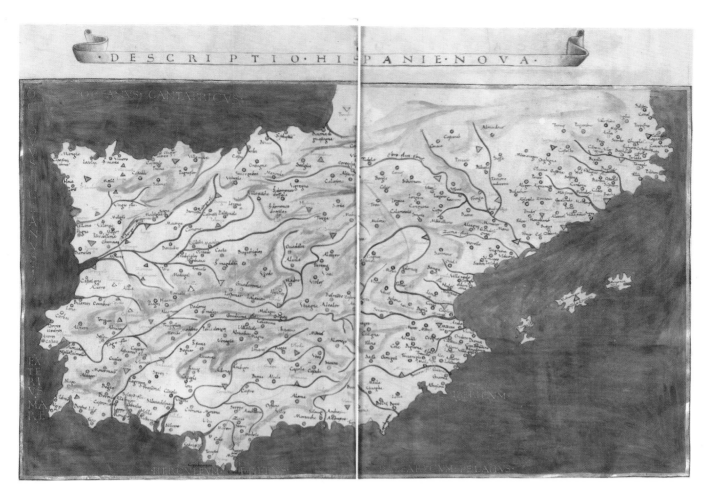

10. *Spagna*, Illuminated parchment in: Ptolemy, *Cosmologia Universalis*, fol. 123v-124r, 1472

Vatican City, Biblioteca Apostolica Vaticana, Urb. Lat. 277

This splendid large format atlas in illuminated parchment was realized in the studio of the Florentine bookmaker Vespasiano di Bisticci. It contains Jacopo Angeli da Scarperia's Latin translation of Claudius Ptolemy's celebrated geographical work, originally composed in Greek in the second century A.D.

The volume includes 27 Ptolemaic tables, 10 plans with bird's-eye views of the principal cities of the world, and 7 modern geographical charts.

The elegant text was prepared by a noted scribe, Ugo Comineaux (Comminelli in Italian) of Mezières, who also copied other important manuscripts including the famous "Bibbia Urbinate" (Urb. lat. 1-2) and another copy of Ptolemy (Vat. lat. 5699) in the BAV collections. The illuminations are the works of the finest artists of the age, including Attavante degli Attavanti, Francesco d'Antonio del Chierico and Francesco Rosselli.

The volume is dated on fol. 70r: "Florentie die quarta Januarii 1472." The codex is opened to fol. 123v-124r, where a map of Medieval Spain is painted with chorographic elements. It is generally attributed to Pietro del Massaio, who was responsible for its drawing but not its illumination. This map is of particular interest because, like the map of France in the same volume, it is among the very first modern maps of the region.

In the drawing the coasts are delineated with black ink; the sea and the rivers are rendered in violet, and the mountains in a yellow-sepia. Small circles indicate populated centers, while triangles denote the most important localities.

GM

ALMAGIÀ, 1944, pp. 99-100; *Die Cosmographia*, 1983; MORELLO, 1987, pp. 17-18; Vatican City, 1975, p. 75, n. 194; Vatican City, 1981, p. 27, n. 24

11. *Exercitia Militaria*, Engraving in: *Vita S. Ignatii Lojola*, fig. 4, Vienna, 1698
Rome, Biblioteca Institutum Historicum Societatis Iesu, 16 B 28

This small engraving is one of twenty-one images added to a revised edition of the 1609 *Vita B. Patris. Ignatii.* The engravings of 1698 are about fifty per- cent smaller and inferior in quality to the images of the 1609 edition. Many of the new engravings deal with miracles and wonders associated with the saint.

Figure 4 shows the young Iñigo training as a swordsman. Much of the early hagiographic writing about Ignatius over-emphasized his military background and training. He was often cast as a professional soldier or a career officer while, in fact, he was neither. The youngest son of thirteen children in a family of petty feudal nobility, three options were open to him: the church, the sea, or the court. One of his brothers, Pero López, chose the church. Hernando sailed for the New World in 1510, and Iñigo's eldest brother Juan Pérez commanded his own ship in the Spanish war against France for the control of Naples, where he died in 1496. Martín García who became the lord of Loyola after his father's death in 1507 fought for the Spanish throne from 1512 until the 1520s. Iñigo's other brothers Beltrán and Ochoa Pérez were also soldiers.

Around the time of his father's death, Iñigo was sent as a page to the house of Juan Velázquez de Cuéllar, the chief treasurer of the Royal Court. He remained there until de Cuéllar's death in 1517. During that ten year interval, he received his training as a "gentilhombre," and would have been in direct contact with the royal court on different occasions. He received training in arms, of course, and gave himself over to dreams of glory on the battlefield. He was also schooled in etiquette, music, and penmanship.

After the death of his patron, de Cuéllar, Iñigo received a pension of 500 ducats and two horses from his widow, as well as letters of recommendation to the Duke of Nájera Don Antonio Manrique de Lara, who was the Viceroy of Navarre. As a gentleman of court he acted as a messenger for the Viceroy and sometimes as a kind of sheriff or justice of the peace (*FN* I, p. 156). In 1521, he fought his last battle.

TL sj

§(IV.)§
Exercitia Militaria.

Dum vario armorum genere exercetur IGNATIUS,
Tenera in ætate illis præludit victorijs,
Quibus omnes orbis, & orci machinas
Aut elidet, aut cludet feliciter.
Imò jam tunc sibi ideam statuit,
Juxta quam conficiat scelera,
Et domesticos domabit hostes;
Ne internam quietem turbent.

DALMASES, pp. 12-38; *FN* I, pp. 153-56; TELLECHEA-IDÍGORAS, 1986, pp. 61-78

12. *The Battle of Pamplona*, Engraving in: *Vita Beati Patris Ignatii*, fig. 2, 1609

Florence, Biblioteca dell'Istituto Stensen, Armadio A

Introduction to the The *Vita Beati Patris Ignatii*

This early pictorial biography of Ignatius was published in 1609, most probably to coincide with his beatification on July 27 of the same year. It was reprinted in various editions at the time of his canonization in 1622.

Authorship of the 74 plates (72 scenes of the life of Ignatius, a title page, and a portrait of Ignatius) is an unresolved mystery. None of the plates are signed, nor are the publisher or place of publication indicated on the title page. Since the eighteenth century, the drawings for ten of the prints in the series (including fig. 64, Cat. 105) have been attributed to Rubens, who had spent the two years just prior to the publication of the *Vita* (1606-1608) working in Rome. The prints attributed to Rubens, with the exception of the title page, all fall in the last part of the book. Held speculates that Rubens contributed his drawings to a series already in preparation (Held, p. 125).

The prints are of varying quality and interest, but all show characteristics of the Flemish school. They have been most frequently attributed to J.B.Barbé or C. Galle (König-Nordhoff, pp. 294-304). The lack of a colophon and printed indication of the city of publication suggests that perhaps the plates were made in Antwerp, and then shipped to Rome for printing and distribution by the Jesuit generalate in conjunction with the beatification celebrations (Held, p. 126).

The series, because of its diffusion and early date, is an important milestone in the establishment of Jesuit iconography. In 1667, Jesuit artist Giacomo Cortese adapted the designs of thirteen of these prints in the tempera panels he painted in the corridor outside the rooms of St. Ignatius in the Roman Casa Professa.

TL sj

On May 20, 1521, Ignatius of Loyola in the service of the Spanish King was engaged in the defense of the citadel at Pamplona in Navarre against its French besiegers. Francis I of France had decided to support the claims of Henri d'Albret to the throne of Navarre which less than a decade before had been incorporated by the Spanish into the Kingdom of Castile. A large French army crossed the frontier in early May and camped near the city walls of Pamplona on May 12. Urgently requested Spanish reinforcements never came. The town capitulated. The small garrison, outnumbered more than two to one by the French forces, decided to quit the citadel. Ignatius, who had just arrived on the scene a few days earlier, refused out of a sense of honor to abandon the struggle. He entered the fortress at the head of a small band of defenders whom he had rallied to the cause. During an attack on the citadel, a cannon ball from a French gun shattered his right leg and damaged the left one. With Ignatius out of the fight, the defenders surrendered.

The wounds that Ignatius suffered were serious and the French chivalrously gave them emergency attention. Then some of his fellow countrymen carried him in a litter to the house of his older brother, the lord of Loyola. The first medical help had been given generously but also hastily and probably without much skill. As Ignatius tells us in his *Autobiography*, the bones "either because they had been badly set or because the jogging of the journey had displaced them, would not heal." The surgeons had to rebreak the bones and "again he went through this butchery, in which as in all the others that he suffered before or after, he uttered not a word nor showed any sign of pain other than the tight clenching of his fists" (*Autobiography*, no. 2).

JP sj

Autobiography, no. 2, 3; DALMASES, pp. 39-41

HELD, 1972; KÖNIG-NORDHOFF, 1982, pp. 294-304

13. *The Vision of St. Peter*, Engraving in: *Vita Beati Patris Ignatii*, fig. 3, 1609
Florence, Biblioteca dell'Istituto Stensen, Armadio A

14. *Scene of the Conversion*, Engraving in: *Vita Beati Patris Ignatii*, fig. 4, 1609
Florence, Biblioteca dell'Istituto Stensen, Armadio A

After the operation on his leg at the family home at Loyola and despite the care and prayers of his family, Ignatius' health declined steadily. So serious was his condition that the physicians in effect urged him to prepare for death by making his confession and receiving the sacraments of the sick. They were sure by June 28, the vigil of the feast of Saints Peter and Paul, that Ignatius would be at the end of his life if his condition did not change for the better within a day.

"As the sick man always cherished a special devotion to Saint Peter, it pleased God that by midnight he should take a turn for the better. So rapid was his initial recovery that within a few days he was declared to be out of danger of death" (*Autobiography*, no. 3). This remark was enough to foster the later tradition that on the vigil of the feast day St. Peter appeared to him and brought him back to health. Engravings such as the one displayed here and other such depictions of the convalescing soldier further popularized the tradition. Ribadeneira's *Life* of St. Ignatius did the same in saying: "And thus it is understood that this glorious apostle appeared to him on that same night of his greatest necessity" (Ribadeneira, *Vita*, I, i in *FN* IV, p. 85).

For a man as active as Ignatius had been all his life, the months of being bedridden must have been as arduous as battle. In order to get through that period of inactivity he thought of reading books of chivalry such as were popular at the time and which he had enjoyed in the household of the nobility that he had served. Somewhat surprisingly, there were no such books in the Loyola manor. The only available texts were the volumes of the *Golden Legend* by Jacobus de Voragine (Cat. 15) and the *Life of Christ* by Ludolph of Saxony (Cat. 16). Since there was no other material available, Ignatius the convalescent took up these books. The reading of them changed him forever.

In an alternation of pious thoughts and worldly dreams, in a growing desire to imitate the deeds of the saints who had followed Christ and about whom he read, Ignatius came step by step to a decisive

E cruris vulnere laboranti, mortiq, iam proximo. S. Petrus in sui peruigilij nocte per quietem apparet, ac sanitatem restituit.

3

resolution to change his life. At this point it was still a very simple and basic resolution. He would make a pilgrimage to Jerusalem where the Lord had died and he would imitate the examples of the saints in their austerities.

His resolutions were confirmed in what Ignatius described as a visitation. "Lying awake one night, he saw clearly the likeness of our Lady with the Holy Christ Jesus, and from this sight he drew for a considerable time very great consolation. Forthwith he felt too great a loathing for the whole of his past life, especially for the things of the flesh, that he seemed to be delivered there and then from all the imagery which had formerly occupied his mind" (*Autobiography*, no. 10).

JP sj

15. *Sts. Francis and Dominic,* Woodcut in: Jacobus de Voragine, *Legendario de sancti vulgare hystoriado,* p. 118, Venice, 1516

Vatican City, Biblioteca Apostolica Vaticana, R.G. Lett. Ital. II, 163

At Loyola in August, 1521, the still bedridden Ignatius asked for novels of chivalry to while away the time. "But," he tells us in his *Autobiography* (no. 5), "in that house none . . . could be found. So they gave him a life of Christ and a book of the lives of the saints in Castilian." Through that reading he was converted to intensive spiritual life.

The lives of the saints which he read were a Spanish translation of those in the still popular *Golden Legend* (*Legenda Aurea,* golden things to be read) of the Dominican Jacobus de Voragine (d. 1298). They were short, ten to twenty pages each, and arranged in the order of the saints' feasts in the liturgical year. In the Spanish translation a preface by the Cistercian Gauberto Vagad told of these "knights of God" and their resplendent deeds in the service of "the eternal prince" Christ Jesus whose banner they were following. Ignatius conceived a desire to do the same and was especially impressed by two, Francis and Dominic (shown here in a woodcut in the 1516 Italian edition).

"Our Lord assisted him . . . for in reading the life of Our Lord and of the saints, he stopped to think, reasoning within himself. . . 'St. Dominic did this, therefore I have to do it; St. Francis did this, therefore I have to do it'" (*Autobiography,* no. 7).

Sometimes, however, he let his thoughts wander for hours on worldly things such as the chivalrous deeds he would do as a knight to win the praise of a king or duke and ladies of the nobility. Then he noticed a difference. The worldly thoughts pleased him while present but afterwards left him dry and dissatisfied. The thoughts of holy exploits and sufferings for Christ consoled him while present and also left him satisfied and joyful afterwards. "Little by little he came to recognize the difference between the spirits that were stirring, one from the devil, the other from God" (*Autobiography,* no. 8).

Here his intimate friend Cámara, to whom he dictated his *Autobiography,* tells us in a marginal note: "This was his first reflection on the things of God; and later, when he composed the *Exercises,* this was his starting point in clarifying the matter of diversity of spirits." He gradually became a master of the art of discernment of spirits, and through his *Exercises* has taught thousands of others how to practice it.

GG sj

16. Ludolph of Saxony, *Vita Iesu Christi*, fol. a, r, Venice, 1507

Vatican City, Biblioteca Apostolica Vaticana, R.G. Vite III, 566

The Life of Christ which Ignatius used at Loyola was the *Vita Iesu Christi* by the Carthusian Ludolph of Saxony (ca. 1300-1377). This classic of devotional literature was a profound book of 1,000 pages containing the best scholarship of the era in Scripture, theology, patrology, and devotional writings. It appeared between 1360 and 1377 and circulated first in many manuscripts. After the first printed edition appeared in 1472, numerous editions were published in French, Italian, Dutch, German, Bohemian, Catalan, and Spanish.

Its introduction presents methods for contemplating events in Christ's life, and its 181 chapters present the Savior's whole life in a manner intended to stir up love and imitation of him. Ludolph presents in sequence the divine generation of the Word in eternity (ch. 1), God's plan for the redemption of the fallen human race (ch. 2), the Annunciation (ch. 5), Nativity (ch. 9), and Hidden Life (ch. 16). Then come 127 chapters on events in his Public Life, 18 on the Passion, 12 on the Risen Life, 1 on praise of God, and 1 on heavenly glory. Thus his book took in God's whole plan for the salvation and redemption of human beings, all that St. Paul called "the mystery of Christ" (Ephesians 3:4-12).

Through Ignatius' prayerful reflections on what he read, Ludolph's presentations profoundly influenced the formation of his spiritual world view. He transcribed many passages into a copybook of nearly 300 pages and took it with him in early 1522 to Manresa, where he derived much consolation from it. There, after his extraordinary mystical illuminations, he began to write his *Spiritual Exercises*.

The same sequence of Ludolph's *Vita* reappeared as the topics of the *Exercises*. In their central core are meditations on God's purpose in creating, the history of sin, the Incarnation, Nativity, Hidden Life, Public Life, Passion, and Risen Life; and in his fifty-one Mysteries of the Life of Christ (261-312), virtually all are in the same sequence which Ludolph used. Hence Ignatius' *Exercises* and whole spirituality are applications of God's plan of creation and salvation for human beings.

For example, in chapter 1, no. 9 Ludolph wrote: "The Son . . . is the highest Wisdom, '*through whom [God] created the Universe* ' (Heb. 1:1), and once it was created, he . . . orders it to his own glory, . . . so that he leaves nothing in this world which is not thus ordered." This and similar passages of Ludolph may well be the source of many characteristics of Ignatius' later *Spiritual Exercises* (23), and his spirituality in general. He wanted all human persons to order their lives to the glory or praise of God. That will become the very purpose of his *Exercises* (21). Concern for the glory of God became his chief motivating ideal, and "the greater glory of God" became his norm for making decisions. He conceived his zeal for God's glory already at Loyola. God, states Ignatius' companion Nadal, "called Father Master Ignatius during his illness, and above all led him to desire, with great devotion, the greater honor and glory of his Divine Majesty" (*FN* I, p. 305).

GG sj

17. *The Vigil at Montserrat*, Engraving in: *Vita Beati Patris Ignatii*, fig. 11, 1609
Florence, Biblioteca dell'Istituto Stensen, Armadio A

18. *Iñigo gives his clothes to a beggar*, Engraving in: *Vita Beati Patris Ignatii*, fig. 10, 1609
Florence, Biblioteca dell'Istituto Stensen, Armadio A

In Æde Montis Serrati tamquam nouus
Christi eques noctem vnam ante aram
Virginis excubat, humanæque arma
militiæ e tholo suspendit.
11

Vestibus pretiosis exutus, ac pauperi
donatis, sacco ac fune præcinctus
Christi domini paupertatem amplectitur.
10

Montserrat, the celebrated mountain near Barcelona, was a very popular place of pilgrimage in the time of Ignatius. The Benedictine monastery there was founded in the eleventh century, but it is surrounded by legends which go much farther back. One such legend located there the ancient castle of the Holy Grail. It is most famous for the "Black Virgin," an image of Our Lady of Montserrat, and for the research carried on by its monks on Catalonian history and culture. Ignatius arrived there, the goal of his first pilgrimage, around March 21, 1522.

In the custom of knights entering into service, described in books of chivalry, he intended to keep a night vigil of arms, giving up his earthly sword as he clothed himself for what he now saw as spiritual combat. Before the vigil, he decided to cleanse himself of sin by a general confession. A French Benedictine, Jean Chanon, received that confession which Ignatius set down in writing and on which he spent three days. It is quite likely that at that time Chanon made available to Ignatius a confession manual such as was commonly used at the time and the small book, *Exercises for the Spiritual Life* written by one of the monk reformers of the abbey, García de Cisneros.

On the eve of the Annunciation, March 25, Ignatius hung up his sword at the altar of the Black

Virgin and, dressed in his pilgrim tunic and rope sandals, engaged in his vigil of arms praying throughout the whole night.

After his vigil, Ignatius, now at the rugged mountain Montserrat, near Barcelona, sought out a beggar in rags. To the astonishment of that man Ignatius gave to him his own expensive garments and put on a pilgrim's tunic of hemp and rope-soled sandals which he had bought, both in the interest of following the poor Jesus and of not making himself noticed by his fine clothes.

Ignatius departed for Montserrat from the family home at Loyola at the end of February 1522, despite the urging of his brother that he carry on his course to the influential career he was surely going to have. After some time at the shrine of the Blessed Virgin at Aranzazu, he went to Navarrete to pay his respects to his old patron, the Duke of Najera. On the way from there to Montserrat, he thought of the great deeds, all external, that he would accomplish in the service of God. How naive Ignatius still was is shown by one such deed that seemed to present itself directly. He encountered a Moor with whom he discussed the virginity of our Lady. The Moor was willing to admit this prerogative before Christ's birth but could not grant it for the birthing itself. After the Moor had gone his own way at a fork in the road, Ignatius thought to himself that he had not sufficiently defended Mary's virginity. He thereupon proposed to himself to "go in search of the Moor and give him a few stabs of his dagger because of what he had said" (*Autobiography*, no. 15). In doubt about what to do, he allowed his mule free rein to take the fork in the road to or from the Moor's direction. Fortunately, the animal chose the latter and Ignatius with clear conscience went on to Montserrat. The incident exemplifies well the naiveté with which Ignatius as yet thought of the following of Christ. So does the exchange of clothes with the beggar, with Ignatius thinking only of following as a pilgrim in poor garments, the poor Christ of the Gospels. It was left to the beggar to explain to the suspicious authorities that he had not robbed the pilgrim of those rich clothes. Fortunately for the poor man, Ignatius could corroborate the story.

JP sj

19. *The Vision at the Cardoner*, Engraving in: *Vita Beati Patris Ignatii*, fig. 20, 1609
Florence, Biblioteca dell'Istituto Stensen, Armadio A

From Montserrat Ignatius went down the mountain to the nearby small town of Manresa "to stay for a few days . . . and also to write some things in the copybook" (*Autobiography*, no. 18), in which he had written passages from Ludolph's *Life of Christ* and Jacobus' *Golden Legend*. He stayed eleven months and his experiences there started him on the composition of the *Spiritual Exercises*. His first residence was a hospital for the poor and sick but he most regularly stayed at the Dominican friary, except when he went for periods of prayer to a hillside cave near the Cardoner river. Ignatius lived in Manresa as a poor pilgrim, at first totally neglectful of his external appearance and engaged in fearful austerities, but later more presentable and more moderate for the sake of his work of charity for the poor and sick and his apostolate of conversing with people about spiritual matters.

His first months were a period of inner tranquillity and joy, "without, however, any clear knowledge of interior, spiritual things" (*Autobiography*, no. 20). In the second period of his stay he was almost overwhelmed with scruples and depression, and at times suicidal impulses. The last third of those months was a time of extraordinary graces, divine enlightenment and interior understanding. It was then that the Spiritual Exercises began to take shape.

Two such extraordinary experiences he recounted vividly. The first took place one day on the steps of the Dominican Church "when his understanding began to be elevated so that, as it were, he saw the Most Holy Trinity . . . and that with so many tears and sobs that he could not control himself" (*Autobiography*, no. 28). The second such experience took place on the banks of the Cardoner. "He sat down for a while with his face toward the river,

which there ran deep. As he sat there the eyes of his understanding began to open. It was not that he saw some vision, but he understood and knew many things . . . This was accompanied by an enlightenment so that everything appeared to him to be new. . . This was such that in the whole course of his life, through sixty-two years, if he gathered together all the helps he had received from God and all the things he had known, and added them together, he does not think that he received as much as he did on that one occasion" (*Autobiography*, no. 30).

JP sj

20. Willem Blaeu, *World Globe*, Papier-mâché, wood, brass, 1622 (?)
Vatican City, Musei della Biblioteca Apostolica Vaticana, Inv. 10157-10157 A

This globe is one of the largest fabricated in the Amsterdam studio of Willem Blaeu, a Dutch student of the astronomer Tycho Brahe. The oldest known celestial globe of Blaeu dates to 1599. His first terrestrial globe dates to 1599, and is 33.7 cm. in diameter. In 1603 he made a celestial globe of the same dimensions. From this point on, paired celestial and terrestrial globes were designed, engraved and printed in Blaeu's printing shop, and, even when produced in different years, were distributed together. Competition with rival engraver Joost d'Hondt (Jodocus Hondius) whose 1613 globes measured more than 55 cm. in diameter induced Blaeu to make larger models. Thus, in 1616 the Dutch cosmographer made a celestial globe measuring 67.6 cm. and in 1622, he produced a terrestrial globe of the same measure. These models enjoyed such wide success that they were repeatedly reprinted with changing dedications and legends.

Our globe of papier-mâché (68.2 cm. in diameter) is hollow, and covered with a thin layer of gesso on which 18 printed strips and 2 printed caps are glued. The strips, cut in half at the level of the equator and ending at 70° latitude north and south, are joined together with the sheets denoting the polar caps.

The meridian circle with the division in degrees through which the axis of rotation is fixed is brass, and the circle of the horizon on which is glued a strip of paper with the signs of the zodiac, the calendar, and the names of the winds is of black wood, as is the rest of the base which supports it. The base consists of four columns which are attached with two cross axes which support a circular compass.

The name of the author "Guiliemus Blaeu" is legible at the end of the dedication and in the note to the reader, both inscribed in architectural decorative motives placed in the southern hemisphere. The year of the printing, however (at the end of the note to the reader), is illegible except for the first number, but the dedication to Maurice Count of Nassau (†1625) suggests that this is the original edition of 1622.

The line of the ecliptic is divided into degrees, the equator is marked with the degrees of longitude, and the tropics and the polar circles are drawn with a double line like the first meridian with the degrees of latitude which passes through Tenerife in the Canary Islands.

There are two roses of the winds with directional lines that circle the globe: one, in the Pacific with the Latin names, and the other, in the Atlantic, with the names in Dutch.

The seas and lakes are painted in a dark blue which is not uniform, and which, in some cases, impedes reading the legends. The continents are painted brown, and houses in the inhabited regions are in red.

Diverse scenes of debarkations dot the seas, which are also decorated with dolphins, flying fish, sea horses, and mythological figures. The interiors of Africa, Asia, and the Americas show native populations, animals, and plants as well as mountain ranges.

The design of the coasts is quite precise for the areas recently discovered: for example, Tierra del Fuego is shown detached from the presumed "Terra Australe." The rendering of less explored zones like the northern Atlantic and Pacific coasts of North America remains more uncertain.

The toponomastic nomenclature is very rich for Europe and central Asia, less so for the other continents, where the focus is primarily on the coasts.

Among the many legends written on the globe are discussions of the numerous attempts to discover a northwestern passage from Europe to Asia, and other notes describing recent geographical discoveries.

AD

LUZIO, 1957, pp. 1-4, 29-40, 47

21. E. Rosselet after J. Stella, *Exercitia Spiritualia S. P. Ignatii*, Engraved frontispiece, Paris, 1644

Vatican City, Biblioteca Apostolica Vaticana, R.G. Vite I, 45

This engraving shows Ignatius in pilgrim garb at Manresa near the River Cardoner. His right leg is shown still bandaged from the wound he had suffered at the Battle of Pamplona more than a year before. In fact, he walked with a slight limp for the rest of his life.

The figure of the Madonna inspiring Ignatius as he began to sketch out the notes which would evolve into the text of the *Spiritual Exercises* is frequently represented. It probably derives from an account of a vision of the Madonna he had at Manresa, and the prominent role which the Virgin Mary plays in the "long retreat," the month-long course of the complete Spiritual Exercises (*Autobiography*, 30).

The text of the *Spiritual Exercises* is not, in itself, a work of literature. Rather, it is a guide book or manual for the person directing the "retreatant" through four "weeks" of meditations and contemplations on the life of Christ. These varied periods and forms of prayer — as many as five per day — aim to conform the retreatant's life to the pattern of the generous life of Christ. The goal of this dynamic process is to enable the retreatant to make a serious decision freed from all attachments to worldly goods, power, or prestige.

Ignatius' own experience of silence, fasting, meditation, and contemplation were the raw materials from which he constructed the durable yet flexible framework of the Exercises, which remain today the central contribution of the Society of Jesus to the spirituality of the Western Church.

TL sj

22. Manuscript edition of the *Spiritual Exercises* with autograph corrections by St. Ignatius, fol. 6v-7r, ca. 1544

Rome, Archivium Romanum Societatis Iesu, Exercitia I

The writings which eventually became St. Ignatius' *Spiritual Exercises* were begun in 1522 at Manresa, shortly after he experienced his extraordinary mystical illuminations. They initially took the form of personal notes which served as aids in his spiritual conversations with others whom he was helping to perform exercises of piety. When he left Manresa he had completed the substance of the *Exercises.* As his experience in giving them grew he added to and revised his notes until 1539. Twenty-five years after their first formulation, he permitted them to be published as the small book which appeared in 1548.

Meanwhile various handwritten copies had been made. To meet the needs of non-Spanish exercitants, a translation into scholastic Latin (designated *P* or *Versio Prima)* was made in Paris between 1528 and 1535, probably by Ignatius himself. Around 1546 a translation into stylistic Latin (later called *V* or *Vulgata)* was made for submission to Pope Paul III, who approved both *P* and *V*. The Latin text *V* was published in 1548 and the Spanish *A* in 1615.

At some time around 1544, Ignatius ordered a scribe to make a new copy of his own latest Spanish text. He used this new copy of 63 folios until his death. On it he wrote in his own hand thirty-two small emendations or additions. For this reason it is called the *Autograph* text, or *A*. This is the precious manuscript displayed here.

Most scholars believe that this autograph text best presents his authentic thought, with the precisions and shadings of his terse, closely-reasoned style.

The *Spiritual Exercises* is the best-known of Ignatius' writings. It contains the heart of his spiritual outlook and most quickly conveys to us the synthesis of his principles and their inspirational force.

It was through the *Exercises* that Ignatius exerted most widely a direct influence upon individuals. During his own lifetime he gave these Exercises continually. By means of them he won and trained the first followers with whom he founded the Society of Jesus, and taught them to carry on this apostolate. Since his day all Jesuit novices have made them for the full thirty days. Probably for most, no other element in their training was more effective in forming their spiritual outlook and apostolic work. According to one plausible estimate worked out in 1948, by then the *Exercises* had been published, either alone or with commentaries, some 4,500 times—an average of once a month for four centuries—and the number of copies printed was around 4,500,000 (*Obras*, p. 225).

The left hand page exhibits the "Principle and Foundation," the long admired starting point of the *Exercises* and synthesis of their principles. Of it the expert Luis de la Palma († 1626) aptly wrote: "It is called a *principle* because in it are contained all the conclusions which are later explained and specifically expounded; and it is called a *foundation* because it is the support of the whole edifice of the spiritual life."

GG sj

Obras, p. 225

TErtium; ad gratiam petendam illud erit, vt poſcamus exploratas habere fraudes mali ducis, inuocata ſimul diuina ope, ad eas vitandas: veri autem, optimiꝗ́ Imperatoris Chriſti, agnoſcere mores ingenuos, ac per gratiam imitari poſſe.

PVnctum primum eſt, imaginari coram oculis meis, apud Campum Babylonicum, Ducem impiorum in cathedra ignea, et fumoſa, ſedere, horribilem figura, vultuꝗ́ terribilem.

SEcundum eſt aduertere, quomodo conuocatos dæmones innumeros per totum orbem ſpargit ad nocendum: nullis Ciuitatibus, et locis, nullis perſonarum generibus, immunibus relictis.

TErtium, attendere cuiuſmodi concionem ha-

beat, ad miniſtros ſuos, quos inſtigat, vt correptis, iniectisꝗ́ laqueis, et catenis, homines primùm trahant (quod ferè contingit) ad cupiditatem diuitiarum, vnde poſtea facilius in mundani honoris ambitionem, ac demum in ſuperbiæ barathrum deturbari queant.

Atꝗ ita tres ſunt præcipui tentationum gradus, in diuitijs, honoribus et ſuperbia fundati, ex quibus in alia vitiorum genera omnia, præceps fit decurſus.

Similiter ex oppoſito, conſiderandus eſt, ſummus optimusꝗ́ noſter Dux, & Imperator Chriſtus.

PVnctum primum erit conſpicari Chriſtum, in amæno campo iuxta Hieroſolymam, humili quidem conſtitutum loco, ſed valde ſpecioſum forma, & aſpectu ſummè amabilem.

23. St. Ignatius of Loyola, *Exercitia Spiritualia*, pp. 47-48, Rome, 1548
Vatican City, Biblioteca Apostolica Vaticana, Rossiano 7229

Shown in their first printed edition of 1548, the *Spiritual Exercises* that Ignatius proposes for those seeking to make or confirm an important decision are a framework of guided meditations that call upon visual imagination more than abstract reasoning or linear thought.

The retreatant begins each major exercise with a "composition of place," a framing or visualization of the scriptural scene or context to be contemplated. Each day ends with an "application of the senses" wherein the insights, graces, and fruits of the day's exercises are seen, tasted, touched or felt rather than analyzed.

One of the central exercises of the whole month-long dynamic is the Meditation on the Two Standards that stands at the crucial hinge point early in the "Second Week" of contemplation of the life of Christ. In the composition of place the retreatant is called to imagine and "see a great plain, comprising the whole region about Jerusalem, where the sovereign Commander in Chief of all the good is Christ the Lord; and another plain about the region of Babylon, where the chief of the enemy is Lucifer...Imagine you see the chief of all the enemy, seated on a great throne of fire...consider how he summons innumerable demons, and scatters them some to one city and some to another, throughout the world, consider the address he makes, how he goads them to lay snares for men...then consider Christ our Lord, standing in a lowly place in a great plain about the region of Jerusalem: his appearance beautiful and attractive. Consider how the Lord of all the world chooses disciples and sends them throughout the world, consider the address our Lord makes to all his friends whom he sends..." (*Sp.Ex*, 38-40)

Rich with overtones of Ignatius' upbringing in a world of feudal relationships, the Meditation of the Two Standards proposes the cities of Jerusalem and Babylon as icons of the tension between the City of God and the City of Man, emblems of the division of the human heart.

TL sj

24. Willem Blaeu, *Nova et accurata totius Europae tabula*, Engraved map with modern overlay showing the journeys of St. Ignatius, 114.5 x 155 cm., 1644

Vatican City, Biblioteca Apostolica Vaticana, St. Geogr. I, 380

To a degree unusual for a man of his epoch, Ignatius of Loyola was a serious traveller. By the time he reached Rome in 1537 he had seen or lived in most of the important cities of Europe.

Although documentary evidence is slight, it can be inferred that Iñigo at least sometimes travelled as a page with his protector the Royal Treasurer, Don Juan Velázquez de Cuéllar, as he followed the peripatetic court of Ferdinand and Germaine de Foix.

After his conversion and the experience of Manresa, Iñigo made the long and perilous sea voyage from Barcelona to Jerusalem in 1523, stopping in Rome to receive a safe conduct from Hadrian VII. Departing from and returning to Italy via Venice, his return to Spain took him through Padua, Ferrara, Parma, and Genoa. During his student years, he visited most of the important cities of Spain and France, and his begging journeys took him to Flanders and London.

Having completed his studies in 1535, he returned to his native Spain to settle his family affairs. He departed from Valencia in 1535, and journeyed to Genoa and Bologna before meeting with his companions in Venice early in 1537. While the other companions preached and taught in the cities of northern Italy, Ignatius, along with Pierre Favre and Diego Lainez, made the final leg of his pilgrim journey as he travelled on foot to Rome via Bologna and Siena in the fall of 1537.

Once in Rome, Ignatius found his missionary field in the streets and churches of the Eternal City. He left the city only very rarely, and for very short journeys in central Italy, in the years before this death in 1556.

TL sj

RAVIER, 1973, pp. 14-15, 29-41

25. *Paris*, Woodcut in: Sebastiano Münster, *Cosmographia Universalis*, pp. 88-89, Basel, 1550

Vatican City, Biblioteca Apostolica Vaticana, R. I., II, 910

On February 2, 1528, Iñigo entered Paris by the Porte Saint Jacques. The city numbered more than 300,000 inhabitants, making it the largest urban population in Europe at the time. Among those inhabitants were more than 4,000 students who were lodged in more than fifty colleges of the University. The University occupied the "Latin Quarter," named for the universal language of scholarly work at the time. The four faculties of the University were theology, law, medicine, and philosophy. Densely populated and in uneasy rapport with the civil government, the university community gave the city a decided international flavor. The largest division, the faculty of philosophy or arts, was divided into four "nations:" Gallic, Picard, Norman and German (which included English and Scottish students). The Gallic "nation" was divided into five provinces, Paris,

Tours, Reims, Sens, and Bourges. Students from Spain, Portugal, Italy, and the eastern Mediterranean were considered part of the province of Bourges.

In spite of its large population, the area of the city was quite restricted: one could walk the circuit of the walls in about three hours. Only a few minutes walk from Ignatius' College Sainte-Barbe was the great convent of the Jacobins (Dominicans), located at the Porte Saint-Jacques, and the Franciscan's center at Les Cordeliers on the city wall near Saint-Germain-des-Prés. Just to the east in the Fauberg Saint-Germain was the "Pré-aux-Clercs," a field for student sports and recreations

TL sj

SCHURHAMMER, 1973, pp. 77-95

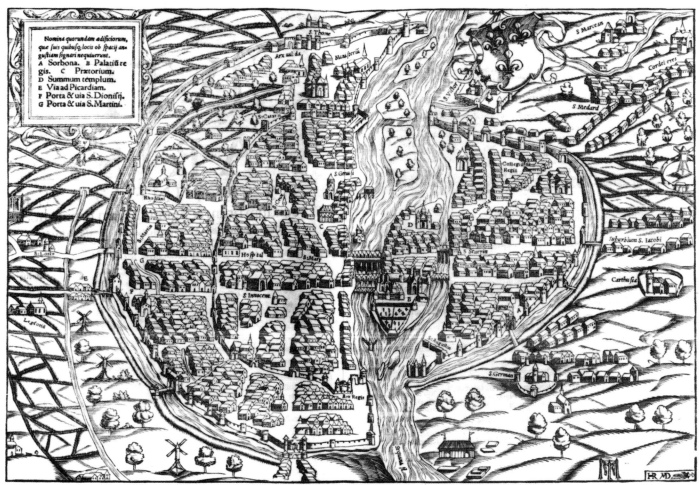

CAT. 25

26. *Diploma of St. Ignatius with the Seal of the University of Paris,* "March 14, 1534"
Rome, Archivium Romanum Societatis Iesu, Epp. NN. 89, 12 (diploma); 89/a, 2 (seal)

The diploma shown here is the fruit of and testimony to Ignatius' seven years (from February 1528 to April 1535) of study at the University of Paris. When he arrived in Paris, he was in his thirty-seventh year. He knew that he had made too little progress in his earlier studies at Barcelona, Alcalá and Salamanca, often because his apostolic activities had interfered. Now he deliberately chose to experience the orderly progress of the "method of Paris."

First he attended for a year and a half the strict and almost archaic College of Montaigu, to improve his knowledge of Latin. He lived in poverty, having to go on begging tours to Flanders, and once to England, during his school vacations. He also gave the Spiritual Exercises to several Spanish students. In the fall of 1529 he entered the College of Sainte-Barbe for the course in the faculty of arts, or philosophy. By and large Ignatius kept his apostolic desires under control in the interest of serious study. But here at Sainte-Barbe he met as fellow boarders the two men who were to be the first of his permament companions, Pierre Favre and Francis Xavier.

In January, 1533 Ignatius received the degree of bachelor of arts. After a further year of study of philosophy he took the two-part examination for the licentiate in arts and passed thirtieth in rank out of one hundred candidates. On March 13, 1533 he received the university license to teach anywhere in the world. The ceremonies cost the candidates a large amount of money for fees and especially for the banquet that the new graduate had to give for his masters and fellow students. Ignatius ran out of money and had to rely on the continuing generosity of friends in Barcelona.

Next came the degree of Master of Arts, in modern terms equivalent to the doctorate. This was even more expensive in the conferral, so Ignatius delayed the reception of that degree for two years. Meanwhile he studied theology with the Dominicans at the College of St. Jacques. With the Master's degree on March 14, 1535 (modern reckoning), Ignatius' name was put on the roll of professors of the University of Paris ("Master Ignatius of Loyola, of the diocese of Pamplona"). Henceforth he could be termed "Master Ignatius," the name by which, as a matter of fact, he was usually called in the future.

JP sj

DALMASES, pp. 106-117

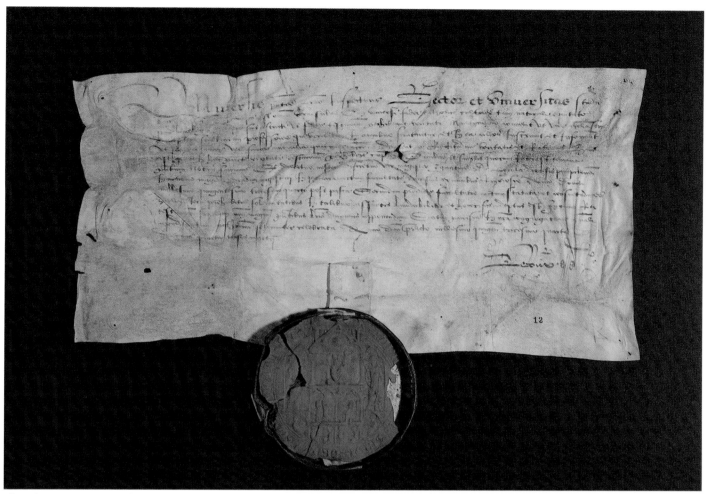

27. *St. Ignatius and his first companions in Paris*, Engraving in: *Vita Beati Patris Ignatii*, fig. 39, 1609

Florence, Biblioteca dell'Istituto Stensen, Armadio A

While in Paris Ignatius met many students, engaged them in conversation on spiritual subjects, and gathered them on Sundays at the Carthusian convent (near what are now the Luxembourg Gardens). In Paris, between 1529 and 1534, he met and won to the following of Christ six men who were to be his first permanent companions.

In 1529, when Ignatius entered the College Sainte-Barbe, he met as his roommates Pierre Favre from Savoy and Francis Xavier from Navarre. Favre was the first to decide explicitly , in the spring of 1531, to join Ignatius. By 1533 Francis Xavier and a young Portuguese, Simão Rodrigues, had also become

companions of Ignatius. Xavier, who by that time was a teacher at the University, was the recruit most difficult to gain. Next came Diego Lainez and Alfonso Salmerón who came from Alcalá to Paris late that same year to continue their studies. At Alcalá they had heard favorable stories about Ignatius, soon met him in Paris and decided to join him. The last of these first seven "friends in the Lord" was Nicholas Bobadilla, also a Spaniard. At the beginning of 1534 Ignatius gave the Spiritual Exercises for a whole month to Favre, who was ordained in May of that year. Later in the spring Lainez and Salmerón and finally Rodrigues and Bobadilla made the Exercises. Xavier only made them later, in September, 1534. "Through prayer [they] had resolved to serve our Lord, leaving behind all worldly things" (*FN* I, p. 100).

Iuuenes ex Academia Parisiensi nouem elegit, ac socios consilij sui destinat.

39

The engraving shown here portrays ten persons, including Ignatius who "chooses nine young men from the University of Paris and makes them companions in his plans." In one sense the engraving is historically inaccurate; in another it is true to what ultimately happened. In Paris between 1529 and 1534 Ignatius and the six other men noted here personally joined themselves to each other. But in April, 1535, Ignatius left Paris to return to Spain to regain his health and to take care of personal and business affairs for himself and his new companions. They all planned to meet again in Venice to embark for Jerusalem. During that interval from 1535 to 1537 the companions who remained in Paris themselves gained three new recruits, a Savoyard priest Claude Jay, a priest from Picardy, Paschase Broët, and Jean Codure from Provence. These nine men together with Ignatius were the first Jesuits, the "first fathers" whose deliberations in Rome produced the Society of Jesus.

JP sj

EppIg. I, p.12; *FN* I, p. 100

28. *The Vows of Montmartre*, Engraving in: *Vita Beati Patris Ignatii*, fig. 41, 1609

Florence, Biblioteca dell'Istituto Stensen, Armadio A

As their studies neared an end in Paris, Ignatius and his companions decided to formalize their relationship with a promise or vow. On August 15, 1534, they gathered in a small chapel of the Virgin Mary on Montmartre and there the seven companions promised to live an apostolic life of service in poverty. They moreover promised to meet in Venice the following year and embark on pilgrimage to Jerusalem.

The exact text of the vow does not exist, so it is impossible to determine whether or not the companions intended to remain in Jerusalem or to return to Europe. What is clear is that they understood the political exigencies of the moment. War between the Turks and Venice often made travel in the eastern Mediterranean impossible. Because of this reality, they included a codicile in their vow which stipulated that if, after a year's wait the pilgrimage were impossible, they would go to Rome and put themselves at the disposal of the Pope. This promise is the foundation of the Society's special vow of obedience to the pope as regards "the missions." Favre called this vow the *fundamentum*, the foundation stone of the whole Society (*FN* I, p. 42).

The vow at Montmartre was not the formal beginning of the Society of Jesus as a religious order or institute. It was, rather, a promise of shared apostolic work and collaboration within the hierarchical church. Thus, it marks an important landmark in the companions' pilgrimage which would lead to the formal approbation of the Society of Jesus in 1540.

TL sj

In æde suburbana B Virginis ipse, ac socij certo se voto obstringunt diuinam vbique gloriam, animarűq salutem in Hierosolymitana præsertim expeditione procurandi, ac palmam inde martyrij sedulo conquirendi, quod votum ibidem quotannis renouant.

DALMASES, pp. 120-122; *FN* I, pp. 36-39, 102-104, 480

29. *Titulus for the priestly ordination of St. Ignatius and Companions*
Rome, Archivium Romanum Societatis Iesu, Epp. NN. 89, fol. 27

The month of June, 1537 proved to be a pivotal one for Ignatius and the first companions in the unfolding of their discernment for their young companionship, for that month saw the reception of Holy Orders by Ignatius and five others. The companions found themselves in Venice, awaiting passage to the Holy Land.

Their preparation for priestly ordination had already been completed. The academic course of studies they had followed in Paris had given them the title of Master of Theology. Pastorally, they had performed ample service on their journey from Paris to Venice, and in the months awaiting passage to the Holy Land, they devoted themselves to pastoral tasks exalted as well as humble, from preaching and academic research (or serving as advisors to bishops) to the instruction of children and work in hospitals.

Two bishops had presented themselves as willing to preside at the ordination ceremonies of the companions: Girolamo Veralli, legate of the Holy See to Venice, and Vincenzo Nigusanti, bishop of Arbe and resident in Venice. Both prelates were learned and concerned about the state of the church. They appreciated the learning and dedication of Ignatius and his companions. In gratitude for the generous offer by two prelates, Ignatius and the companions asked Nigusanti to perform the ordination rite, while Veralli received their vows.

In this document is the resolution of the question posed to the companions whether they wished to be ordained on the title of sufficient learning or of voluntary poverty, or both. They chose both, and Girolamo Veralli gives his dispensation forthwith in this letter. The letter recognizes the preparation of the companions both academically and spiritually for priesthood, and in it, Veralli accepts "in his hands the perpetual vows of poverty pronounced by Ignatius of Loyola."

It is of note that the early Society of Jesus would be distinguished by its learning and by its poverty even at the moment of its inception as a priestly order. This vow of poverty is especially significant in that it manifests Ignatius' desire to form a company of priests who would be freed from the obligations of benefices or endowed masses for their maintenance and daily living. This would protect the incipient order from undue dependence on certain families for endowed support, and it would free the companions to travel on mission as they were assigned without worry of benefice obligations at various altars or to any particular diocese.

PT sj

DALMASES, pp. 145-146; *FD*, pp. 529-532.

30. *The Ordination of St. Ignatius and Companions,* Engraving in: *Vita Beati Patris Ignatii,*
fig. 49, 1609

Florence, Biblioteca dell'Istituto Stensen, Armadio A

Six of the ten companions (except for Favre, Jay and Broët who were already priests, and Salmerón who had to wait because he had not yet reached the minimal canonical age of twenty-three) were ordained priests in 1537 in Venice.

In January of that year all ten of these friends in the Lord had come together in Venice, where Ignatius had spent all of 1536, to prepare for their pilgrimage to the Holy Land. To go there required permission of the pope and all but Ignatius went to Rome in April to receive it. The zeal and the learning of these men made such an impression on Pope Paul III that he not only gave them permission to go to Jerusalem but he also gave them permission to preach and to hear confessions anywhere, and to those who were not yet priests, permission to be ordained. With the pilgrimage document in hand, the year which they gave themselves to set out for Jerusalem began.

After ordination, they decided to prepare for several months to celebrate their first masses, to do works of mercy and to preach in the city squares as much as their minimal knowledge of Italian allowed. Ignatius, accompanied by Favre and Lainez, went to Vicenza, where they lived for months in an abandoned and ruined monastery, S. Pietro in Vivarolo, and spent the first forty days in solitude, prayer and such continuous and extraordinary gifts of God that he once referred to it as a second Manresa.

By October, 1537 the group was together again in Venice. All except Ignatius had by now celebrated their first masses; he still hoped that he might be able to do so in Bethlehem, a hope never to be realized. (He finally offered that first mass at midnight on Christmas, 1538 at the altar of the Nativity in S. Maria Maggiore in Rome.) They now decided to preach in several Italian cities while still awaiting the chance to go to Jerusalem. When the question arose among them what they might reply to people who asked them who they were, they decided that "seeing that they had among themselves no head except Jesus Christ whom alone they desired to serve . . . they would call themselves the "Company of Jesus" (*FN* I, p. 204).

JP sj

In Italiam reuersus Venetijs socios e Gallia
excipit, vnaq cum illis sacerdotio initiatur, tam
coelesti voluptate perfuso Episcopo, vt non nisi
diuinum quid in nouis Sacerdotibus praesagiret.
                                                    49

31. Dirk Theodor Helmbreeker, *The Vision at La Storta*, Oil on canvas, 48.7 x 64.3 cm., mid-17th century

Vatican City, Pinacoteca Vaticana, Inv. 692, Mag. 12 B

While in Venice, seven of the companions, including Ignatius, were ordained on June 24, 1537. Thereupon Ignatius, Favre, and Lainez went to Vicenza, where they spent forty days in prayer and preaching. "At Vicenza," he tells us, "he had many spiritual visions and many quite regular consolations; the contrary happened when he was in Paris. In all that traveling he had great supernatural experiences like those he used to have when he was in Manresa" (*Autobiography*, no. 95).

With their pilgrimage thwarted, in late October they set out for Rome to offer their services to the pope. Ignatius traveled with Favre and Lainez. "On this journey he was visited very especially by God" (*Autobiography*, no. 96).

In a small wayside chapel at La Storta on the outskirts of Rome he was favored with a mystical vision which was as important for this period of his life as his outstanding illumination at Manresa had been in 1522. During the journey he had been "praying Our Lady to deign to place him with her Son. One day, a few miles before reaching Rome, he was at prayer in a church and experienced such a change in his soul and saw so clearly that God the Father placed him with Christ his Son that he would not dare to doubt it" (*Autobiography*, no. 96).

He told other details of this vision to his companions who soon spread them to others in the Society. Ignatius "told me," Lainez wrote in 1559, "that it seemed to him that God the Father had impressed on his heart the following words: 'I shall be propitious to you in Rome' . . . then another time he said that it seemed to him that he saw Christ carrying a cross on his shoulder and the eternal Father nearby who said to Christ: 'I want you to take this man for your servant.' And because of this, conceiving great devotion to this most holy name, he wished to name the congregation the 'Company of Jesus'" (*FN* II, p. 133).

Thus this vision at La Storta, which became a staple element in Ignatian iconography, had a profound confirming effect on the foundation of the Society and the shape it took. Its members should be intimately united to Jesus in prayer and enrolled under the banner of the cross, to labor in a corporate manner for the glory of God and the welfare of their neighbors. These are the ideas which Ignatius was to express at the very beginning of his First Sketch of the Institute of the Society of Jesus.

GG sj

DALMASES, pp. 151-153

Cat. 31

32. Pietro del Massaio, *Firenze* and *Roma*, Illuminated parchment in: Ptolemy, *Tabulae Geographicae*, fol. 126v-127r, 1469

Vatican City, Biblioteca Apostolica Vaticana, Pal. Lat. 5699

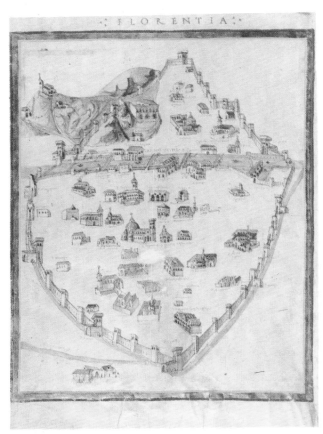

CAT. 32, FOL. 126V

A pair of maps of Florence and Rome illuminated by Pietro del Massaio in Jacobo Angeli's deluxe edition of Ptolemy shows the topographical relationship between the city centers and the mendicant foundations of the thirteenth to early fifteenth centuries. The map of Florence shows the circuit of the new walls (the "sesta cercia") built between 1284 and 1333. The most important early mendicant foundations, the Dominicans' S. Maria Novella (1221, center right) and the Franciscan complex at S. Croce (1226-1228, "S.†", upper left) stood just outside the perimeter of the wall that the Comune had built between 1173 and 1175. Those large complexes were built opposite one another at the city gates, and at points equidistant from the center of the city (the Cathedral/Palazzo della Signoria axis).

The newly founded preaching orders needed space for a large church and *piazza* for their preaching activities, and desired sufficient space for traditional cloister complexes. Large pieces of downtown property were prohibitively expensive. The space was to be found only on the fringe of the tightly packed urban grid. The successive foundations of the Servites' SS. Annunziata (1248), the Carmelites' S. Maria del Carmine (1250) and the Silvestrinis' S. Marco (1299) continued this pattern, maintaining a measured distance from one another and from the densely inhabited center of the city.

The major concentration of population in Rome from the time of the fall of the Empire until the Renaissance was found in the bend of the Tiber, centered around the Campo dei Fiori and Piazza Navona. The measure of the *abitato* at the middle of the thirteenth century is likewise indicated by the placement of the mendicant foundations of the thirteenth century. S. Sabina on the Aventine (freely rendered in the upper center right) was given to St. Dominic in 1219. His Order of Preachers rebuilt S. Maria Sopra Minerva (ca. 1280) next to the Pantheon following the plan of S. Maria Novella in Florence. Open fields stood between the church and the Via del Corso. In 1250, the Franciscans began rebuilding S. Maria in Ara Coeli that clung to the slopes of the rural Campidoglio. Built as an *ex voto* offering for the cessation of the Black Death in 1348, the great flight of stairs was constructed with marble recycled from the Temple of the Sun. The route of the Via del Pellegrino from S. Pietro and Castel S. Angelo to the Campidoglio is shown passing "Campus Floris" (Campo dei Fiori), "Area Iudea" (the Jewish quarter), and "Sto. Angelo," "where fish are sold."

TL sj

FANNELLI, 1988, pp. 24-28, KRAUTHEIMER, 1983, pp. 275-276 287

ROMA:

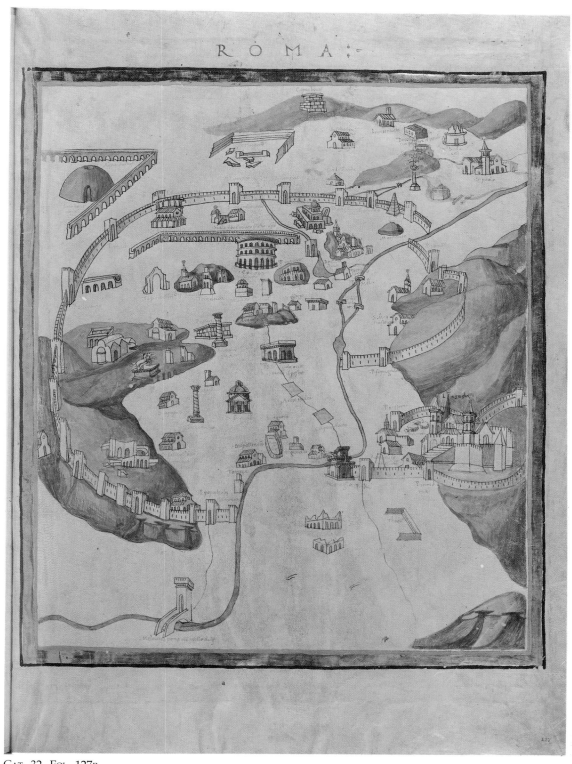

33. After Paolo da Venezia, *Roma*, Illuminated parchment in: *Compendium*, fol. 270, 1334-1339

Vatican City, Biblioteca Apostolica Vaticana, Vat. Lat. 1960

This plan of Rome is one of several maps found in a manuscript which was composed between 1334 and 1339. The codex contains a number of works by the Franciscan Friar Paolino, born in Venice ca. 1270-1274. After holding various public offices, he was named bishop of Pozzuoli in 1324. Paolino also prepared the plan on display, an integral part of his *Compendium* (also called the *Chronologia Magna*) which he completed in 1320.

The untitled plan was drawn on parchment in pen and ink (now much faded) by the same hand which transcribed the codex. The scribe seems little practiced in cartographic rendering. The map is coarsely colored: the hills, some gates and posterns in red, Castel S. Angelo and other gates in brownish yellow, and the Tiber which flows through the circuit of the city walls in cerulian. This elliptical circuit is circumscribed by fortified walls with eleven gates and thirty posterns. The plan is oriented with the east to the top, the west to the bottom, north and south respectively to the left and right. The buildings, many of which are shown as turreted and crowned with battlements, are not all drawn according to this orientation. The topography is sometimes in error, for example, in the case of several gates and Monte Mario "Monte Malis," placed to the right instead of the the left of S. Pietro. Only a few of the ancient monuments are named.

Within the city walls, streets on the perimeter of the city are indicated more than those in the center. Between the Porta Nomentana and the Porta Labicana, the so-called "Tempio di Minerva Medica" is represented as a round edifice surmounted by a cross and, in the area of the Viminal Hill, a barrel is drawn, the so-called "botte dei termine," the great basin of water which fed the Baths of Diocletian. In the Piazza of S. Giovanni in Laterano are still seen the statue of Marcus Aurelius (which in 1538 was transferred to the Campidoglio) and fragments of the head and hand of the Colossus of Nero (also known as the statue of the sun). The hand is drawn without the globe it held, a globe called "the ball of Samson" in the Middle Ages. A little lower, the Colosseum is represented as covered with a cupola, and still further down the page is the Pantheon with the inscription "S.M. Rotunda."

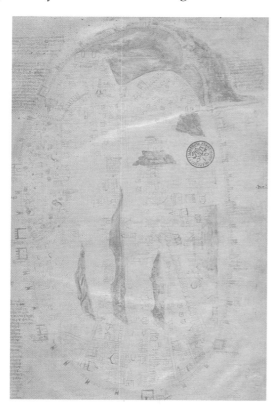

The most remarkable image, however, is a hunting scene that takes place in an enclosed circus in the area called the "Prati di Castello," where the ancient Naumachia Vaticana stood. Slightly above is Castel S. Angelo, in front of which is drawn the only bridge which crosses the Tiber. At Trastevere (where another gate is represented) the river divides into two streams which reunite once they have passed the "Isola Tiberina."

A series of toponymical indications and other written information complete the map. They are written on the margins of the sheet and surround the plan, beginning, in the upper left, with the names of the thirty principal streets of Rome. On the right margin, outside the walls, one can see the churches of S. Paolo, S. Sebastiano, S. Stefano and S. Lorenzo (the only one of the four identified by name).

AD

FRUTAZ, 1962, I, pp. 120-122

34. Giacomo da Fabriano, *Roma*, Illuminated initial in: St. Augustine, *De Civitate Dei*, fol. 2r, 1456

Vatican City, Biblioteca Apostolica Vaticana, Reg. Lat. 1882

Giacomi da Fabriano illuminated this edition of St. Augustine's *The City of God* in 1456. The first initial (the "I" of "Interea") of Augustine's theological and philosophical reflection on the meaning of history is illustrated with a precisely drawn miniature of the center of Medieval Rome. The Campidoglio with its long flight of stairs leading to the Franciscan church of the Ara Coeli and the diminutive Palazzo del Senatore behind it mark the outer perimeter of civilization. An immense greensward separates the city from S. Giovanni in Laterano, the cathedral church of Rome with its abandoned papal palace. Small houses are huddled between the base around the Pantheon and the bend of the Tiber at Castel S. Angelo.

Written while the civilized world still reeled from the trauma of the first barbarian sack of Rome in 410, Augustine's masterpiece is both polemical and reflective. He forcefully argued against the pagan intelligentsia who attributed the fall of the Empire to the rise of Christianity and the overthrow of the pagan gods, yet he never directly identified Rome with the City of Man nor the church with the City of God. Rather, a philosophy of history emerges that reads human experience as a constant dialectic between faith and unbelief, "love of God proceeding to disregard of self and love of self proceeding to disregard of God" (XVI, 28).

This theme would be central in the dynamic of Ignatius' Spiritual Exercises. For Augustine, the inevitable fall of decadent Rome prefigured the escatological battle between good and evil; for Ignatius the struggle between Jerusalem (the Kingdom of Christ) and Babylon (the Kingdom of Satan) at the center of the "election" meditations of the second week of the Exercises, is an icon for the struggle for the conversion of the human heart.

TL sj

FRUTAZ, 1962, I, p. 134

35. Jacopo Filippo Foresti, *Urbs Roma*, Woodcut in: *Supplementum supplementi chronicarum*, p. 66v, Venice, 1513
Vatican City, Biblioteca Apostolica Vaticana, R.G. Storia II, 463

36. Michael Wohlgemuth and Wilhelm Pleydenwurff, *Roma*, Woodcut in: Hartmann Schedel, *Liber Chronicarum*, pp. LVIIv-LVIIIr, Nuremberg, 1493
Vatican City, Biblioteca Apostolica Vaticana, Stamp. Ch. S. 176

37. Christoph Stimmer, *Romanae urbis situs*, Woodcut in: Sebastian Münster, *Cosmographiae Universalis*, fol. 150-151, Basel, 1550
Vatican City, Biblioteca Apostolica Vaticana, R.G. Geografia II, 112

Three woodcuts taken from Renaissance encyclopediae give a clear indication of a shift towards precision in cartographic rendering at the end of the fifteenth century.

The first edition of Fra Jacopo Filippo Foresti's *Supplementum Chronicarum* was published in Venice in 1486. In it, both Rome and Genova were illustrated with the same small block print of a port city. In Foresti's second edition of 1490 the *Urbs Roma* (the 1513 edition, Cat. 35) appeared. The panoramic print (north to the right) is more like a line-drawing for an illuminated capital than a usable map; like the Giacomo da Fabriano initial from the *City of God* (Cat. 34), landscape is here as important as cityscape.

Sixtus IV's new Ponte Sisto links the old Medieval core of the city to Trastevere, while the area at the foot of Ponte S. Angelo (where Paul III would construct his trident) is undeveloped. The Pantheon has been reoriented eastwards, and to the left of its portico the crenellations of the Barbo family's Palazzo S. Marco appear under S. Maria in Aracoeli and the Campidoglio.

The flourishing presses of Nuremberg produced Latin and German editions of Hartmann Schedel's *Liber Chronicarum* in 1493. Included in that volume was a large woodcut of Rome by Michael Wohlgemuth and Wilhelm Pleydenwurff (Cat. 36). The image focuses on the Vatican side of the Tiber: the hospital complex of Santo Spirito, Castel S. Angelo, the old Basilica of S. Pietro, the Papal Palace, and the Belvedere. The Aurelian Wall and the Quirinal and Pincian Hills block most of the view of the center of

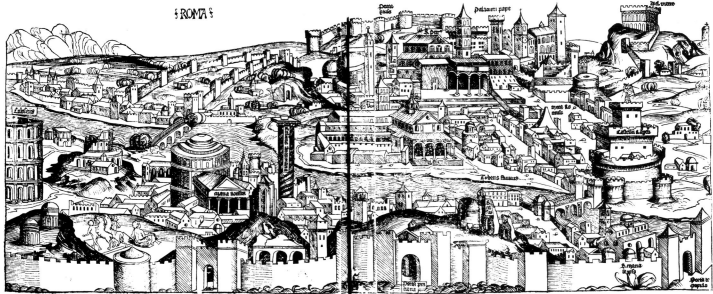

CAT. 36

98

CAT. 35

Rome itself. Dominating the center of the cityscape are the Colonna Antoniana and the Pantheon, whose facade is reoriented towards the viewer. The area between the Pantheon and the Colosseum is disproportionately small and imprecisely drawn.

Christoph Stimmer's 1490 woodcut of Rome (Cat. 37) was inserted in Sebastian Münster's *Cosmographiae Universalis*, printed in Basel in various editions in the 1550s. The panorama shows the city as its center began to reconsolidate towards the end of the fifteenth century. The equestrian statue of Marcus Aurelius, moved to the Campidoglio by Paul III in 1538, can still be seen in front of the Lateran Palace, which was abandoned as a papal residence because of its dangerous isolation from the heart of the city.

The area between the Pantheon and the Campidoglio appears densely populated, and the *abitato* has begun to spread eastwards again (here, towards the bottom of the woodcut), encompassing the Via del Corso and moving towards Monte Cavallo, the Quirinale. Although some antiquities are drawn with care, others are omitted where inconvenient: the "narrowness of the site" excluded the rendering of the Colosseum (G).

TL sj

FRUTAZ, 1962, I, pp. 148-150, 156-157

38. Philippe de Soye after Titian, *Portrait of Paul III*, Engraving, 24.5 x 16.5 cm., ca. 1568
Vatican City, Biblioteca Apostolica Vaticana, Stampe II. 228, 25r

Pope Paul III approved the founding of the Society of Jesus, first verbally at Tivoli on September 3, 1539, and then officially, on September 27, 1540, with the promulgation of the Bull "Regimini Militantis Ecclesiae." This portrait of the pontiff comes from the studio of Philippe de Soye, a Belgian engraver and student of Cornelis Cort, who worked in Rome between 1566 and 1572.

The engraving (with the legend at the bottom "PAULUS. III. PONT. OPT. MAX.") is one of 27 portraits that illustrate the short but accurate papal biographies written by Onofrio Panvino. This work, entitled *XXVII. Pontificum Maximorum Elogia et imagines accuratissime ad vivum aeneis typeis delineatae*, was published by Antonio Lafréry in 1568. When an index of the prints for sale in Lafréry's studio was compiled (before 1572), the series ended with the figure of Pius V signed "Philippus Soius fecit." Gregory XIII was later added. The following note is found in that index, at lines 587-589: "Images of the eighteen pontiffs created after the return of the Apostolic See from Avignon to Rome, with the descriptions of their lives by Onofrio Panvino, together with Gregory XIII." A copy of this series can be found in the Library of the Monastery of San Lorenzo del Escorial.

Philippe de Soye, to whom six other plates of the series and perhaps all those which contain ornamental dedicatory plaques can be attributed, most likely used as a model for this engraving one of the many highly expressive portraits by Titian, specifically the painting of Paul III which was considered the official portrait of the Pope. Indeed, the similarities between this engraving and the Titian (Naples, Museo Nazionale di Capodimonte), painted in Bologna in the spring of 1543, are evident in spite of minor variations such as the position of the arm and hand and the border of the fur cuff on the Pope's robes.

AD

HOLLSTEIN, 1983, p. 240; WETHEY, 1971, pp. 122-124

39. Giuseppe Vasi, *Palazzo S. Marco della Sereniss. Rep. di Venezia*, Engraving in:
　　Delle magnificenze di Roma antica e moderna, 29 x 41.5 cm.,Vol. 4, Rome, 1754
Private Collection

40. Giuseppe Vasi, *Chiesa di S. Marco*, Engraving in: *Delle magnificenze di*
　　Roma antica e moderna, 29 x 41.5 cm., Vol. 6, Rome, 1756
Private Collection

The late Cinquecento Gesù complex was built back-to-back with a major papal landmark dating from the previous century: the Palazzo Venezia. Known as the Palazzo di S. Marco, after the ninth-century church (which replaced an Early Christian basilica) around which it was built in the second half of the Quattrocento, the palace was used during much of the Cinquecento as a papal summer residence. Even after it had been turned over to Venice in 1564 to become the residence of the Venetian ambassador, the Palazzo S. Marco, renamed Palazzo Venezia at that time, was frequently requisitioned by the pope for his own use. By the early Seicento however, the expanding Renaissance city had enveloped it, and the popes shifted their attention to the higher and more suburban Quirinal palace (Coffin, p. 33).

The Vasi engravings show two of the three principal sides of the *palazzo* as well as the Palazzetto and the Tower of Paul III on the Campidoglio linked to it by an elevated passageway. Between 1455 and 1464 the Venetian Pietro Barbo, titular cardinal of the Church of S. Marco, rebuilt the episcopal palace attached to the east flank of that church. This early section of the palace is the part which appears on the extreme right of Cat. 39. When Cardinal Barbo became Pope Paul II in 1464, the modest building began to be enlarged into a papal residence. Thus the southern corner of the *palazzo* was raised (1465-1470) so as to become the massive tower visible in both prints. At the same time the hanging garden, surrounded by a double tier of arcades, to be known as the "Palazzetto Venezia" later when its arcades were walled up, was built almost as a separate unit tenuously attached to the southern corner of the main *palazzo* by a short interface. In Cat. 40, four of the lower level arches are shown as being still open, so that we can get an idea of the lightness of the original structure.

The unusual siting of the arcaded garden formalized the irregular space on the south and east sides of the palazzo by creating two distinct *piazze*:

Piazza Venezia (Cat. 39) and Piazza S. Marco (Cat. 40). The irregular quadrilateral plan of the garden building is a revealing example of the blend of formality and adaptation to be found so often in Renaissance planning. Its two principal facades form precise right angles with the two sides of the *palazzo* they encounter. But its other two facades, not parallel to the former, are clearly determined by the odd angling of the two pre-existing streets upon which they front. In turn, one of these angled facades (Cat. 39) was to determine the direction of Paul III's elevated passageway to the Campidoglio.

Two maps of Rome reveal an interesting link between Piazza Venezia and Piazza S. Marco. Both Bufalini, in his plan-map of 1551 (Cat. 48) where Piazza Venezia is still called "Platea Divi Marcii" and Maggi, in his view-map of 1625 (Cat. 74), depict an open passage connecting the right-angled corners of the two piazzas. Rather than a gap between the *palazzo* and the garden building, this refers to a covered corridor passing under the garden. The garden level of the "giardino pensile" as Vasi calls it, was one story above ground level, corresponding approximately to the first string course on the facade. This left the ground level open for use as store rooms and stables, and allowed room for the corridor linking the two piazzas. Access doors to this corridor are visible in both Vasi prints. Nolli's 1748 plan of the city shows the corridor clearly, but by this time it had been converted into a long narrow chapel dedicated to the Blessed Virgin.

By the time of Paul II's death in 1471, the Piazza Venezia facade had been lengthened to the corner of Via del Gesù (modern Via del Plebiscito). The cross-mullioned windows of the *piano nobile* in this new section, being more widely spaced than in the older part which housed the pope's private quarters, reveal the grander scale of the rooms at this end of the building. This increased scale, reflecting the ceremonial character of the new rooms, appears also in the

CAT. 39

new long wing on the Via del Gesù built between 1471 and 1491 by Cardinal Marco Barbo, Paul II's nephew. The names of new rooms in this wing (Sala del Concistoro, Regia) clearly indicate the intention of turning the Palazzo S. Marco into a key papal residence (Casanova Uccella, p.122). This wing houses the main entryway and stairway (rebuilt in 1930) for the whole complex. With the completion of the rectangle enclosing the great courtyard by the end of the century, the *palazzo* had completely surrounded the Church of S. Marco. Even its facade had been covered by the two-level benediction loggia (Cat. 40), which also shows the twelfth-century bell tower as the only visible element of the Medieval church.

Pope Paul III Farnese, head of the family that was to provide much support for the Jesuit order, continued the enhancement of the *palazzo* in the late 1530s when he ordered the building of a covered passageway on arches connecting the garden building to the Campidoglio. This walkway spanned two city streets: Via di S. Marco (the arch is visible in Cat. 40, no. 2) and Via della Pedacchia, before meeting the side of the Capitoline hill. This enabled the pope to pass through the upper arcades of the hanging garden (accessible only from the pope's private apartment in the *palazzo*) thence along the raised passageway to a ramp which led up to the gardens of the Ara Coeli monastery. Between 1540 and 1542 the pope had a tower built on the monastery grounds (Cat. 40, no. 2; Coffin, p. 31). The west facade of this tower had a two-tiered loggia facing a garden, thus giving it a less martial air than the narrower northern facade. The sequence of *palazzo*, elevated passageway and tower recalls, on a smaller scale, the Vatican palace, *passetto*, Castel S. Angelo sequence.

Palazzo Venezia is an early example of a common Roman palace type: irregular plan and elevations whose variations in design depend upon both accretion over time and response to surrounding urban characteristics. A later example, strikingly

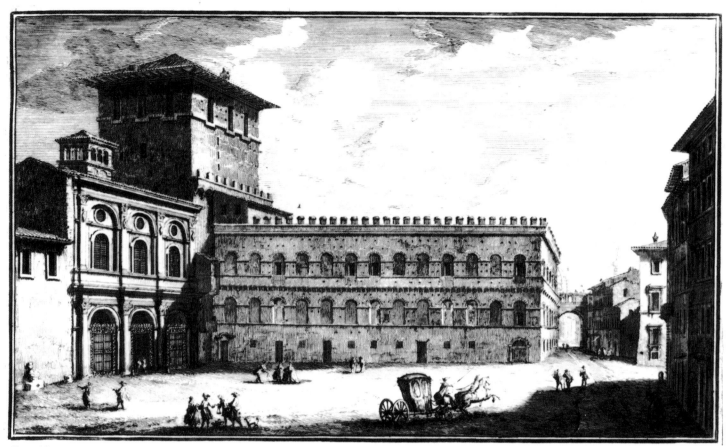

CAT. 40

similar in the fact that it too faces in three directions, is Palazzo Borghese. Palazzo Venezia also belongs to a smaller group of Roman buildings which incorporate an important church in their overall perimeter. A near contemporary of this type is the Cancelleria, where the Church of S. Lorenzo in Damaso was demolished and rebuilt as an internal element of the *palazzo*, virtually invisible from the exterior. Other examples of this group (eg: Palazzo Colonna, Palazzo Doria, Palazzo Pamphilj) do not engulf the church but are still closely tied to it. It should be apparent that both the Gesù-Casa Professa complex and the nearby Collegio Romano-S. Ignazio grouping belong to the latter type.

AC

CASANOVA UCCELLA, 1980; COFFIN, 1979; SCALABRONI,1981

41. *City Plans,* Illuminated parchment in: *Corpus Agrimensores Romanorum,*
   fol. 90, Fulda, 9th century
Vatican City, Biblioteca Apostolica Vaticana, Pal. Lat. 1564

42. Leon Battista Alberti, Manuscript edition of *Descriptio Urbis Romae,* fol. 3, ca. 1450
Vatican City, Biblioteca Apostolica Vaticana, Mss. Chigiana, M. VII 149

43. *Homo in circulo,* Woodcut in: *Virtruvius per Iocundum solitio castigatior factus,*
   p. 22, Venice, 1511
Vatican City, Biblioteca Apostolica Vaticana, Cicognara V, 696

44. *City Plan,* Woodcut in: Vitruvius, *Architettura con il suo commento e figure in volgar
   lingua raportato da Gianbattista Caporli,* p. 41, Venice, 1536
Vatican City, Biblioteca Apostolica Vaticana, Stamp. Barb. K.V, 76

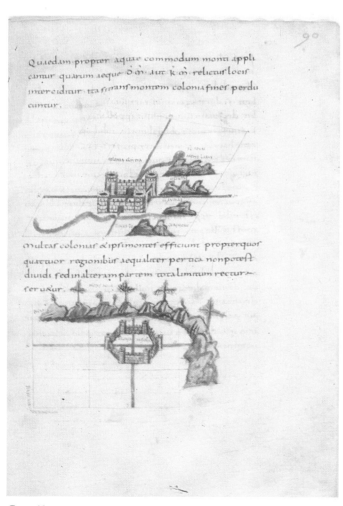

CAT. 41

A precipitous decline in urban populations followed the "barbarian" invasions and the fall of the Roman Empire in Western Europe, yet cities continued to be built and rebuilt. Where new construction was undertaken, Roman models of urban planning were more or less taken for granted, and, where possible, applied. The basic Roman grid pattern which, ironically, was to be found almost everywhere *except* in Rome, was readapted as cathedrals and the municipal palaces took the place of imperial temples and fora in the cities of Christian Europe.

The *Corpus Agrimensores Romanorum,* the handbook of the ancient Roman guild of surveyors, exerted great influence and was widely used in the late Middle Ages and the early Renaissance. It provided practical information on principles of surveying and design, as well as instructions for constructing the simple tools needed for plotting a site. The ninth-century copy of the *Corpus* on display here (Cat. 41), illustrated with particularly fine illuminations, shows the basic cross-grid layout of *cardo* and *decumanus* which marked the center of Roman towns and military camps (Guidoni, pp. 133-134).

In 1414, humanist Poggio Bracciolini rediscovered the text of Vitruvius' *De architectura.* The book served as a rich mine for the humanist architects and aestethicians of the early Renaissance, particularly for Leon Battista Alberti. As Alberti studied the architectural and design principles of the Augustan Age in Vitruvius' wide-ranging and often difficult text, he sought to interpret the buildings in Rome, and indeed the very urban fabric itself, according to Virtruvian rules of proportion and beauty. As official architect to Pope Nicholas V, Alberti sought to interpret the ancient city in light of the renewed papacy which was beginning to reestablish its hold on Rome after the "Babylonian Capitivity" in Avignon and the Conciliar Crisis (Stinger, pp. 66-67).

Alberti's *Descriptio Urbis Romae* (Cat. 42) is an attempt to describe how to draw an accurate map of Rome. He proposed using an astrolabe-like device mounted on the Campidoglio to make angular measurements on a disk divided into 48 equal segments.

His choice for the center of his map is of primary importance. He recognized the center of the city as the Campidoglio and not the Basilica of S. Pietro or S. Giovanni in Laterano. Not only did his choice of the Campidoglio provide him with a convenient platform from which to make his measurements of the city walls, the monuments of antiquity and the Christian landmarks, but it also shows that the center of gravity had begun to shift back towards the traditional civic and cultic center of the *Umbilicus Mundi*.

Two illustrations from early printed editions of Vitruvius (Cat. 43, 44) show how laws of perfect proportionality governed Augustan and Renaissance sensibilities. The center of the human being is the umbilicus, which stands as center of harmonic relationships which define the human body. If Renaissance man served as the measure of all things, then the human body had to be understood as a perfectly proportional form which exemplifies the perfection of nature. The Renaissance city is conceived as the body politic, the incarnate form of human interchange. For Alberti and for Vitruvius, the city should be no less well-proportioned than the human body: its streets radiate from the civic center which is oriented in proper relationship to sun and wind to assure the health of the body (Vitruvius, I, vi-vii).

TL sj

GUIDONI, 1978, pp. 133-134; MARCONI, 1973, pp. 30-35, 52-53; STINGER, 1985, pp. 66-67

CAT. 43

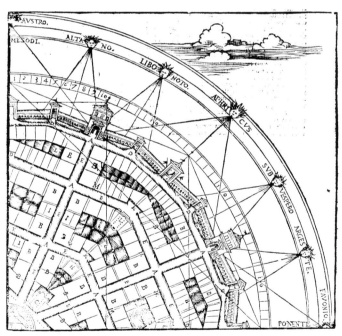

CAT. 44

45. *Plan for Troop Deployment* in: Giovanni Maggi,
   Della fortificazione della città , pp. 108v-109, Venice, 1583
Vatican City, Biblioteca Apostolica Vaticana, R.G. Scienze I, 82

46. *Plan for a Military Camp* ("Alloggiamento di Alloggiare accanto a una collina
   e presso un fiume"), Colored woodcut in: Girolamo Cataneo,
   Dell'Arte Militare, , fol. 78, Brescia, 1571
Vatican City, Biblioteca Apostolica Vaticana, R.G. Scienze IV, (1) 2467

Although Ignatius of Loyola was not a professional soldier, his life as a gentleman-at-arms introduced him to the military world of the Renaissance. He was familiar with arms, having fought in a number of skirmishes for the Viceroy of Navarre. His conversion followed an injury he sustained in an artillery barrage at Pamplona in northern Spain (Cat. 12).

By the beginning of the sixteenth century, the development of firepower irrevocably changed the

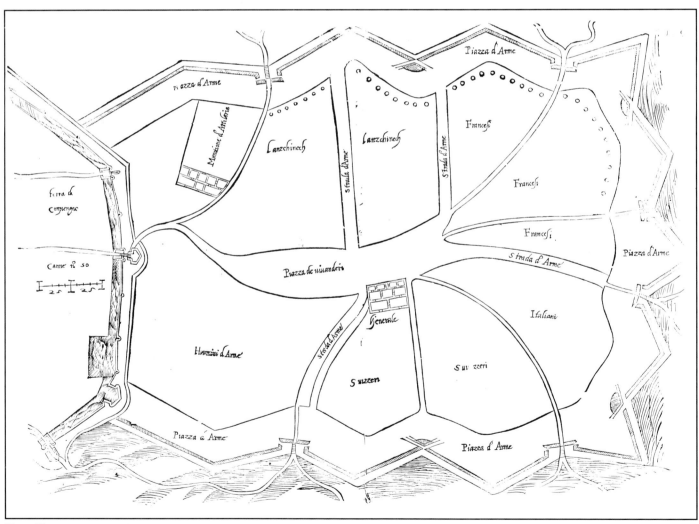

CAT. 45

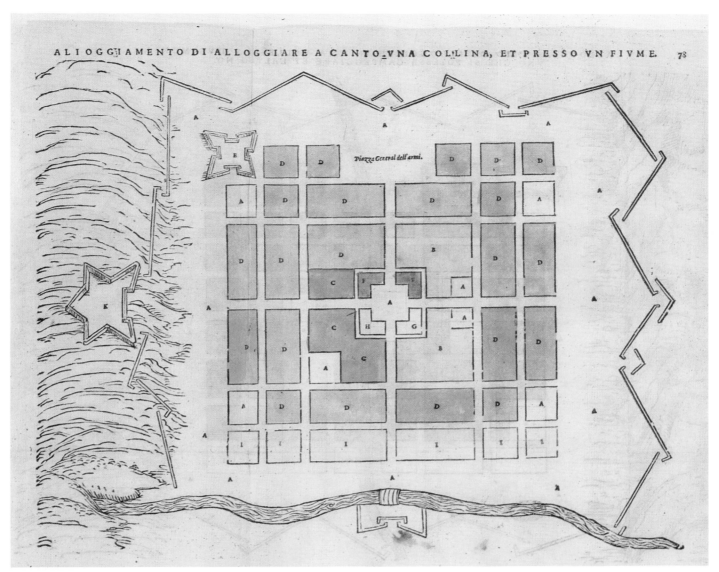

CAT. 46

rules of warfare. A whole school of defensive military engineering evolved in response to the use of the cannon. What remained constant from Roman times, however, was a concern that the commanding general be located at the very center of the city or fortress. The Roman *castrum* was laid out for maximum efficiency: straight streets linked gates and outlying troop concentrations to the central crossroads where the commander's headquarters was located. Comparing two military treatises published shortly after Ignatius' death with his choice of a centrally located headquarters in downtown Rome, one can argue that Ignatius' choice of a central location for his headquarters might have been influenced by his military experience.

In Cataneo's design for an ideal camp (Cat. 46), letter "A" indicates the central plaza with the headquarters of the general at the center. Letter "F" denotes the quarters of the gentlemen-at-arms who act as the general's adjutants. Maggi's design (Cat. 45) shows a similar disposition for a camp made up of regiments of different nationalities. The general is located at the center of the field of action so that he can oversee the diverse sectors of his army and overlook the surrounding countryside.

TL sj

GUIDONI, 1982, pp. 9-29

47. Anonymous, *The Campidoglio*, Engraving, 37.3 x 50.5 cm., first half of the 16th century

Vatican City, Biblioteca Apostolica Vaticana, Stamp. Barb. X, I, 13A, fol. 18

A short distance from the house in which St. Ignatius lived from 1544 until his death on July 31, 1556, rises the Capitoline Hill. When Paul III (Farnese) was elected pope in 1534, the Campidoglio was in a state of miserable neglect and abandonment. This state was especially in evidence during the preparations for the visit of Emperor Charles V in 1536. In order to renew this area of the city which was considered the symbol of the grandeur of Rome and the center of civil life, the Pope turned to Michelangelo. But neither the pontiff nor the great artist saw the realization of this work of urban renewal which, for lack of funds, proceeded at a snail's pace.

This engraving, one of two published by Antonio Lafréry in the various editions of the *Speculum Romanae Magnificentiae,* shows the Capitoline Square ("Sic Romae Capitolio") as it appeared around 1565. In the center, the statue of Marcus Aurelius stands within an oval area three steps below the level of the *piazza.* Paul III had the statue transferred from the Lateran to the Campidoglio in 1538 and changed the inscription. To the left, where today we find the Palazzo Nuovo, one can see a wall with a large niche in the center, where later the Fountain of Marforio would be built. Behind the wall, constructed in 1539 to support the terrace bordering S. Maria in Aracoeli,

one can see the palm tree planted from a seed brought from the Holy Land, the porch, and the wide stairway leading to the convent. In the background is the Palazzo del Senatore with its bell tower and double stairway. Below the niche are two statues of the Nile and Tigris Rivers, the latter shown before its transformation into an allegory of the Tiber.

The construction of Michelangelo's ramp was begun in 1547 together with the restoration and transformation of the facade of the palace. The work seems to have been overseen by Tommaso Cavalieri, friend of Michelangelo and deputy of the Capitoline workshops. Whereas the stairway was completed in 1554, the facade was finished only around 1565, after continuous prodding by Pius IV who had visited the Campidoglio on November 5, 1561. On the right is the Palazzo dei Conservatori, the facade of which would be substituted by one of Michelangelo's design in 1565; under the first arch, note the colossal bronze head of the Emperor Constantine, given by Sixtus IV to the *popolo romano* in 1471.

AD

PECCHIAI, 1950, pp. 4, 12-13, 35-36, 84, 87-89; PIETRANGELI, 1976, pp. 22-28, 96

SIC ROMA CAPITOLIO

48. Leonardo Bufalini, *Plan of Rome*, Woodcut, fol. H, 42 x 30 cm., 1551

Vatican City, Biblioteca Apostolica Vaticana, St. Geogr. I, 620

49. Alan Ceen, *Rectification of the Bufalini Plan of 1551* based on
Giambattista Nolli's, *Plan of Rome*, 1748

Vatican City, Biblioteca Apostolica Vaticana, St. Geogr. S 528

50. Alan Ceen, *Bufalini distortion grid* (This grid represents the distortion of a 4 x 4 cm.
grid drawn on the Nolli plan when it is transferred to the Bufalini plan)

The plan of Rome by Leonardo Bufalini was first printed in 1551. No copies of this edition survive, and only two complete ones of the 1560-1561 reprint from the same wood blocks are known: the copy from the Biblioteca Apostolica Vaticana (exhibited here) and another in the Map Room of the British Museum (S.I.R. 1). It is the first plan-map (orthogonal, ichnographic projection as opposed to the oblique projection of a view-map) of the contemporary city since the early second-century marble plan, the *Forma Urbis* of Septimius Severus. Indeed, it is the *only* plan-map of the Renaissance city drawn in the whole of the Cinquecento. As such it is the earliest clear image of the layout of Renaissance Rome available, the first to show streets and squares and the relative locations of churches, palaces and ruins.

Bufalini was one of a group of architects and military engineers assembled in Rome by Paul III Farnese, under the direction of Antonio da Sangallo il Giovane, for the purpose of rebuilding and redefining the city walls (Lanciani, II, p.104). It is not surprising then to find both the ancient Aurelian walls and the Renaissance replacement sections shown in detail, with distances marked for each stretch of wall, and for each tower and bastion. This may well have been the original purpose of the map: to serve as an overall working drawing for the relation of the ancient walls to the terrain, as well as to record recent changes in the urban circuit of walls. Roads penetrating the walls would be a necessary part of such a map, and it is tempting to speculate that what started out as a study of the city walls and related streets eventually developed into a depiction of the street-net of the whole city.

Distortion and scale variation make the Bufal-

ini difficult to use in a consistent way. Perhaps that is why details of the map are frequently reproduced but rarely made part of coherent topographic analysis. In Bufalini straight streets sometimes bend, whole city blocks are often unevenly expanded or compressed, and angles between streets are frequently wrong. But he usually takes care to depict street intersections accurately, especially in the less densely built-up parts of the city. This allows for rectification of his plan over a precise base-map such as the Nolli plan-map of 1748 (see Cat. 49).

The 1551 date of the map assures the inclusion of the flowering of urban planning under the Renaissance popes, from Alexander VI's Borgo Nuovo, to Julius II's Via Giulia and Via Lungara, to the Piazza del Popolo Trivium of the Medici popes, completed by Paul III, to whose reign also date the Via Trinitatis, the Banchi Trivium; the Via dei Baullari and the Via Capitolina. It is also easy to trace the Via Papale, the Medieval papal processional route linking the Vatican to the Lateran, and to discern the Renaissance variations to that important way through the city (see Cat. 73, Tempesta, and Cat. 74, Maggi; Ceen, p.167).

St. Ignatius chose a remarkable site for his first church when he obtained S. Maria della Strada ("S.M. Alteriorum" on this map). This was the point on the Via Papale where the recently cut Renaissance section of that route ("Via Capitolina") diverged from the Medieval path, which, passing from the "Forum Alteriorum" (the future Piazza del Gesù) to Piazza di S. Marco, skirted the foot of the Captoline hill on its way to the Roman Forum (Cat. 72). Paul III's Via Capitolina formed part of a carefully planned urban sequence which culminated in the Piazza del Campi-

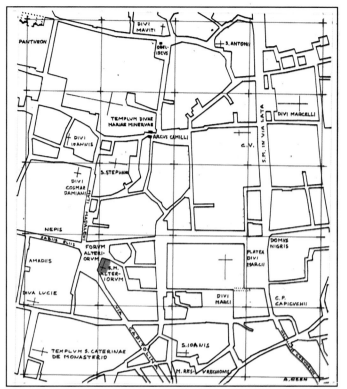

CAT. 50 DETAIL OF SHEET G/H OF BUFFALINI'S 1551 PLAN SHOWING S. M. ALTERIORUM (COLOR), SITE OF THE FUTURE CHURCH OF THE GESU'. THIS DETAIL IS ORIENTED TO MAGENETIC NORTH, AND GRIDDED TO CORRESPOND WITH THE GRIDPOINTS ON CAT. 49, THE NOLLI-BASED RECTIFICATION OF THE PLAN. THE GRID REVEALS THE DISTORTION OF THIS PLAN WHICH, IN OTHER RESPECTS, IS FULL OF USEFUL TOPOGRAPHICAL INFORMATION MUCH OF WHICH IS UNAVAILABLE ELSEWHERED

CAT. 49 RECTIFICATION OF THE 1551 BUFALINI PLAN BASED ON THE MORE ACCURATE 1748 PLAN OF ROME BY G.B. NOLLI. DETAIL SHOWING S. M. ALTERIORUM (COLOR). GRIDPOINTS OF THE RED GRID HAVE BEEN RELAYED TO THE ORIGINAL BUFALINI PLAN (CAT. 50) SO AS TO OBTAIN THE DISTORTION GRID ON THAT MAP.

doglio which Michelangelo was reshaping at the time Bufalini's map was first printed (see Cat. 47). The Pope, by rerouting the processions over the Campidoglio which, since the early Middle Ages, had been the seat of the secular government of Rome, symbolically asserted his temporal authority over the city. The positioning of the future Chiesa del Gesù literally blocked the old papal route and redirected it toward the Campidoglio.

The usefulness of this map in studying the Jesuit impact on the city lies in the fact that it depicts the city shortly after the Society had settled in the Piazza Altieri, and therefore enables us to obtain a clear idea of the contemporary urban context chosen by St. Ignatius for his work. Comparison with later maps reveals how the Jesuit foundations transformed this part of the mid-Cinquecento city to form what might be termed a Jesuit *quartiere* in Rione Pigna (see Cat. 72).

AC

CEEN,1986; EHRLE, 1911; FRUTAZ, 1962; LANCIANI, 1902-1912

51. *The Preaching of St. Ignatius*, Engraving in: *Vita Beati Patris Ignatii*, fig. 60, 1609

Florence, Biblioteca dell'Istituto Stensen, Armadio A

Preaching the word of God and teaching catechism ranked very high among the many apostolic works in which Ignatius and the early Jesuits engaged throughout the city of Rome. From the earliest days of his conversion, Ignatius engaged in the ministry of the Word. He himself says of his time at Manresa that "he sometimes spoke with spiritual persons who respected him and liked to talk with him, and...he showed such fervor in his talk and a great desire to go forward in the service of God" (*Autobiography*, no. 21). Everywhere he went in those early years Ignatius engaged increasingly in spiritual conversation, in the teaching of catechism, and in preaching. It was such spiritual conversation that gained him his first adherents and at times got him into trouble with the Inquisition. It was such preaching and teaching in Rome and other cities of Italy that so favorably impressed Pope Paul III and the papal court.

Even before the formal foundation of the Society, the early Jesuits preached and catechized everywhere with startling success. They engaged, too, in other ministries of the Word such as teaching in the universities, serving as theological advisers at the Council of Trent, and, in the case of Francis Xavier, going off to spread the Gospel in the mission lands of Asia.

In Rome itself, the first Jesuits and their rapidly growing numbers of recruits engaged in a widespread urban apostolate, preaching, teaching, and catechizing in the streets, squares, and churches of the city (see Cat. 54). Ignatius himself concentrated on giving the Spiritual Exercises far and wide in Rome and on administering the sacrament of Penance.

How central to the Jesuit vocation such ministry of the Word was in its various forms is shown clearly in the foundational document of the Society of Jesus, the *Formula of the Institute* which states that it is to defend and spread the faith and help men and women grow in Christian Life "by means of public preaching, lectures and any other ministration whatsoever of the Word of God, and further by means of the Spiritual Exercises, the education of children and unlettered persons in Christianity and the spiritual consolation of Christ's faithful through hearing confessions and administering the other sacraments (*Formula of the Institute* incorporated into *Constitutions*, no. 3).

JP sj

Const. no. 3; DALMASES, pp. 140, 169, 179

Sacramentorum, piarumq concionum ʋſū Romæ renouat, ac rationem pueris tradendi doctrinæ christianæ rudimenta Romanis in templis, ac plateis inducit.

60

SANCTÆ MARIÆ DE STRATA QVÆ IN TEMPLO FARNESIANO
NOMINIS IESV ROMÆ COLITVR VERA EFFIGIES
ANTE QVAM S. IGNATIVS SOCIETATIS IESV FVNDATOR
ET EIVS SOCII SACRVM SÆPIVS FECERVNT.
Petrus Miotte Burgundus Sculp:

52. Pierre Miotte, *The Madonna della Strada with Sts. Ignatius and Francis Xavier*,
Engraving, 37 x 27 cm., after 1638
Rome, Archivio della Congregazione dei Nobili del Gesù

At the very center of the Rione della Pigna stood a small chapel called "S. Maria Alteriorum" on the Bufalini plan of the *piazza* located on the Via Papale (Cat. 48). This chapel was more commonly know as Santa Maria della Strada, and dates at least to the eleventh century, when it appeared in the *Liber Censuum* as "S. Maria Hastariorum." In documents of the thirteenth century it was called "S. Maria Astariis" and in the fourteenth century , "S. Maria de Astara." It most probably owes its name to the Astalli family, one of the most important families of the Rione della Pigna, whose Gothic ancestors can be traced in Rome to at least the middle of the tenth century. At least two Astallis were cardinals during the twelfth century. The small church that was granted by papal concession to the Jesuits in 1540 had served as a funeral chapel for the Astalli family from the late thirteenth century (Tacchi Venturi, p. 26).

Pietro Codacio, the first Italian Jesuit, had served as *maestro di camera* to both Paul III and his predecessor Clement VII. He left the papal court at Palazzo S. Marco to join Ignatius and his companions in 1539. The practical Lombard was immediately charged with the duties of "minister" of the community, coordinating the practical details of everyday life. In November of 1540, six weeks after the written approval of the Society, Codacio used his influence in the papal court to obtain the benefice for S. Maria della Strada for himself as pastor. The companions moved to rooms rented from the Astalli family next to the chapel early in 1541. Later that same year, Codacio transferred the parish in perpetuity to the superior general of the Society.

Early documentary evidence clearly indicates that Ignatius and the first companions chose S. Maria della Strada not because of its buildings, but because of its strategic location at the center of Renaissance Rome (FN III, 178). At least three times the Jesuits enlarged the chapel, including the addition of a separate wing or *penitenceria* for the sacrament of reconciliation (*EppIg.* XII, 6094). The chapel was used until 1568, when it was in large part demolished to make room for the *Templum Farnesium,* the present Chiesa del Gesù. Its apse served as a sacristy until the building of the new Casa Professa contiguous to the church in the early 1600s.

The late fifteenth- or early sixteenth-century image of the Madonna della Strada (anonymous, Roman school) probably decorated the side of the church which faced Via Capitolina (Dionisi, p. 10). It was removed from the wall, placed in the Chiesa di S. Marco for safekeeping during the construction of the Gesù, and then installed in the round chapel to the left of the high altar of the Gesù. The chapel is a favorite center of Marian devotion for the citizens of Rome. The engraving displayed here dates from the mid-seventeenth century, after the Madonna was solemnly crowned by the Chapter of S. Pietro on August 14, 1638. It shows Ignatius and Francis Xavier in prayer before the Madonna and Child.

TL sj

DIONISI, 1982, pp. 9-11; FABRE, 1887, p. 441; TACCHI VENTURI, 1899, pp. 21-29

53. *Sentence of the Governor of Rome against the detractors of Ignatius and his companions,* November 18, 1538

Rome, Archivium Romanum Societatis Iesu, Hist. Soc. 1b, no. XIX, fol. 35

With the failure of the early companions to find passage to the Holy Land, they travelled to Rome to await both papal approval and papal missions for their apostolic works. As in the Veneto, in Rome they engaged in various forms of ministry which in a priestly context now included the celebration of mass, confession, and most importantly, preaching. One cannot underestimate the importance of preaching in the context of Renaissance church practice; preachers were enormously influential and had their own followings.

After receiving the proper faculties from the authorities on May 5, 1538 Ignatius and his followers began preaching publicly from the Roman churches. What they discovered, however, was opposition from various people in Rome who began to spread rumors of unorthodox theology, either of the Alumbrados form, of which Ignatius was suspected many years earlier in Spain, or of the Lutheran form as German Reformation theology began to be countered by the Catholics.

Ignatius immediately realized that his fledgling company's effectiveness as an apostolic organization would be seriously undermined by these rumors. He sought and received a speedy hearing and exoneration from the Roman Curia which found the early Jesuits to be teaching nothing but the most orthodox of Catholic teachings.

In this judgment of Governor Benedetto Conversini, we find the statements which not only declared Ignatius and his companions free from doctrinal error, but which also praised the good works they were accomplishing in the church in Rome. The governor states that after extensive public testimony from "Spain, Paris, Venice, Vicenza, Bologna, Ferrara, and Siena where...Ignatius and his companions

CAT. 53

preached,...and after examining their morals and doctrine and lives," he found that "every speculation and accusation and rumors against them were without any support whatsoever."

Conversini stated that he could find nothing of infamy in their teaching, but rather found their accusers to be far from the truth given that men of serious bearing had testified instead in the most favorable manner on behalf of the early Jesuits.

Such a clear and favorable pronouncement was necessary for Ignatius to continue his apostolic work of reform and renewal in the church. It is ironic that one of the great champions of the Catholic reform should come under suspicion of upholding Lutheran theology.

Having spent one and a half years in spiritual preparation and free to continue his growing ministry without suspicion, Ignatius now celebrated with greater joy his first mass at the Basilica of S. Maria Maggiore on Christmas Eve, 1538.

PT sj

DALMASES, pp. 157-163; FD, pp. 556-558

54. The Urban Mission, Engraving in: *Vita Beati Patris Ignatii*, fig. 63, 1609

Florence, Biblioteca dell'Istituto Stensen, Armadio A

Publica Romæ pietatis opera instituit: coenobia mlie-
rum male nuptarum: virginum S. Catherinæ ad funa-
rios: puellarum SS. quatuor coronatorum: puerorū item
qui orbi parentibus per Vrbem vagi mendicant: Cathecume-
norum: aliorumq̃ collegia magna orum admiratione, fructuq.
63

The early Society's positive decision to perform a wide range of social, pastoral, and educational ministries in the urban context determined Ignatius' deliberate choice of a downtown location for his headquarters in Rome. While the preaching and teaching works of the Jesuits are well documented, less known but no less important for understanding Ignatius' urban strategy were the works of charity which the Jesuits performed on behalf of the emarginated, the outcasts, and the underprivileged.

The first charitable work at the house on Via dei Delfini (the establishment of a soup kitchen for the poor during the very severe winter of 1537-1538) was followed by a number of social and pastoral initiatives which were directed towards those on the fringes of society. In an era when the Jewish community was treated with prejudice and suspicion, Ignatius organized an outreach to his neighbors in the Jewish quarter (which Paul IV transformed into a walled ghetto in 1556, the year of Ignatius' death). With the assistance of members of the Farnese family, he founded two houses for Jewish catechumens near the Campidoglio, and obtained papal concessions for their protection. He also cooperated in the foundation of orphanages for boys and girls at the Piazza Capranica near the Pantheon.

Perhaps the most radical of Ignatius' initiatives were those addressed to women: as early as 1543, he proposed a new model of ministry for reformed prostitutes, a kind of "half-way house" which sought not only their conversion but also their reintegration into society. Earlier houses for the *convertite* had emphasized severe penance for past waywardness; Ignatius' *Compagnia della Grazia* which was located at the Church of S. Marta (in modern Piazza Collegio Romano) stressed rehabilitation and helped the women to regain their self-esteem. Because of the very large number of courtesans in Renaissance Rome, Ignatius also founded the *Compagnia delle Vergini Miserabili*, a home for the daughters of prostitutes. This work, centered at S. Caterina dei Funari near the della Strada Chapel, sought to assist young women by providing shelter and support, including dowries, which could enable them to avoid economic pressures which drove many women to prostitution (*EppIg.* I, 119).

Ignatius' favored model for such foundations was the "confraternity," a religious association of lay people organized and directed by the Jesuits in its early phases. Many of these works were turned over to the lay direction after they had been firmly established.

TL sj

DALMASES, pp. 179-185, 188-189

55. Pedro Ribadeneira, *Vita del P. Ignatio Loiola*, pp. 190-191, Venice, 1587
Vatican City, Biblioteca Apostolica Vaticana, R.I. V. 1162

For the biography of Ignatius of Loyola and for the history of the early Society of Jesus, the *Life* by Pedro Ribadeneira is an extremely important document.

Ribadeneira was born in Toledo, Spain in 1527 and was received into the Society of Jesus by Ignatius himself on September 18, 1540. Ribadeneira was not yet fourteen years old and the Society was nine days from its formal approval by the pope on September 27, 1540. He spent the next seventy-one years as a Jesuit and died in Madrid on September 22, 1611, the very last survivor of the first generation of Jesuits.

In his youthful years in Rome he came to know intimately the daily life of the Jesuits in the first house of the Society. In 1549 he went to Palermo to teach rhetoric for three years, then returned to Rome and went to Belgium in 1555 to establish the Society there. Subsequently he became provincial of one of the Italian provinces, commissary in Sicily, twice general assistant in Rome, and superior of several Roman houses. In 1574 he went to Spain where he lived and worked until his death.

In 1572 the first Latin edition of his *Life of Ignatius Loyola, Founder of the Society of Jesus* appeared in Rome. Ribadeneira had apparently completed the original manuscript in Spanish in 1569, thirteen years after the death of Ignatius. The book was a widespread success. In less than thirty years Latin editions appeared in Madrid, Antwerp, Lyons and Cologne, and it was reprinted in Vienna as late as 1744. Most importantly, it was rapidly translated into Spanish, after some retouching by the author. Some would maintain that the corrections were made at the request of the then-General Claudio Aquaviva, in order to give a more formal, less personal portrait of Ignatius as Jesuit superior general.

Over the next several centuries the *Life* was translated in various editions in Spanish, in Italian (Cat. 55), German, French, English, Flemish, Greek, Polish, Czech, and in 1886, in Basque.

In some ways Ribadeneira produced the first full written portrait of Ignatius and the early Society, just as the early engravings displayed in this exhibit produced an iconography for Ignatius and the Society. This portrait was to influence for centuries the understanding of the founder, the lives of later members of the Society, and the progress of Jesuit historiography. Indeed, it has only been with the ongoing publication over the last ninety years of critical, scholarly editions of the works of Ignatius and of the early Jesuits (in the *Monumenta Historica Societatis Iesu*) and the publication of more popular works based on those editions that we have begun to know Ignatius in the fullness of his personality.

JP sj

FN IV, pp. 3-54

56. Ugo Pinard, *Urbis Romae Descriptio*, Engraving, 53.5 x 86 cm., 1555
Vatican City, Biblioteca Apostolica Vaticana, Riserva 7, fol. 3

This view-map shows the city as it might appear from a point above the Janiculum hill looking toward the east. Its emphasis on the city street, which appears as a distinct entity for the first time in this type of map, suggests the influence of Bufalini's plan-map of 1551 (Cat 48). Compared to this, a near contemporary view-map by Pirro Ligorio (1552) shows the city as the traditional collection of buildings and monuments, where the few streets shown within the dense part of the city appear as mere left-over spaces between the houses. Pinard instead uses the buildings to define Rome's major streets, which are shown in exaggerated width and clarity, and which mark unencumbered paths connecting the different parts of the city.

Unlike Bufalini, Pinard does not show every street and city block. He telescopes areas such as the blocks between the Pantheon and the Corso, so that we get a rather summary image of the city. Like Ligorio he makes certain monuments stand out by outsizing them with respect to their neighbors. Thus the Pantheon dwarfs its neighborhood, and the Palazzo del Senatore, and indeed the whole Capitoline hill, tower far higher over the Forum than they do in reality. But he breaks with tradition by including contemporary *palazzi* in the group of outsized notable monuments. We see the incomplete Palazzo Farnese (No. 82 on the map and its index), the Cancelleria (No. 80) and the boxy Palazzo Venezia (No. 79) rising high above their modest *quartieri*. Angular distortion is used by the map-maker in order to enable us to view some major elements more clearly. Thus the Vatican complex is skewed around to face south (instead of east) so that the *piazza* and the facade of old St. Peter's can be clearly seen.

Rather than in topographic completeness or precision, the value of Pinard's view-map lies in the overall image it gives of the extent to which the shrunken Medieval town had expanded by the mid-Cinquecento. By 1555 the Renaissance city had just begun to extend eastwards across the Corso towards the hills. To north and south it had reached out toward Piazza del Popolo and the Campidoglio with new, straight streets (Via Leonina-Ripetta and Via Capitolina-d'Aracoeli). The built-up Renaissance city is given relief by the contrastingly empty areas, scat-

tered here and there with ancient ruins and a few churches, stretching to the distant boundary of the third-century Aurelian walls. Indeed this empty part of town is depicted as being more uninhabited than it really was at the time: Bufalini reveals that the areas around S. Maria Maggiore and the Lateran were not nearly as devoid of human habitation as Pinard shows them.

The definition of the Renaissance city afforded by Pinard's map helps to understand the choice of location for St. Ignatius' community. He chose Rione della Pigna, on the edge of the city in an area much more lightly built than populous *rioni* such as Ponte and Regola along the river. Consequently property values in this neighborhood were not as high as in the denser areas. But it was in a part of town which was rapidly expanding as witnessed by the recently built Via Capitolina (modern Via Aracoeli) and the large new Quartiere del Pantano laid out in the 1560s on reclaimed swampy ground which covered the Imperial Fora. Finally it was near two centers of papal authority: Palazzo Venezia and the Campidoglio (Cat. 39, 40, 47).

The site of the future Church of the Gesù appears directly in front of the Palazzo Venezia. Conforming to the summary nature of Pinard's work, the cluster of four small city blocks which constituted the area upon which the church and the Casa Professa were to be built appears on the map as a single unit with an element projecting to the left which may be interpreted as being S. Maria della Strada. While its schematic depiction does not allow for precise topographic or architectural analysis, the two-storey building attached to the church may well represent the early Casa Professa. Less conclusive is the depiction of the block along the Corso between Palazzo Venezia and S. Maria sopra Minerva (No. 68) which contains within it the site of the future Collegio Romano/S. Ignazio complex. Pinard's view-map shows us St. Ignatius' Rome just before the beginning of the Jesuit building program and thirty years before the transformation of the empty area of the city by Sixtus V.

AC

FRUTAZ, 1962

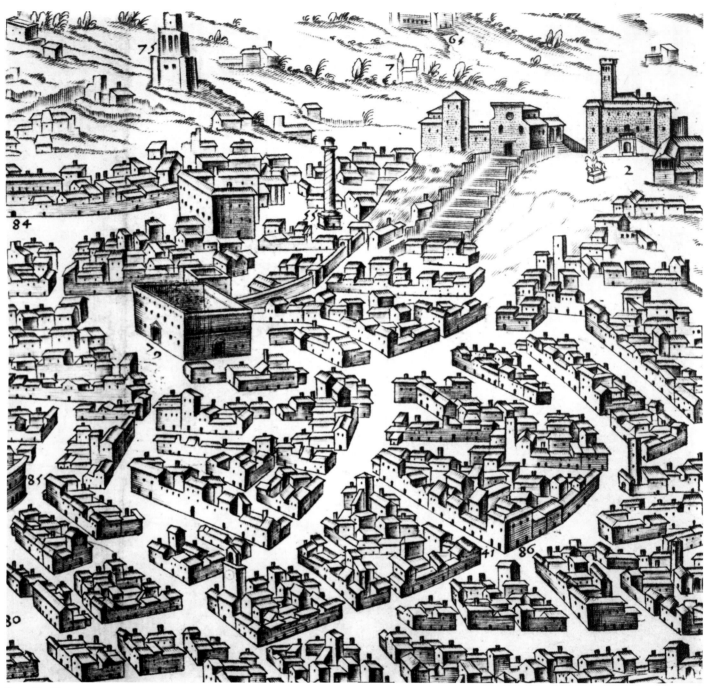

CAT. 56, DETAIL

119

57. Anonymous, *Paul III approves the Society of Jesus*, Oil on canvas, 235 x 281 cm., mid-17th century

Rome, Church of the Gesù, Antesacristy

This mid-seventeenth century painting telescopes into a single scene Ignatius' presentation of the foundational documents of the Society to Paul III and the aged pontiff's formal approval of the Society of Jesus which was given at the Palazzo Venezia on September 27, 1540. In the group behind Ignatius are Pierre Favre and Diego Lainez, the companions who had accompanied Ignatius on his journey to Rome in 1537. The older man with the white beard behind the pope can be identified as Pietro Codacio, the first Italian Jesuit. Codacio had left the papal court to join Ignatius in 1539. Between Ignatius and Paul III stands the Cardinal Nephew Alessandro Farnese, an early supporter of the Society and the major benefactor of the Church of the Gesù.

The portraits of the pope and Cardinal Alessandro are based on copies of the famous Titian paintings of the Farnese family. The facial characteristics of Ignatius, Lainez, Favre and Codacio are similar to those found in early portraits from the late sixteenth century. This large painting, along with its pendant which represents the Cardinals Alessandro and Odoardo Farnese (Cat. 81), was almost certainly commissioned by the Jesuits in gratitude for the generosity of the Farnese family towards the order in the early years of its history.

MPD'O

Moroni, 1844, XXIII, p. 211; Ravier, 1973, pp. 128-129

58. *Regimini Militantis Ecclesiae*, in *Summorum Pontificum Paulii III...indulta ad conformatione instituti Soc. Iesu pertinentia*, p. 1, Rome, 1584
Vatican City, Biblioteca Apostolica Vaticana, R.I., VI, 274

Regimini Militantis Ecclesiae is the bull by which Pope Paul III officially approved the Institute of the Society of Jesus on September 27, 1540.

In an audience of late November, 1538, Ignatius and his nine companions offered themselves and their services to Pope Paul III, as they had vowed at Montmartre. The pope thought of sending them, singly or in small groups, to Italian cities, and it seemed that their group would be dispersed. Hence they wondered: Should they, to retain some form of unity, elect one of their number as a superior, and vow to obey him? Should they form themselves into a new religious order? In mid-March, 1539, they began deliberations about the pros and cons and by June 24 they reached unanimous affirmative conclusions.

The first step toward giving juridical structure to their group was to compose a summary of the nature and characteristics of the new institute for approval by the pope. Ignatius was charged to do this, with help from the others. He soon produced a document containing "Five Chapters" or sections of 200-400 words each, entitled "A First Sketch of the Institute of the Society of Jesus." The sketch is permeated with the founder's ideas. The very first words, for example, reflect his enthusiasm over his vision at La Storta and his desire to be associated with Christ as still living in the Church: "Whoever desires to serve as a soldier of God beneath the banner of the cross in our Society, which we desire to be designated by the name of Jesus, and in it to serve the Lord alone and his vicar on earth, should, after a solemn vow of chastity, keep what follows in mind. He is a member of a community founded chiefly to strive for the progress of souls in Christian life and doctrine, and for the propagation of the faith by means of the ministry of the word, the Spiritual Exercises, and works of charity ..."

In early July Ignatius entrusted these Five Chapters to his friend Cardinal Gasparo Contarini, who on September 3, 1539, read them to the pope. "The finger of God is here," Paul III remarked. He orally approved the Chapters and ordered the preparation of an official document. This led to a year of discussions in the papal Curia. Then the Five Chapters, revised only in a few small details, came back to Ignatius, encased within one paragraph of Introduction and another of formal approval, in the bull

Regimini Militantis Ecclesiae, a later edition of which is exhibited here. Ignatius and his companions were now a new religious order of clerics regular in the church, the Society of Jesus. The "Five Chapters" were its papal law and the Society's fundamental Rule. On April 6, 1541, the companions elected Ignatius as their superior general, by unanimous vote except for his own.

GG sj

Const., pp. 14-21; DALMASES, pp. 169-172

59. *Autograph text of the vows of 1541*

Rome, Archivium Romanum Societatis Iesu, Hist. Soc. 1A, fol. 14-15

After the companions had received papal approval for their enterprise in the form of the papal bull *Regimini Militantis Ecclesiae*, it was necessary to establish the constitutional forms of the religious life, elect a superior, and take vows. The young Company was already dispersed: Xavier and Rodrigues in Lisbon, Favre on his way to Germany, and four others (Broët, Jay, Lainez, and Bobadilla) in the cities of Italy on papal missions.

Lainez, Jay, and Broët joined Ignatius, Salmerón, and Codure in Rome at the beginning of Lent, 1541. During the month of March, 1541 Ignatius and Codure drafted provisional constitutions based on their first deliberations in 1539. After those constitutions were signed by all present, and after three days of prayer, they voted to elect their superior general. Before leaving for Portugal, Xavier and Rodrigues

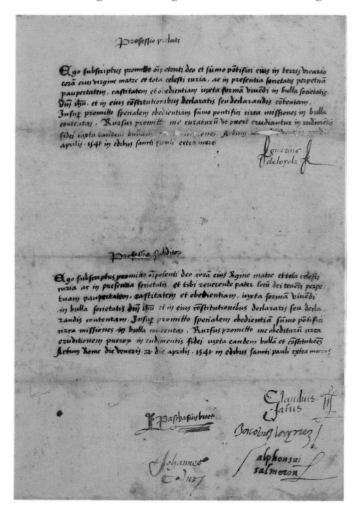

had left behind sealed ballots. Favre sent his from Germany. Eight of the nine votes cast on April 5 were for Ignatius. The text of Ignatius' ballot read "Excluding myself, in regard to there being a superior I give my vote in our Lord to him who will receive a majority of votes for that office. I have given my vote indeterminately, considering that as good" (*Scripta*, II, p. 5, n. 4).

Ignatius implored his companions to allow him to refuse the election, "because of his many faults and bad habits, past and present, with many sins, and other faults and miseries" (*FN* I, 18). After a week's deliberation another scrutiny was held, and the results were the same as the first. Ignatius went to S. Pietro in Montorio and there put himself in the hands of his confessor, Franciscan Teodosio da Lodi. Fra Teodosio convinced him to accept the election.

On April 22, 1541 the newly elected superior general celebrated mass for his companions at the Basilica of S. Paolo Fuori le Mura. Just before communion he pronounced his vows, and his companions did the same. The text of the formula (Cat. 58), signed by Ignatius and his companions, reads as follows:

"I, the undersigned, promise to Almighty God and the Supreme Pontiff, his vicar on earth, in the presence of his Virgin Mother and the whole heavenly court, and of the Society, perpetual poverty, chastity, and obedience, according to the manner of living which is contained in the bull of the Society of our Lord Jesus and in its Constitutions adopted or to be adopted. Moreover, I promise special obedience to the Supreme Pontiff in regard to the missions as contained in the bull. I likewise promise to procure that children be instructed in the rudiments of the faith in accordance with the same bull and Constitutions" (*FN* I, pp. 20-21).

At the end of the Eucharist, the companions exchanged the kiss of peace with one another "with no lack of devotion, feeling, and tears" (*FN* I, p. 22). That day they made the round of the Seven Churches of Rome, traversing on foot the city they had vowed to serve.

TL sj

DALMASES, pp. 172-178; *FN* I, pp. 15-22; *Scripta de Sancto Ignatio*, 1904-1918, II, p.5, n. 4

122

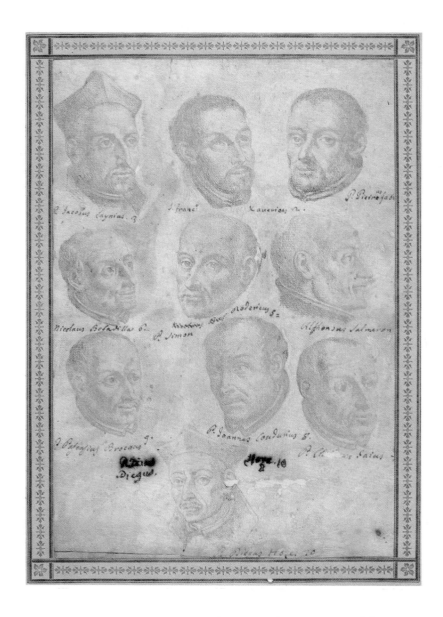

60. *The first companions of St. Ignatius*, Red chalk, 26.2 x 17.4 cm., late 16th century (?)
Rome, Archivium Romanum Societatis Iesu, Armadio 12

According to oral tradition, this drawing is the earliest known representation of the first companions of St. Ignatius. It shows Diego Lainez, Francisco Javier, Pierre Favre, Nicholas Bobadilla, Simão Rodrigues, Alfonso Salmerón, Paschase Broët, Jean Codure, Claude Jay, and Diego de Hoces. No documentary evidence has been found to assist in dating the sheet.

A close comparison of this image, however, with the medallion portraits of the first companions by Andrea Pozzo in the corridor next to the rooms of St. Ignatius at the Casa Professa in Rome, suggests very strongly that Pozzo had this drawing in hand when he was decorating the corridor in the 1680s. The archives of the Society at that time were located in the Casa Professa, and it is not unreasonable to speculate that Pozzo had access to the visual materials contained therein.

TL sj

RAVIER, 1973, pp. 303-304

61. *The Original Seal of the Superior General of the Society of Jesus,* Engraved brass,
diameter 4 cm., ca. 1550

Rome, Archivium Romanum Societatis Iesu, Sigilli 1

Ignatius himself sealed legal documents with this seal, the first of many engraved for the superior general of the Society of Jesus (see fig. p. 11).

The seal shows the monogram of the name of Jesus in lower-case letters, with the bar of the "h" serving as the upright of a Latin cross. This form of the monogram was popularized by St. Bernardino of Siena, and was widespread in Italy at the time. Ignatius chose the name of Jesus for his official seal, and he also instructed that the monogram be placed over the doors of Jesuit houses (*Epplg.* II, no. 551, 554) to underscore his intention that the Society be known as the "Companions of Jesus" and not "of Ignatius."

There are different interpretations of the sun,

moon, and stars which appear on the seal. For some, the sun is a symbol of Christ and the moon and stars are figures of the Virgin Mary. Others see in this iconography a reference to the Christological hymn in Philippians 2:3-10, which extols the "name above every other name, so that at the name of Jesus every knee must bend in the heavens, on the earth, and under the earth, and every tongue proclaim to the glory of the Father that Jesus Christ is Lord" (see Cat. 112).

TL sj

Acta Sanctorum, 1749, VII, p. 532

62. Manuscript of *The Constitutions of the Society of Jesus* ("Textus B")
with autograph corrections by St. Ignatius, ca. 1550

Rome, Archivium Romanum Societatis Iesu, Inst. 1b, fol. 38v-39r

This manuscript is St. Ignatius' personal and final copy of his *Constitutions of the Society of Jesus* which he used from 1552 until his death in 1556. Because of many small corrections or marginal additions in his own hand it is called the Autograph text, or Text B.

The bull *Regimini* of 1540 authorized the general and his associates to compose statutes applying this fundamental papal law to extensive further details. The Latin word *constitutio* can mean a statute. These *Constitutions of the Society* are a collection of such statutes, in four separate books gradually composed after 1540 and contained in the manuscript displayed: (1) the *General Examen,* explaining the Society for candidates and their examiners; (2) the *Declarations of the Examen,* further explanations of some passages of the *Examen*; (3) the central core of legislation, the *Constitutions* proper; (4) their explanatory *Declarations.*

In January, 1551 Ignatius submitted a rather complete draft of his Constitutions, called Text A, to a council of Jesuits in Rome. They suggested a few emendations and approved the four treatises for experimental promulgation. Another, Text B, incor-

porated these emendations and was ready in 1552. From then through 1555, Father Jerónimo Nadal carried Text B and explained these Constitutions to Jesuit communities in Sicily, Spain, Portugal, Germany, and Austria.

Meanwhile Ignatius had his own copy (Textus B), on which he made further small corrections until his death in 1556. In 1558 the Society's First General Congregation approved both this Spanish text and a Latin translation of it. Thus his *Constitutions* became juridically valid.

Since then the *Constitutions* have been and still are the governing law of the Society. They are the application of Ignatius' inspiring concept of God's plan of salvation to the organization, inspiration, and government of his world-wide religious institute.

Ignatius' *Constitutions* are a manual of discernment, guiding superiors and members to apply Ignatius' criterion for choice among options: choose what is likely to result in greater praise or glory to God. The criterion informs all decisions about apostolic works and the choice of locations for such activities. The text displayed (in the printed *Constitutions* 622, D, 3) reads: "The more universal the good is, the more is it

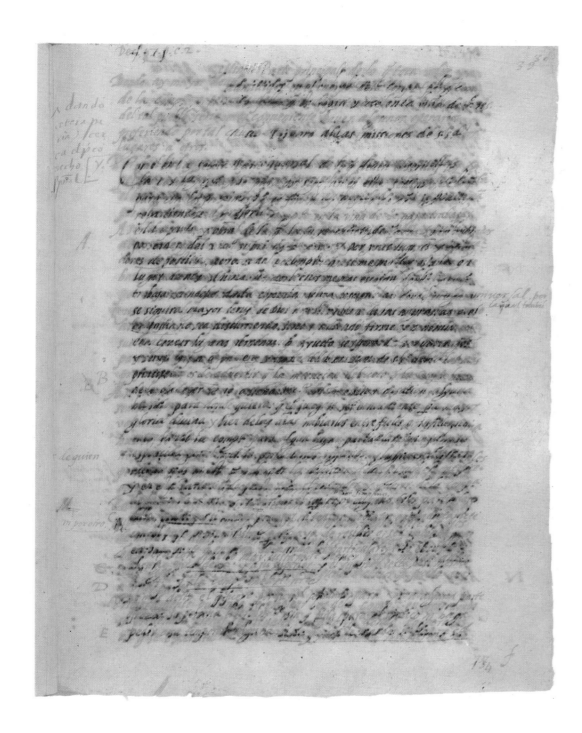

divine. Therefore preference ought to be given to those persons and places which, through their own improvement, become a cause which can spread the good accomplished to many others who are under their influence or take guidance from them. For that reason, the spiritual aid which is given to important and public persons ought to be regarded as more important, since it is a more universal good . . .

Preference ought to be shown to the aid which is given to the great nations such as the Indies, or to important cities, or to universities, which are generally attended by numerous persons who by being aided themselves can become laborers for the help of others."

GG sj

63. *Constitutiones Societatis Iesu*, Rome, 1570

Vatican City, Biblioteca Apostolica Vaticana, R.G. Storia V, 4111

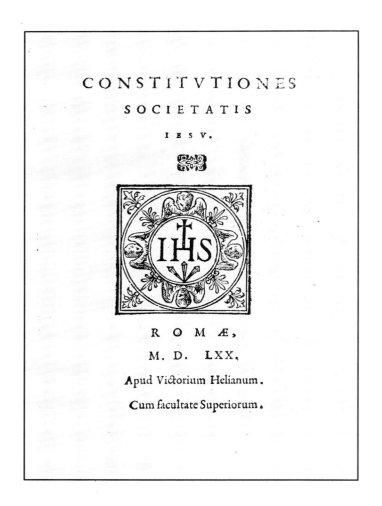

The Latin translation of St. Ignatius' original Spanish *Constituciones* was made chiefly by his capable secretary, Father Juan de Polanco, partly before and partly after Ignatius' death in 1556. Of the two texts approved by the First General Congregation, the Spanish and the Latin, the Latin was the more necessary. It was the language of the Universal Church and could be used in the many countries where the Society already existed. Hence, under General Diego Lainez the work of printing the Latin text quickly began. It soon appeared in print in the form of four separate books: the *General Examen* and the *Constitutions of the Society of Jesus* in 1558, the *Declarations on the Examen* and the *Declarations on the Constitutions* in 1559.

However, on the occasions when the *Examen* or *Constitutions* referred the reader to a declaration, many found the task of turning to a separate book and searching for it there inconvenient. During the generalate of Francis Borgia a new edition was published in 1570. It wove the previous four books into one. All the declarations were printed immediately under the passage of the *Examen* or *Constitutions* which referred the reader to a declaration. The text of the *Examen* and *Constitutions* was printed in Roman type, and the *Declarations* in italic type. That arrangement has been followed in virtually all later editions. A copy of the 1570 edition is displayed here.

GG sj

Const., pp. 39-59

64. Roman School, *St. Ignatius*, Oil on canvas, 98.5 x 84.5 cm., early 17th century (?)

Rome, General Curia of the Society of Jesus

Never before published, this half-length portrait of the saint represents Ignatius displaying a book on whose open pages one reads "Ad Maiore Dei Gloria / Regulae Soc. Iesu" (For the greater glory of God / Rules of the Society of Jesus). He is clothed in the cassock and black cape of the Society, without the four-cornered biretta characteristic of other images of the period.

The painting is part of a group of idealized portraits executed after the death of the saint (July 31, 1556), and actively maintains the somatic and skeletal characteristics of the prototypical portraits of Rome (Jacopino del Conte, 1556) and Madrid (Alonso Sanchez Coello, 1585). In comparison with the Madrid image, based on the death masks and of the recollections of Pedro de Ribadeneira, Jacopino's painting, based on sketches made of Ignatius' face on the day of his death, transmits a more faithful image of Ignatius' physignomy. The painting on display shows marked similarities to the prototype of Jacopino, while the crystalline quality of the execution and the geometric regularity of the facial planes relate the work to the calligraphic clarity of line found in a canvas of the same subject conserved in Louvain in the Residence of the Jesuit fathers.

The presence of the luminous halo (which a recent close study of the painting showed to be original) argues for a dating close to the time of Ignatius' canonization in 1622. Dating the painting to the years of the first veneration of Ignatius (ca. 1600) or the time of his beatification (1609) would be premature, given the architectural background and the chromatic density of the minor areas of the painting inspired by the softness of the early baroque palette.

GC

Technical information

The painting is executed on canvas which, between the end of the sixteenth and the beginning of the seventeenth centuries, definitively supplanted the use of heavier and less flexible wooden supports. The priming of the canvas with a red gesso and glue clearly highlights the rather wide weave of the canvas, conferring on it the characteristic grid common in seventeenth century paintings.

The rendering of the image, achieved by the laying of a noticeably thick color field, shows confident brushwork. The observable progress of surface cracks gives unmistakable evidence that the painting was executed in oil.

MDL

De Hornedo, 1956; Künstle, 1926, pp. 327-29; Tacchi Venturi, 1929b

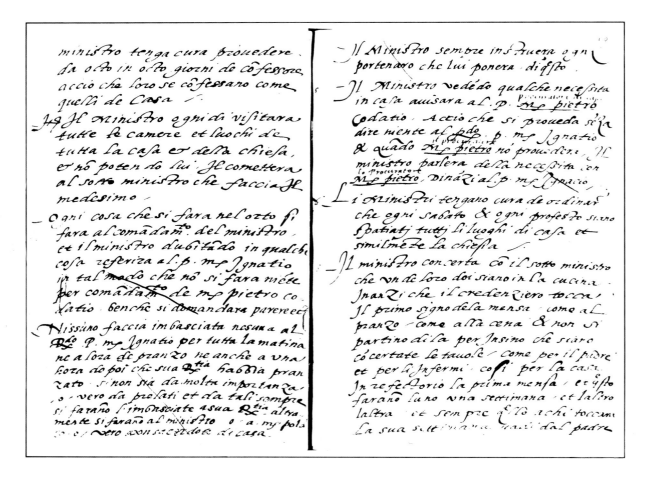

65. Manuscript of the *Regulae Communes Romanae*, 1549
Rome, Archivium Romanum Societatis Iesu, Inst. 38a, fol. 18v-19r

St. Ignatius foresaw in the *Constitutions* that, in addition to the *Constitutions* and their *Declarations* (that have the same juridical value and are concerned with "immutable things that universally must be observed"), other "ordinances which can be accommodated to diverse times, places, and persons" are also necessary. In the language of the Society of Jesus, these are referred to as the *Regulae* or Rules.

Displayed here are the Rules of the house of Rome that St. Ignatius himself composed and that went into effect in 1549. In the Italian manuscript displayed here, traces of Spanish, Ignatius' mother tongue, appear in the text: "yo reservo" in Rule 40, the conditional particle "si" and the reflexive "se," as well as the characteristic use of the gerund. The author of the critical edition of the Rules in the *MHSI* has argued that the author is none other than St.

Ignatius, even though some other father might have taken part in the redaction.

The rules are called "common" because they are to be followed by all those who live in the house they govern. Other particular rules follow in the text which pertain to determined persons or offices, for example, the minister, the sacristan, the cook, the janitor, etc.

Often re-edited and republished in subsequent generalates, Ignatius' common rules of the house were the model for centuries of domestic legislation in the Society of Jesus.

MR-J sj

Regulae, 1948, pp. 5*ff.

66. *Ratio atque Institutio Studiorum*, Rome, 1586

Vatican City, Biblioteca Apostolica Vaticana, Rossiano 6230

In the years following the death of Ignatius not all Jesuits agreed that operating schools was a proper activity for the Society of Jesus; it was a debate that lasted well into the seventeenth century. Nevertheless Jesuit involvement in education continued to grow at a rapid rate. Of the 40 schools that Ignatius had personally approved, at least 35 were in operation when he died, even though the members of the Society numbered only about 1,000. Within forty years, the number of Jesuit schools would reach 245. Ignatius' *Constitutions* had promised the development of a document describing common principles for all Jesuit schools. With the rapid increase in schools and enrollment, formulation of such a document became a practical necessity.

Successive Jesuit superiors encouraged an exchange of ideas based on concrete experiences so that, without violating the Ignatian principle that "circumstances of place and persons be taken into account," a basic curriculum and pedagogy could be developed that would draw on this experience and be common to all Jesuit schools.

The first drafts of a common document were, as Ignatius had wished, based on the "Rules of the Roman College." An international committee of six Jesuits was appointed by Superior General Claudio Aquaviva; they met in Rome to adapt and modify these tentative drafts on the basis of experience in other parts of the world. In 1586 (Cat. 66) and again in 1591 this group published more comprehensive drafts that were widely distributed for comments and corrections. Further conversations, commission meetings and editorial work resulted in the publication of a definitive *Ratio Studiorum* in 1599.

The records of the meetings of the committee of six that prepared the first *Ratio Studiorum* in 1586 state that "the spirit of Ignatius presided over the deliberations." They often consulted Loyola's guidelines set forth in the book of the *Spiritual Exercises*, in the *Constitutions*, and in his letters. Throughout these writings and in the formulation of the *Ratio*, one finds a stress on means as well as ends in education. His own painful educational experience had proven to Ignatius that enthusiasm was not enough for success in study. *How* a student was directed, the method of

teaching employed was crucial. The dynamic of the Exercises has been described as "radically pedagogical," and the system of Jesuit schools that grew from them shared with them a concrete world view, a focus on individual responsibility, and the need for following well-tried means to reach the end, which is always Christ.

VD sj

CHARMOT, 1943, pp. 150-152; DONOHUE, 1963, p. 16

67. *Manuscript of a Letter of St. Ignatius* (Instructions for those sent to Modena), 1551
Rome, Archivium Romanum Societatis Iesu, Inst. 117a, fol. 140v-141r

In the Society's early years, Ignatius was compelled to give specific direction to those he sent out on mission to new cities and works. The numbers of new recruits was very large and the proportion of fully "formed" fathers, those who had taken final vows and who had received training directly from Ignatius or one of the other companions, was extremely small. Given the inexperience of the leaders of the new missions as well as the youth of most of those sent, Ignatius worked out a series of strategic directives which came under the rubric of "nuestro modo de proceder," or "our way of proceeding." These guidelines stake out three important areas of edification (literally, "building up") which focus the works of the new communities. Displayed here is a typical document of this type, an instruction for those sent to Modena in 1551.

The spiritual and moral edification of the religious community was to be obtained by the ordinary means of prayer, the sacraments, and the corporal and spiritual works of mercy. As in the foundational documents the "way of proceeding" directives placed special emphasis on the ministries of preaching and teaching. These instructions suggest that Jesuits should work in close collaboration with the local nobility and ecclesiastical hierarchy, "pleasing them in every way, according to what is Godly." Where possible, the Society should work in those pious works which are closest to the hearts of the civic leaders.

The instructions also give practical guidelines for the management of resources and acquisition of property. In order to preserve its spiritual authority, the community should "avoid any appearance of cupidity" by having its lay friends look after business or temporal affairs. Finally, the community is instructed "to have special care to obtain a good site that is spacious, or that can be enlarged in the future, that is sufficiently large for a church and a residence, and if at all possible that is not far removed from the dialogue of the city ("non troppo discosto da la conversatione della città"), and having bought that, it will be a good beginning for all the rest." The Society, then, is imagined in active conversation with the city, a city which it serves from the inside out.

TL sj

EppIg . IV, 411-412

68. *Canon 11 of the First General Congregation*, in: *Canones Congregationum Generalium*, p. 3, Rome, 1581
Vatican City, Biblioteca Apostolica Vaticana, R.G. Storia V, 4164

The supreme governing body of the Society of Jesus is the General Congregation, a body composed of professed members from all the provinces and regions. The General Congregation is the Society's ultimate legislative body, and as such is charged to update and clarify Constitutions as the times and circumstances demand. General Congregations do not occur with fixed regularity, but rather are called for the election of a new superior general, or if deemed necessary, for other motives by a group of "procurators" or representatives of the various provinces who meet every three years.

The first General Congregation (1558) was held two years after Ignatius' death in the room in which he died at the Roman Casa Professa. The *Constitutions* he had written were approved for the whole Society, and Diego Lainez, one of his first companions, was elected the second superior general. Among the "canons" or directives of that congregation, the eleventh dealt directly with the question of building. "It is decreed that the manner of the building of our houses and colleges, both for habitations and the

CAT. 67

CAT. 68

dem sepeliuntur, acquirant.

Tit.6. d.41. Declaratur in 4.Cõg. d.72.	9 In morte principum, quando pro eis exequiæ publice fieri solent per Ecclesias ciuitatis, possunt in nostris Ecclesiis huiusmodi exequiæ celebrari cum pheretro sine pompa; celebrando scilicet missas, vel si vsus patriæ habet, etiam recitando officium defunctorum modo nostro simplici, vt fieri solet in sepulturis nostrorum.	P.4.c. 1.§.4.
Tit.6. d.55.	10 Non expedit, vt Capellaniæ, quibus inseruiñt Clerici seculares, quos nostri possint eligere, in nostris Ecclesiis erigantur.	P.4.c. 2.§.4.
Tit.6. d.34. Can.9. Cõg.2.	11 Modus imponatur ædificiis Domorũ, & Collegiorum, quod in nobis est, vt sint ad habitandũ, & officia nostra exercendũ vtilia, sana, & fortia, in quibus tamen paupertatis memores esse videamur; vnde nec sumptuosa sint, nec curiosa. De Ecclesiis tamen nihil dictum est.	P.4.c. 2.§.5.
Tit.6. d.19.	12 Nostris præscribẽdum nõ est, vt omnes in eundem locum, orationis causa conueniant; quod de ordinaria oratione intelligitur, non de extraordinaria, quæ pro re nata publice ad tempus institui potest.	P.4.c. 4.§.3.& 4.
Ex 4. Cõg.d. 70.	[Cum Nouitijs tamen in oratione ante cœnam dispensari poterit, vbi Præpositus Generalis expedire indicauerit.]	

CONGREG. GENERALIS. 3

---

exercise of our ministries, is to be serviceable, healthful, and strong (utilitia, sana, et fortia); in these buildings, we should also appear to be mindful of poverty, and thus they should be neither sumptuous nor novel (nec sumptuosa sint nec curiosa). However, nothing is decreed about churches."

This canon codifies the practical experience and style of Ignatius, who insisted on simplicity and dignity in Jesuit construction. Until the end of his life, however, Ignatius spent freely to restore and enlarge the Chapel of the Madonna della Strada next to his Roman headquarters (EppIg. X, 6197), and twice had plans drawn to replace it with a large and splendid building. Ignatius had in fact been stung by local criticism when the first residence was completed: "Some say that we built ourselves a palace and we do not care for the church, even though those who say so are in error, for we have spent much since the beginning on the church and the properties [adjacent to it]" (EppIg. II, 366). In his urban vision, the church was the fulcrum of the ministries of the Society, and so no expense was to be spared on its construction or decoration.

The second General Congregation (which elected St. Francis Borgia as third superior general in 1565) enacted legislation which followed another of Ignatius' practices. Canon 9 insisted that the "forma et modus," the plan and the manner of all construction must be overseen directly by the superior general. Detailed descriptions of property and plans of new buildings were to be sent to Rome for approval. A large collection of drawings of Jesuit buildings was assembled in the central archive of the Society in Rome, which was dispersed with the suppression of the Society in 1773. 1,222 of these plans, purchased by a French bailiff of the Knights of Malta at a sale at the Collegio Romano, are now in the Cabinet des Estampes of the Bibliothèque Nationale de Paris.

TL sj

VALLERY-RADOT, 1960, 3*-7*

69. *Litterae Apostolicae et varia privilegia*, p. 73, Rome, 1606
Vatican City, Biblioteca Apostolica Vaticana, R.I., V, 2198

The rapid and simultaneous growth of the mendicant communities at the beginning of the thirteenth century had serious implications for the urban scene as well as for the local church organization. Older centers of ecclesiastical influence, the cathedral and the traditional parish, were rivaled and often supplanted by enormous new mendicant foundations which served in large part the pastoral needs of the growing mercantile classes. For centuries diocese and parishes had relied on feudal agricultural holdings. The return of a currency-based urban economy made large building projects feasible, and the mendicant foundations were often the beneficiaries of the newly-won wealth of the mercantile class.

The rapid mendicant expansion was not, however, achieved without difficulties and rivalries. Pools of resources were abundant in the urban landscape of the thirteenth century, but far from bottomless. Almost immediately conflicts arose between Franciscans and Dominicans, and sometimes within the religious families themselves over the siting of new churches and convents. Overcrowding of neighborhoods with new foundations caused serious drains on available resources.

As early as 1239, papal documents were promulgated to regulate the distance between new convents and churches. In 1265 Clement IV established a standard distance of 300 *canne* (one *canna* averaged about 2.5 meters) between mendicant foundations, although this was often reinterpreted according to the size of the town in question. By the sixteenth century, the measure was standardized to 140 *canne* (Guidoni, p. 85). Generally speaking, Franciscans, Dominicans, and Augustinians tended to site their establishments in a triangular pattern more or less equidistant from the recognized town center, either the *palazzo del comune* or the cathedral.

With the advent and rapid expansion of the Jesuits in the mid-sixteenth century, the mendicant orders, in many cities already established for more than three hundred years, fought to keep the Jesuit churches and colleges at a safe distance. In Ignatius' correspondence, more than twenty-five letters deal with the issue of the "rule of the cannae." The Jesuits were usually exempted from the rule by an oral judgment from the local ordinary who wanted the Jesuits as teachers and preachers in his city. Enough appeals came to Rome, however, that the Jesuits asked for and received a papal brief from Pope Pius IV. This document, dated April 13, 1561, gave the Society by papal authority a "decree, confirmation, concession, indult, license, faculty, and absolution" to build wherever and at whatever distance from mendicant foundations they chose. This *motu proprio* underscores the papal conviction that the Society's churches and colleges were important Catholic centers of worship and learning in the early period of the Counter Reformation.

In spite of this clear papal proclamation, the Jesuits were often called before local ecclesiastical tribunals. After the Jesuits' building projects caused them to be excommunicated by local authorities in some cities of Spain and Mexico, further appeals to the Holy See led Gregory XIII to publish a "Confirmation and Extension" of these same privileges in 1576. Nevertheless, even into the eighteenth century the Jesuits were required to defend their building programs against the mendicant charges of incroachment (see Cat. 78).

TL sj

GUIDONI, 1977, pp. 70-73, 82-86; *Litterae Apostolicae*, 1578, pp. 73, 156-166

70. *Medal of Ignatius of Loyola*, Bronze, 42mm., 1556 (?)
Obverse: Bust of Ignatius, *"IGNAT. SOCIET. IESU. FUNDAT."*
Reverse: *"OBIIT PRID. KAL. AUG. ANN. MDCLVI AET SUÆ LXV. CONFIR. VERO SOCIET. IESU XVI.*
Rome, Archivium Romanum Societatis Iesu, Medaglie dei Santi e Beati (see p. 33)

ROMA.

DOMVS AC PIETATIS OPERA, QVÆ B. P. IGNATIVS ROMÆ FACIENDA CVRAVIT, QVÆQ. SOCIETAS SVÆ CVRÆ COMMISSA HABET.
A. *Domus Patrum Profeſſorum*. B. *Collegium Romanum*. C. *Colleg. Pœnitentieria*. D. *Nouitiatus*. E. *Orphanorum atque orphaniarum domicilia*. G. *Catechumeni*. H. *S. Marthæ, tunc mulierum pœnitentium perfugium* I. *S. Catherina de Funarys Virginum in lubrico verſantium portus*. K. *Coll. Germanicum* L. *Anglicanum*. M. *Seminarij Romani*. N. *Maronitarum*.

71. Studio of Mallery/Galle, *Roma Ignaziana*, Engraving in: Pedro Ribadeneira, *Vita Beati Patris Ignatii Loyolae*, 27 x 36 cm., Antwerp, ca. 1610

Rome, Archivium Romanum Societatis Iesu, Armadio 4

The "Roma Ignaziana" map of the early seventeenth century shows the dramatic impact of the Society of Jesus on the Roman urban landscape during the Society's first seventy years of existence. This engraving was originally inserted in an illustrated life of Ignatius, the *Vita Beati Patris Ignatii Loyolae*, published shortly after the beatification in 1609. The engraving from the studio of Flemish engraver Cornelis Galle superimposes the principal Jesuit installations directly on the 1575 plan of Braun, Novellanus, and Hogenberg, which itself derived from the 1555 plan of Ugo Pinard. The erroneous placement of some of the installations (e.g. S. Caterina dei Funari, the Roman Seminary, and the House of Catechu-

mens) suggests that the engraver was probably working in Antwerp from second-hand information.

The title of the plan ("Domus ac pietatis opera quae B. P. Ignatius Romae facienda curavit, quaeq. Societas suæ curæ commisa habet") is significant, for it gathers together under the rubric of works of mercy *(pietatis opera)* all of the works of the first generations of Jesuit labor in Rome. Education was seen as work of charity no less than work with reformed prostitutes, catechumens, or orphans.

This piece of triumphalistic hagiographic propaganda makes an early and powerful visual statement about the urban theological vision of Ignatius. It portrays him (with the faint halo granted him as a *Beatus*) surrounded by fellow religious and a layman, in the heart of the urban fabric whose texture was changed emphatically by the explosion of Jesuit building that began with the first Casa Professa in 1543. By the time Galle's studio set about transforming the Pinard-Braun maps (which had clearly shown the first Jesuit house built under Codacio's supervision) that house, with the exception of Ignatius' rooms which were preserved, was already being replaced by the imposing bulk of the Casa Professa (1599-1623) adjoining the Church of the Gesù.

From the Jesuits' point of view at least, Rome had become an urban theater in which the Ignatian *Opera Pietatis* could be performed, with his well-trained troupe occupying center stage. In the plan of Pinard and those derived from it, Palazzo San Marco dominated the area at the foot of the Campidoglio. In the "Roma Ignaziana" the towering facades of the Gesù and the Collegio Romano occupy the absolute center of the field of vision, and the Palazzo San Marco disappears entirely.

In general, the works established and buildings erected during the life of Ignatius tended to be located within a narrow radius around the Gesù (Casa Professa, Santa Marta, House of Catechumens, Santa Caterina dei Funari) while works with which he collaborated (for example, the hospitals of Santo Spirito and S. Giacomo) and those built after his death (the Novitiate at S. Andrea, the Penitenzieria Apostolica, the English, Greek, and Maronite Colleges, and the Orphanage at SS. Quattro Coronati) tended to be more distant from his chosen center.

TL sj

FRUTAZ, 1962, I, p. 199; INSOLERA, 1985, pp. 161-162

72. Ambrogio Brambilla, *Plan of Rome*, Engraving, 39.5 x 52 cm., 1593

Vatican City, Biblioteca Apostolica Vaticana, St. Geogr. I. 630

This view-map of 1593 is derived directly from the 1575 view-map by Mario Cartaro, including the first 69 index entries, which are identical. Frutaz notes that, despite some differences, the Cartaro map is basically similar to the Pinard map (Frutaz, I, p. 184). Thus we can trace a line from Ugo Pinard's view-map, dating from 1555 (Cat. 56), through Cartaro to the Brambilla map. Like Pinard, Brambilla gives an oblique view of the city taken from a point above the Janiculum hill looking toward the east. The major streets are given the same importance as in Pinard, and in some cases are even more clearly defined. The convention of enlarging major monuments is retained, but Brambilla emphasizes obelisks rather than contemporary *palazzi*.

The emphasis on obelisks gives a clue to the theme of this map: it is an image of the city showing the impressive urban changes which had been just completed under Pope Sixtus V Peretti, who died in the same year (1590) that the map was drawn. This pope was responsible for the relocation of the four obelisks shown towering over the churches at Piazza S. Pietro, Piazza del Popolo, Piazza dell'Esquilino (behind S. Maria Maggiore, where the dome of Sixtus V's chapel is visible) and Piazza S. Giovanni in Later-ano. Equally emphasized on the map are the ancient columns of Trajan and of Marcus Aurelius, which Sixtus V had crowned with bronze statues of St. Peter and St. Paul. The emphasis on the obelisks is reminiscent of the fresco by an anonymous hand over the entrance to the Biblioteca Vaticana (see p. 42). The column of Trajan and three of the obelisks (Popolo, S. M. Maggiore, and Lateran) are the anchor points for the vast network of new arrow-straight streets which had been laid out in the empty quarter of the city under Sixtus V. Interestingly, Brambilla shows Sixtus V's new, and perhaps unfinished, streets bordered by dotted lines. This is in contrast to the graphic convention used for another recent street in that part of town: the Via Pia (Via del Quirinale/ XX Settembre) which is defined by solid lines. Even more intriguing is the presence of a straight street (never built) from S. Maria Maggiore to the Piazza del Quirinale, drawn with the same dotted-line convention, which is not one of the streets usually assigned to the urban plan of Sixtus V.

Brambilla's Rome has expanded considerably in the thirty-five years separating his map from that of Pinard. The Popolo Trivium has filled up with houses, and that neighborhood has spilled over on to

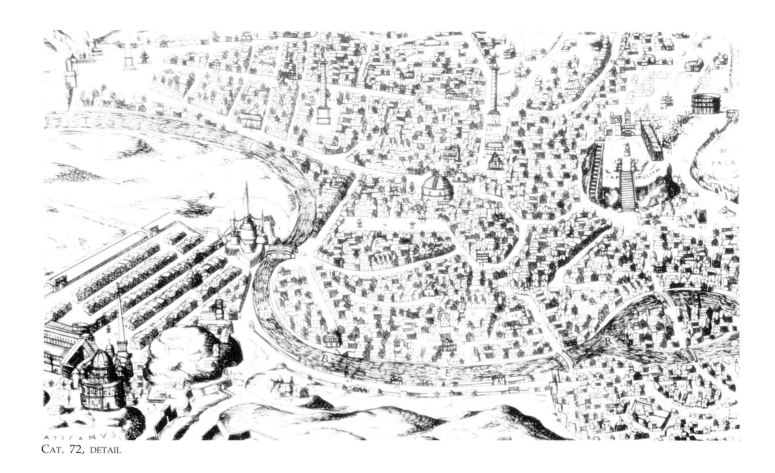

CAT. 72, DETAIL

the other side of Via del Babuino and sent a tentacle toward the future site of Piazza Barberini (next to the "M" of "M. QVIRINALIS" on the map). The quartiere del Pantano, built over the Imperial Forums in the 1560s and 1570s is shown schematically between the Roman Forum and the semi-circle of the Markets of Trajan.

Two Jesuit buildings are named in the index at the bottom of the map. The Church of the Gesù (No. 33: "Ecc[lesia] Societatis Iesu") appears on the map as an almost free-standing building surrounded by much more open space than it ever had in reality. This dramatic isolation, coupled with its dominating position on the Via Papale on its way to the Campidoglio, indicates the importance accorded by the map-maker to this recently completed church. The facade, though only sketchily represented, clearly corresponds to the two-level late Renaissance church front designed by Vignola and Della Porta. It is curious to note that in his map, Cartaro had depicted the Gesù as a columned and pedimented classical temple. The cluster of small buildings attached to the

church include the old Casa Professa and together constitute the site of the new Casa Professa begun in 1599.

The other Jesuit structure in the Brambilla index is the Collegio Romano (No. 92: "Collegium Societatis Iesus"). The number 92 on the map is placed on a city block corresponding to the site of the Collegio, but so schematically drawn that the 1580s structure is not readily recognizable. More than an actual representation of the building, it is an acknowledgement of another element of what might be referred to as the Jesuit *quartiere* of the city. The early 1600s would see an important addition to this grouping with the building of the Church of S. Ignazio. Whereas at mid-century this Jesuit *quartiere* was on the edge of town, by 1590 Rome's eastward expansion had caused it to be in the quick of the shifting center of the city.

AC

FRUTAZ, 1962; GAMRATH, 1987

135

73. Antonio Tempesta, *Plan of Rome*, Engraving, fol. 3, 40 x 54 cm., 1593

Vatican City, Biblioteca Apostolica Vaticana, St. Geogr. I, 621

At first glance this large (109 x 245 cm., in 12 sheets) image of Rome is a view-map belonging to the series starting in 1555 with Pinard (Cat. 56) and continuing through to the 1593 map by Brambilla (Cat. 72). The same characteristics of emphasis on the street network, enlargement of major buildings and monuments, eastward orientation with the view taken from a point above the Janiculum hill, and representation of all buildings and city blocks in oblique projection are present in this map. Like Pinard (but not Brambilla), Tempesta distorts the map to show something of the facade of the complex of structures at S. Pietro. However, closer examination of this remarkably detailed work reveals that, unlike most of its predecessors, it is really a combination of view-map and plan-map (Borsi, p.16). In this respect, Tempesta was following a technique used by Cartaro in his large map of 1576 and by Duperac in 1577. Using a vertically compressed street pattern of an ichnographic plan, almost certainly Bufalini's 1551 map, Tempesta represents each city block and each building in that block in oblique view. To avoid hiding streets and overlapping blocks, the author had to exaggerate the width of the streets and to reduce the vertical scale of most of the buildings (with the exception of the major monuments).

The result of this effort is an image which reveals the city's street system more completely and coherently than most earlier view-maps of Rome. At the same time, the large scale of this map allows for the inclusion of greater detail in the depiction of individual buildings than its two close predecessors, Cartaro 1576 and Duperac 1577. The theme of Sixtus V's urban planning noted for the 1593 Brambilla (see Cat. 72) is also very evident in Tempesta. Via Felice, Via Panisperna and Via di S. Croce in Gerusalemme are all clearly defined, and what was the empty quarter of the city is represented as an integral extension of the older, denser *Rioni*. There is a noticeable affinity between Tempesta's treatment of the Sixtine expansion of Rome and that of the anonymous painter of the fresco representing Sixtus' urban plan in ideal form, located over the entrance of the Biblioteca Vaticana (see p. 42). In both works S. Maria Maggiore is given considerable prominence by size, breadth of the surrounding empty space, and system of radiating streets. The fresco predates the map, so that it could have been an influence on Tempesta's work.

The similarity between fresco and map ceases however, when it comes to the depiction of individual buildings and monuments. An outsized Porta del Popolo marking the left edge of the fresco is balanced by an equally enlarged oblique view of the Chiesa del Gesù near the right edge. The anonymous painter renders the facade of the church in standard late Renaissance two-level form, with single pilasters and simple volutes, interchangeable with so many other contemporary church facades in Rome. Tempesta, on the other hand, captures every major particularity of that important facade: paired pilasters, double-curved volutes and even the segmental pediment over the main door breaking up into the heavy horizontal band of the upper level. It is an individualized portrait of the Gesù, and not a schematized multiple replicating other contemporary churches. Following the Pinard/Brambilla tradition of enlarging major buildings, Tempesta has the Gesù towering over its neighborhood to the point of dwarfing and partially hiding the neighboring Palazzo Venezia, which, by comparison is given rather summary treatment.

The church, with its lettered title ("T[emplum] Societatis Iesu"), is placed squarely in the path of the Via Papale, the papal processional route shown as a wide street approaching its impressive front from the west (see Cat. 48, Bufalini, and Cat. 73, Maggi). The wide facade, only partly visible at a distance from the narrower street, gradually opened out to the view of the processions as they drew closer, until it appeared in its entirety as they entered the Piazza del Gesù. This element of dramatic, gradual disclosure must have played an important part in the siting and careful angling (not quite perpendicular to the axis of the street) of this, the major Jesuit church. Consistent with the rest of the map, comparatively less attention is given to the cluster of small houses to the right of the church containing the Casa Professa and other buildings which were being gradually acquired for the new building which was to be begun six years after this map was published.

The other major building of the Jesuit *quartiere*, Valeriano's Collegio Romano (labelled "Collegium Societ[atis] Iesu") appears in detailed and outsized side view. The *piazza* in front of the main

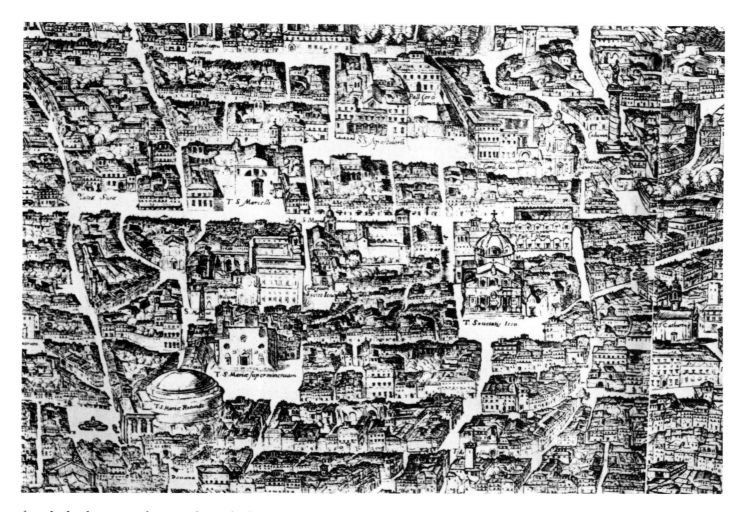

facade had not yet been enlarged: the Palazzo Salviati, which appears above the word "Collegium" would not be demolished to make way for the large *piazza* we see today until 1659. To the left of the unfinished back section of the Collegio is the Church of the Annunziata ("Nu[n]ciato" on the map) which was to be absorbed by the building of S. Ignazio in the seventeenth century.

More is known about Tempesta than about most of the other sixteenth-century map-makers. He was a Florentine landscape painter, who, upon coming to Rome, was drawn into the circle of Cardinal Alessandro Farnese, the great patron of the Jesuit order (Borsi, p.10). He was one of the painters commissioned by the order in the 1580s to work on the cycle of frescoes at S. Stefano Rotondo.

AC

BORSI, 1986; EHRLE, 1932; FRUTAZ, 1962

74. Giovanni Maggi, *Plan of Rome*, Woodcut, fol. 8, 38 x 54 cm., 1625
Vatican City, Biblioteca Apostolica Vaticana in: *Le Piante Maggiori di Roma dei secoli XVI e XVII*. Facsimile edition, 1933

This gigantic (224 x 428 cm.) view-map, composed of 48 sheets, is the largest image of Rome published before the 20th century. There are no known surviving copies of the original edition so we have to rely on the 1774 reprint edited by Carlo Losi (Frutaz, 1962, I, p. 208). The copious detail permitted by its large size, as well as the oblique projection based on an ichnographic plan of the city suggest that this map is a direct descendant of the Tempesta 1593 view-map (Cat. 71). The length to width ratios of the two maps are remakably close, with the vertical compression in Maggi being slightly less than that in Tempesta.

There is considerably less distortion in Maggi. His streets, while clearly visible, do not have the exaggerated and arbitrary width of Tempesta's streets. Maggi does not skew the complex of S. Pietro to reveal its facade as does Tempesta (like Pinard, Cat. 56). In this respect, Maggi is closer to Brambilla (Cat. 72). The enclosing boundary line of the third-century Aurelian walls is rendered with far greater accuracy by Maggi: for example the two ends of the wall where they meet the river at the right edge of the map are shown to be offset, as they were in reality, whereas Tempesta shows them as being directly opposite each other. Also Maggi includes the Sangallo bastion which replaced part of the Aurelian wall at the time of Paul III, while Tempesta does not. Less obvious is the subtle shaping of each city block by Maggi. Tempesta tends to standardize the shapes of the blocks.

This is not to say that the Maggi map is free of distortion. Any view-map (as opposed to orthogonal, ichnographic plan-maps), by its very nature, is distorted. But the minimization of distortion in the Maggi image makes it the most useful of all the view-maps for the topographical analysis of Rome, with the possible exception of Falda (1676). Part of the readability of the map is due to fact that, unlike his predecessors, Maggi does not excessively overscale the major buildings and monuments in order to make them stand out. Rather, he gives them relief by using a different graphic convention from the one used for surrounding buildings. Thus the tight weave of curves defining the drum and dome of the Pan-

theon, and the relatively blank treatment of the facade of the Church of S. Maria sopra Minerva provide the contrast with neighboring structures which gives both of these significant landmarks prominence in their Rione.

The clarity noted above makes the Maggi map ideally suited to the purpose of following coherent routes or paths through the city. A good example of this is the Via Papale, the processional route from the Vatican to the Lateran. The first part of this route was used as an access into the city for papal processions to various churches on their feast days. The whole route was used for the elaborate procession of the *Solenne Possesso* which occurred a week after each pope's coronation, when the new pontiff would publicly "take possession" of the Lateran, which, as the seat of the Bishop of Rome, ensured his title as temporal as well as spiritual ruler of the city.

The name "Via Papale" applied not only generically to the whole route between the Vatican and the Lateran, but also specifically to the middle third of that route between the Via de' Banchi and the Church of the Gesù . Most of this section appears on the Piazza Navona/Campidoglio sheet of the Maggi map (Frutaz, II, tav. 315). Starting at the lower left, Maggi labels it "Via di Parione" (modern Via del Governo Vecchio), and shows it passing through Piazza "Pasquino" on its way to the recently completed Theatine church of S. Andrea della Valle, three blocks beyond which a right hand turn joined it on to the wide street leading up to the facade of the Gesù. At this point, the Jesuit church, placed squarely over the Medieval route of the Via Papale (see Cat. 48, Bufalini), deflected the processions onto Paul III's Via Capitolina (Via d'Aracoeli). The new Casa Professa, which encapsulated St. Ignatius' rooms, shows clearly on this sheet with its bent facade which helped to funnel the processions toward the distantly visible Campidoglio (Ceen, p. 157).

Maggi's perfect illustration of the dramatic siting of the Jesuit complex on the Via Papale helps to illuminate the special relationship which existed between the Jesuit order and the pope. Midway on his progress between the Vatican and the Lateran each new pope was tangibly, visually reminded of

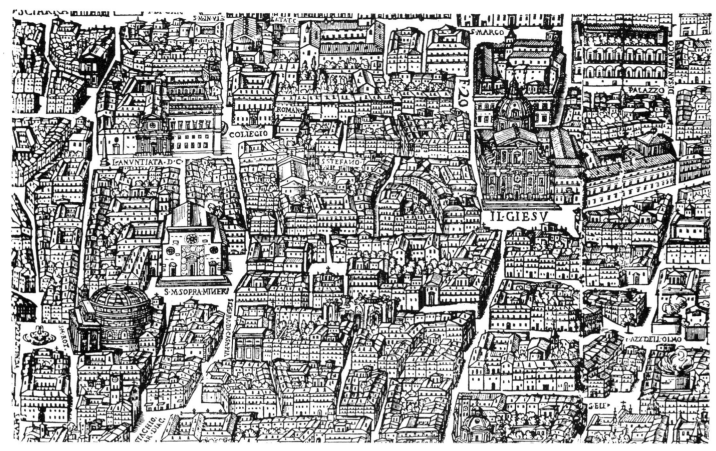

this group of militant supporters, the "Companions of Jesus." Apart from the terminal basilicas, the Gesù was the only major church along the whole papal route until S. Andrea della Valle was built. Except for the Palazzo del Senatore on the Campidoglio, the Gesù is the only major building approached frontally by the processions along the Via Papale. Its impressive approach gives a foretaste of the equally impressive urban sequence of square-street-*piazza-cordonata* which links the Gesù itself to the Piazza del Campidoglio.

The Gesù was scarcely finished before it became the model for a major church built nearby by another one of the reform orders. The Theatines, when they built S. Andrea della Valle starting in the 1590s, imitated not only the architecture but also the procession-related positioning of the church on the Via Papale. Maggi shows the facade as set back from that street and canted slightly toward the direction from which the processions came. S. Andrea replaced S. Sebastiano de Via Papae, which Bufalini shows as fronting directly on the street (Cat. 46). Pulling the facade of the new church back from the Via Papale provided an open space in front of it as well as a position of greater visibility. This apparent imitation of the urban siting of the Gesù suggests contemporary awareness of the innovative character of the Jesuit complex within the framework of the city.

AC

CEEN, 1986; EHRLE, 1915; FRUTAZ, 1962

75. *Catalogue of the Society of Jesus*, Broadsheet, 70 x 46.5 cm., 1626
Rome, Archivium Romanum Societatis Iesu, Armadio 8

76. *Imago Primi Saeculi Societatis Iesu a Provincia Flandro-Belgica eiusdem Societatis repraesentata*, pp. 246-247, Antwerp, 1640
Vatican City, Biblioteca Apostolica Vaticana, Stampe Barb. H. V, 89

By 1626, four years after the canonizations of St. Ignatius and St. Francis Xavier and 70 years after the death of its founder, the Society of Jesus had experienced phenomenal growth. This broadsheet catalogue, surmounted by images of the new saints, gives a demographic and geographic breakdown of the Jesuit organization at that time.

At the time of Ignatius' death in 1556 there were approximately 1,000 Jesuits in about one hundred different residences in 12 provinces. In 1626, there were 15,535 members in 36 provinces and 2 missionary "vice provinces." From a single residence on Via dei Delfini in Rome, the Society had multiplied into 26 *domus professae*, 443 colleges, 44 novitiates, 228 residences and 56 seminaries.

The *Imago Primi Saeculi* (Cat. 76) is a large celebratory volume published by the Jesuits of Antwerp to commemorate the first centenary of the foundation of the order. The work is a rich compendium of Jesuit history, poetry, panegyrics, engraved emblems, and lore.

It is divided into six books: "Societas Nascens," a history of the foundation of the order; "Societas Crescens" on the diffusion of the Society throughout the world; "Societas Agens," an exposition of Jesuit apostolic works; "Societas Patiens," a catalogue of the persecutions and obstacles the Society confronted in its first century of existence; "Societas Honorata," a directory of important friends of the Society and the wonders attributed to its saints; "Societas Flandro-Belgica," a history of the works of the two Belgian provinces that produced the work. Each book ends with a series of engraved allegorical emblems that provide the inspiration for Latin and Greek poems on subjects relating to the teachings, works, and aspirations of the Society.

The second book contains an important catalogue of the provinces, houses, colleges, and seminaries, based on the broadsheet catalogue of the Society in 1626 (Cat. 75). Moreover, it provides an interesting "update" that details the new foundations established in the 14 years between 1626 and the publication of the *Imago* in 1640: 153 new works, including 85 colleges and seminaries.

TL sj

Synopsis, 1950, col. 34, 170

CATALOGVS PROVINCIARVM SOCIETATIS IESV,

Domorum, Collegiorum, ac Seminariorum, Sociorumq; qui in vnaquaque Prouincia sunt.

CAT. 75

77. *Horoscopium Catholicum Societ. Iesu*, in: Athanasius Kircher, *Ars Magna Lucis et Umbrae*, p. 553, Rome, 1646

Vatican City, Biblioteca Apostolica Vaticana, Cicognara VI 842

Mathematician, physicist, Egyptologist, geologist, student of optics, alchemy and metaphysics, and founder of the Collegio Romano's famous natural history museum, Jesuit Athanasius Kircher began his almost half-century tenure as professor of mathematics and physics at the Collegio Romano in 1634.

His *Ars Magna Lucis et Umbrae*, a massive, brilliant, and often flawed study of the properties of light and optics, is typical of his voracious curiosity —it studies and seeks to understand visual phenomena from sunspots to fireflies. Four of the ten books are devoted to timekeeping. He also considers the difficult navigational problem of establishing longitude without an exact chronometer.

His research led him to invent a universal clock or *Horologium Catholicum* whose purpose was "to tell the time everywhere, but especially in the Colleges of the Society of Jesus, scattered throughout the world. This cannot be done without a knowledge of longitudes, and to find these I have spent a great deal of time in study. I have used information supplied to me by Jesuit mathematicians who made observations of eclipses in Europe, Eastern India, China, Peru, Brazil, Canada and Mexico, and used these to determine longitudes. Knowing the differences between the time when an eclipse was observed, for example, in Nanking in China, from that of the same eclipse observed in Goa in India, Mozambique in Africa, Pernambuco in Brazil and in several other stations, it was possible, though not without difficulty, to calculate the longitudes of each of these places, as well as of other places lying between them. Using this infomation, then, we were able to construct the timepiece for the whole Jesuit Order."

The clock, dedicated to General Vincenzo Caraffa, is dated January 7, 1646. It represents the Society as an olive tree ("like an olive tree bearing fruit in the House of God") whose leaves are inscribed with the names of particular cities where the Society had houses in 1646.

TL sj

REILLY, 1974, pp. 83-84

HOROSCOPIVM CATHOLICVM SOCIET. IESV

SICVT OLIVA FRVCTIFERA IN DOMO DEI

Iconismus XX. inferendus folio 555 artis magna lucis et umbræ.

78. Jean-Battiste Gillis (?), *Plan of the Church of the Society at Cuzco, Peru*, Pen and ink, 58 x 47 cm., ca. 1650

Rome, Archivium Romanum Societatis Iesu, F.G. Col, 1407, 7, fol. 2

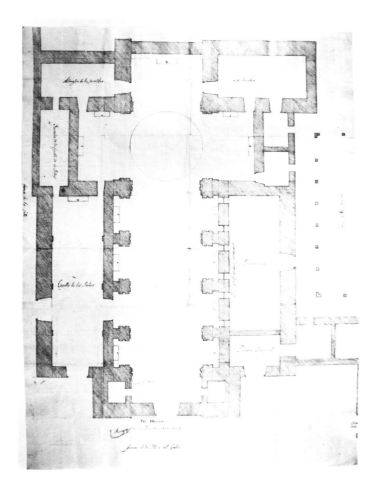

In 1571, the Jesuits arrived in Cuzco, the former capital of the Inca empire. Their first church, attributed to Jesuit Gerónimo Ruiz de Portillo, was located in the Plaza Mayor. At the time of the church's foundation, the canons of the nearby Cathedral began—in vain—legal proceedings in order to prevent the Jesuits from locating their church and residence on the site. A small church was nevertheless built there.

After a disastrous earthquake levelled the building in 1650, the Jesuits began their reconstruction almost immediately, ignoring once again the opposition of the canons (Wethey, p. 59). The "Capilla de los Indios," also known as the Capilla de Nuestra Señora de Loreto, was designed and constructed by J-B. Gilles, a Flemish Jesuit, and dedicated in 1653. The rest of the building, one of the finest examples of Spanish colonial architecture, was completed in 1668.

The large single nave with four shallow chapels, a domed transept, and shallow presbytery recall the floorplan of the Gesù, although regional variations are also evident. A choir stands over the entrance, and two large lateral spaces flank the nave: the "Capilla de los Indios," a distinct chapel for the native American population, and the "Penitenceria."

Among the ministries of the Society specified in its fundamental documents, the sacrament of Penance is given particular importance. Early in 1556, St. Ignatius ordered Jesuit architect Giovanni Tristano to design and build a distinct space for the celebration of the sacrament at S. Maria della Strada in Rome, because the crowds coming to popular Jesuit confessors overwhelmed the small church (*EppIg.* X, 6094). At Cuzco, penitents remained in a hall beside the church and confessed through a grille in the wall to priests who flanked the side altars, thus reducing traffic in the nave of the church. Such an arrangement was also used in southern Spain and other parts of the Americas (Lamalle, p. 461).

TL sj

EppIg. X, 6094; LAMALLE, 1960, pp. 461-462; WETHEY, 1949, pp. 56-60

79. Anonymous, *Perspective view of the Collegium Clementium, Prague,*
    Pen and ink with red and blue washes, 28.5 x 38 cm., 1631
Rome, Archivium Romanum Societatis Iesu, F.G. Col, 1541, 4, fol. 57

80. Anonymous, *Plan of the Collegium Clementium, Prague,*
    Pen and ink with red wash, 26 x 41 cm., ca. 1696
Rome, Archivium Romanum Societatis Iesu, Boh 200

The capital of the Kingdom of Bohemia and definitively part of the Hapsburg empire from 1525, Prague was one of the most cosmopolitan and culturally, economically, and politically lively centers of continental Europe. Perhaps there more than elsewhere, the advance of the Reformation acquired overtones of national resistance and political insubordination that directly threatened imperial power. To defend, consolidate, and reestablish the supremacy of the Catholic Church (and with it his own hegemony), Ferdinand I invited the Jesuits to Prague in 1554. Under Peter Canisius as the first rector, they established themselves in the former Dominican convent in the Old City. The Emperor granted a university charter to their institute, the "Clementium," which had faculties of theology and philosophy. Thus a Jesuit "Universitas Ferdinandea" counterbalanced the famous "Alma Mater Carolina," the oldest university in Central Europe. After a failed attempt on the part of Ferdinand II, the two institutes were amalgamated in 1654.

In the most difficult phase of "re-catholicizing," the "Clementium" served as a frontline outpost of the Catholic Counter Reformation. After the victory of the imperial troops at White Mountain (1620) it became the principal theological, cultural, and scientific center of the country.

The architectural complex of the Jesuits' most important center in the country was located near the Charles Bridge, covering an area of almost two hectares. It included six courtyards (four large and two small), three churches, and other oratories. The diverse sacred spaces, organized for the populations of various nationalities present in large numbers on the banks of the Moldau, were entrusted to fathers chosen specifically for these ministries. The largest church, St. Savior's (constructed *ex novo* beginning in 1578) served as the Czech national church. St. Clement's (located on the foundation of the prior church, rebuilt only in 1711-1715) was destined for the German population of the city, while a small oval edifice (constructed in the area between the two large churches betwen 1590 and 1600) served as the Italian Chapel, directed by a Marian sodality founded in 1575 by the very numerous Italian population. Later ethnic needs of the metropolis led to the institution of a French chapel and a Latin oratory, expressions not only of the international character of the Hapsburg state but also of the trans-national universality of the Society of Jesus.

The perspective drawing of the college exhibited here (Cat. 79) shows a project for the general organization of the complex proposed by an anonymous architect in 1631. St. Savior's, in that year almost completed, appears still in its original form, lacking the cupola added to the crossing in 1648 and still fronted with the simple facade which preceeded the solemn portal of 1653. Between the two towers the small cupola of the Italian Chapel appears, while an orientation perpendicular to the pre-existing edifice is already planned for the Church of St. Clement, from whose roof a small tower rises. The organization of the facades of the college with arched double and triple mullioned windows is also interesting, a feature frequently found in late Renaissance Central European construction (for example, in the Jesuit college in Graz). A small loggia tops the entryway to the left of the facade of St. Savior's.

As the plan exhibited here clearly shows, the architectural project of 1631 was profoundly transformed by the successive phases of work, begun in 1654 and executed by Carlo Lugaro and Domenico Orsi after the Thirty Years War. This drawing, datable to about 1696, shows, to the left of St. Savior's, the wings of the college constructed in the course of the second half of the seventeenth century. It also shows the immense summer refectory ("Triclinium"),

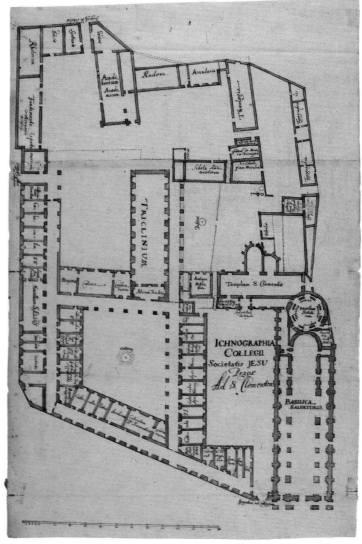

CAT. 80

a magnificent space realized in 1669, as well as the areas designed for the use of the college's own press ("Typographia"). The entire eastern part of the school buildings, the library and the new Church of St. Clement would be rebuilt in the eighteenth century.

RB

FRANZ, 1962, pp. 86 , 211, n. 3; LAMALLE, 1960, pp. 494-496; MERTEN, 1967, pp. 144-162; SCHMIDL, 1747; VALLERY-RADOT 1960, pp. 316-319

81. Anonymous, *Cardinals Alessandro and Odoardo Farnese*, Oil on canvas, 235 x 281 cm., ca. 1610 (?)
Rome, Church of the Gesù, Antesacristy

This commemorative painting recalls the two cardinals of the Farnese family who particularly distinguished themselves in their munificence to the Jesuits, Alessandro (1519-1589, grandson of Paul III), and Odoardo (1574-1626, great-grandson of Paul III). As the inscription on the original frame recounts, the cardinals were, respectively, the generous benefactors and donors of the Church of the Gesù and the Casa Professa. These monuments are represented in the painting with meticulous precision, and serve the dual function of memorial and background for the portraits.

The unknown artist gracefully resolved the challenge of this complex subject-matter. For this double portrait, he used a compositional model which derived from sixteenth-century portraits and which was still widely used in the next century. He depicted the two prelates Alessandro and Odoardo in full-length portraits, seated on two high armchairs facing one another and turned towards the center. On the left, Alessandro holds a letter addressed to him, to the right, the younger Odoardo, and behind their shoulders, the interior of the church.

In order to render the immensity of Vignola's project, the painter followed the example adopted by Sacchi (Cat. 109) in his centenary painting "Pope Urban VIII's visit to the Church of the Gesù:" he eliminated the facade and replaced Sacchi's coaches with the two large-scale portraits. In order to complete the description of the church and the Casa Professa, he placed in the foreground, flanking the cardinals, prie-dieus covered with draperies embroidered with the Farnese coat of arms. On top of these, large drawings of the floorplans of the buildings are held in place by models of the respective facades.

The painting, whose author and original location are yet to be determined, was probably commissioned by the Jesuits. According to Strinati (oral communication) the influence on this anonymous painter of Zuccari and Passignano suggests a date between the first and second decades of the seventeenth century. The painting provides important evidence of the prior decoration of the pendentives done by Andrea Lilio, which are clearly visible here.

MPD'O

PECCHIAI, 1952, p. 278

82. Nanni di Baccio Bigio, *Plan for the Church of the Gesù and the first Casa Professa* (photograph), original ca. 1553

Paris, Bibliothèque Nationale, Cabinet des Estampes Hd4 D, fol. 82

Codex Hd4 D, fol. 82 of the Cabinet des Estampes at the National Library of Paris contains a plan of the Casa Professa and the Church of the Gesù which merits special interest and study. The design (photo shown here) has been dated by Bösel to ca. 1553, that is, before a statement (Jan. 7, 1554) by Bigio about this, his second, design for the Gesù, and after the Jesuits renounced their objective of using the northern side of the insula which borders on Via del Plebiscito (Bösel, II, pp. 161-163, 175).

Before 1568, and thus before Vignola's design for the church, two other architects were assigned the task of designing the church, Nanni di Baccio Bigio in 1550 and 1553, and Michelangelo Buonarroti in 1554.

The architect chosen to begin the project and provide its rough outlines, both in preliminary models and the final documents of approval, was, it seems, Nanni di Baccio Bigio, even though Vignola's name does appear on one of the rough drafts. This conclusion is based not only on the documents and licenses, but also on Master Nanni's declaration of himself as author.

The importance of Nanni di Baccio Bigio's design is considerable in many respects. From the artistic point of view, it demonstrates that the idea of a church of longitudinal design, with apse and transept and with chapels instead of lateral naves, was already adopted a full 18 years before Vignola took over and added his own brilliant touches to the imposing building. The plan of ca. 1553 does not differ substantially from the plan of 1568. The only details which differentiate the two are the two bell towers which Nanni placed at either side of the facade, and one single door instead of three, with two side doors located in the transepts.

The document also complicates the question as to the origins of baroque architecture. The fact that the general outline of the Gesù in Rome was determined in its essentials as early as ca. 1553 leads us to the question: was Nanni working from his own personal ideas or did he merely put into practice directives which had been given to him? We lean toward the second hypothesis, all the more given the fact that the fundamental concepts were adhered to with exceptional fidelity and constancy, through many interruptions and changes, a fact that cannot be explained without good reason.

It is important also for the history of Jesuit building. In the design of Master Nanni we have a comprehensive and unified plan for a large residence connected to a large church, destined to serve as a model for other houses and other churches of the order. It was completed under the watchful eye of St. Ignatius and probably not without his personal inspiration, since the building projects of the Society, especially in Rome, were under his direct care.

(Text taken from Pirri, 1941, pp. 181-182 emendations based on Bösel, 1986, II, pp. 162-163, Doc. 1, p. 175; see also Vallery-Radot, 1960, p. 21)

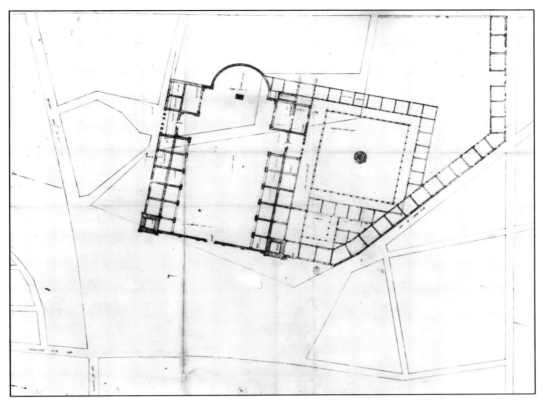

CAT. 82

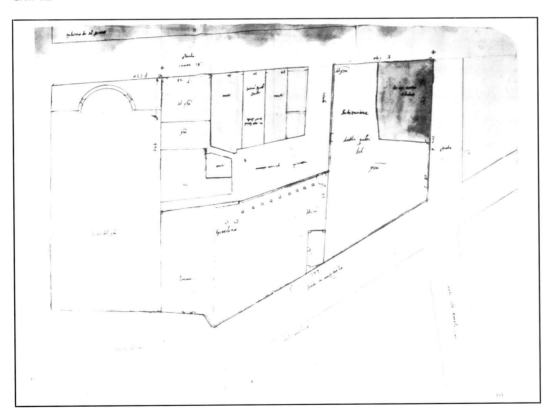

CAT. 83

149

83. Anonymous, *Plan of the Church of the Gesù and the first Casa Professa,*
Ink with washes, 53 x 43, ca. 1578-1582

Rome, Archivium Romanum Societatis Iesu, Rom 143 II, fol. 544

This plan of the Gesù and the original Casa Professa, drawn between 1578 and 1582, indicates the Jesuits' situation as the construction of the church was nearing completion. Considered in relation to the ca. 1553 plan of Nanni di Baccio Bigio, this plan clearly shows how the Jesuits had made serious progress in their attempts to consolidate the trapezoidal block that would eventually be filled with the new Casa Professa/Chiesa del Gesù complex. Already two complete blocks (formerly occupied by the Astalli and Altieri families), three small streets, and a *piazzetta* had been covered by the imposing bulk of the church. The facade of the church, according to the expressed desires of the Jesuits' patron Alessandro Farnese, was oriented squarely on the former Piazza Altieri, now Piazza del Gesù. The chapel of the Madonna della Strada had been largely demolished, and only its apse remained standing for use as the sacristy of the new church.

Before the construction of the church, three lanes diverged from the small *piazza* located at the center of the block. After the construction, two of those alleys dead-ended into the southern wall of the church, and only one remained open onto Via degli Astalli.

Shaded areas on the plan indicate the properties that the Jesuits had not managed to obtain before 1582. The Muti family (who had successfully blocked Ignatius' construction of the church) fought the Jesuits during the construction of the Gesù over the closing of the lanes, apparently attempting to drive up the value of the property that the Jesuits needed to complete their holdings around the church. The Jesuits enlisted powerful friends including Antonio Borghese, and were eventually able to buy up the remaining Muti property in 1582-1583. They did not obtain the last corner of the block from Curtio de Rossi until 1618, nineteen years after Odoardo Farnese laid the cornerstone for the new Casa Professa.

TL sj

LAMALLE, 1960, p. 420; PIRRI, 1955, pp. 228-229; TACCHI VENTURI, 1899, p. 53

84. Francesco Villamena, *Robertus Bellarminus,* Engraving, 35.5 x 22.5 cm.,
Rome, 1604

Rome, Archivium Romanum Societatis Iesu, Armadio 4

Ths 1604 portrait of St. Roberto Bellarmino, one the first Jesuits to be named cardinal, is of particular interest because of its background. The stern figure of Bellarmino at his desk is bracketed by two images: a picture within the picture of St. Ignatius and a view out the open window of the Gesù complex. This engraving is perhaps the very first to show the new Casa Professa designed by Jesuit architect Giovanni de Rosis. After the flood on Christmas Eve, 1598 had weakened the foundations of the original Casa Professa, Cardinal Odoardo Farnese and General Claudio Aquaviva laid the cornerstone of the new headquarters on July 6, 1599. The sober entrance to the Casa, to the right of the church in the engraving, was the result of long negotiation between Aquaviva and Farnese, a compromise between the Jesuits' rule of simplicity and Farnese's desire to build "splendidamente e nobilmente" (Pirri and Di Rosa, pp. 28-29).

The house built by Ignatius and Codacio in 1543-1544 was razed except for the apartment where Ignatius and the generals after him had lived and worked. Those rooms were underpinned with a massive system of double vaults and then knitted into the fabric of the new building. Work progressed quickly on the facade facing Piazza del Gesù and Via Aracoeli. On July 31, 1605 (the 49th anniversary of the death of Ignatius), Aquaviva celebrated mass in the shrine created in the founder's simple rooms.

CAT. 84

Close study of the engraving shows that the Casa Professa was far from complete in 1604. Indeed, the last corner, where Via degli Astalli meets Via delle Botteghe Oscure was not obtained until 1618, and construction continued until 1623.

TL sj

KÖNIG-NORDHOFF, 1982, p. 73, n. 582, fig. 150; PIRRI and DI ROSA, 1975, pp. 25-30

85. *Medal from the laying of the cornerstone of the Church of the Gesù,*
Bronze, 49.25 mm., 1568
　　Obverse: Bust of Alessandro Farnese facing left,
　　　　"ALEXANDER•CARD•S•R•E•VICECAN. F.P"
　　Reverse: Facade design by Vignola for the Church of the Gesù,
　　　　"NOMINI　•I.E.S.U. SACRUM/ AN•MDLXVIII ROMAE"
Rome, Church of the Gesù, Sacristy (see p. 37)

86. *Medal from the Holy Year 1575 showing the Della Porta Facade of the Church of the Gesù,*
Bronze, 38.55 mm., 1575
　　Obverse: Bust of Alessandro Farnese facing right, "ALEXANDER • CARD •
　　　　S • R • E • VICECAN. IO. V. MILLION."
　　Reverse: The Della Porta Facade of the Church of the Gesù,
　　　　"FECIT ANNO-SAL•MDLXXV, ROMAE"
Vatican City, Biblioteca Apostolica Vaticana, Numismatica (see p. 37)

87. Antonio Lafréry, *Plan of the Church of the Gesù*, Engraving from:
Speculum Romanae Magnificentia, 20.5 x 35 cm., ca. 1600
Private Collection

88. Giovanni Franscesco Venturi, *Section of the Church of the Gesù*, Engraving in:
Giovanni Giacomo de Rossi, *Insignium Romae Templorum,*
fol. 21, Rome, 1684
Vatican City, Biblioteca Apostolica Vaticana, R.G. Arte-Arch., S 282

CAT. 87

The spatial conception of the Gesù is considered one of the most significant creations of Counter Reformation architecture and a point of departure for sacred construction in subsequent centuries. Its floor plan (Cat. 87) in the form of a Latin cross results from the combination of two very distinct entities: a vast longitudinal hall (accompanied on each side by three small chapels) and a central plan edifice in the form of an inscribed greek cross. This latter element consists of the crossing crowned by a tall cupola, four arms (the presbytery is closed by the apse) and in the angles of intersection, four subordinate spaces. Two of these spaces serve as small chapels and two serve as lateral entrances; together with the three portals of the facade, they guarantee an orderly flow of worshippers. All of the lateral spaces are intercommunicating, that is, it is possible to visit the single lateral chapels without disturbing the faithful gathered in the nave. At the end of these passageways, small spiral staircases that provide access to the "coretti" or small choirs over the chapels are set into the thick wall of the facade.

The unified effect of the great nave or "aula" is clear from a study of the floorplan and from the proportional relationship between the depth of the chapels and the width of the nave, an effect which is perceived even more clearly *in situ*. This effect is virtually uninterrupted by the slight projection of the pilasters of the crossing, and, indeed, it is accentuated by the majesty of the cupola. Spatial continuity characterizes the entire internal longitudinal axis from the main entrance to the high altar, which, according to the exigencies of the reformed religious architecture of the period, needed to appear in a most visible form at the center of the vision of the whole.

The longitudinal section of the Church of the

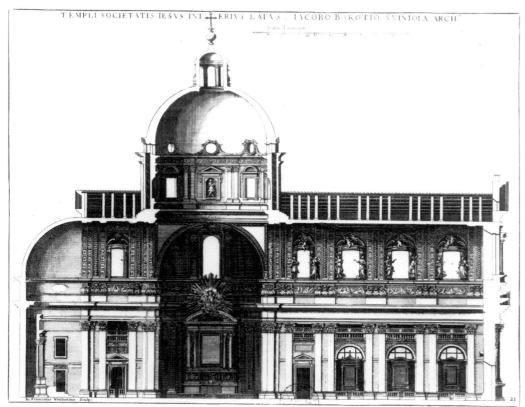

Cat. 88

Gesù (Cat. 88) indicates the monumental, unitary and complex structuring of its interior. It renders visible the volumetric development formed by the spacious barrel-vaulted ceilings and a crossing surmounted by a tall cupola. The wall treatment in the church is broken by a composite order of double pilasters supporting a trabeation interrrupted only over the great pilasters of the cupola. Subordinate to this is the combination of openings arranged in two levels: below, the arcades of the chapels as well as (in the bays before and after the transept) the doors of the vestibules and small chapels; above, framed between the capitals, the low, wide windows of the *coretti*, closed by balustrades and grilles. In the nave, the sequence of three large spans (corresponding to the lateral chapels) and one narrower span (the vestibules, which are nothing other than two of the four angular elements of the cross) confirms the principle of combination which is the basis of the entire interior spatial arrangement.

The "suture" between the combined longitudinal and central-plan schemata evident in the study of floorplan is perceivable between the last of the chapels and the vestibules.

This demarcation, however, is not underscored in the articulation of the elevation; in fact, the uninterrupted trabeation binds entirely the bays of the vestibules to the nave in an indivisible manner, decreasing at the same time the logical correlation with the analogous bays beyond the transepts. From this emerges not only a particular asymmetry in the wall composition of the nave, but moreover a striking ambiguity between the concept of pure combination in the floorplan and the spatial formation which stresses the appearance of organic unity.

This final perception was later underscored by the rich pictorial and sculptural decoration and ornamentation of the vaults executed by G.B. Gaulli beginning in 1672. In this way, the nave is thus definitively interpreted as a self-sufficient entity: an apparent symmetry is suggested by the extension of frescoes over the two central spans, enclosed between the first and last bays.

RB

ACKERMAN, 1972; BÖSEL, 1985, I, pp. 160-179; PECCHIAI, 1952; SCHWAGER, 1977; STANKOWSKI, 1981

89. Mario Cartaro, *Facade design for the Church of the Gesù by Vignola*,
   Engraving, ca. 1573, from: Giovanni Giacomo de Rossi,
   Insignium Romae Templorum, 35.5 x 22.5 cm., fol. 38, Rome, 1684
Private Collection

90. Valerién Regnard, *Facade and interior perspective of the Church of the Gesù*, from
   Giovanni Giacomo de Rossi, *Insignium Romae Templorum*,
   fol. 20, 35.5 x 22.5 cm., Rome, 1684
Private Collection

It was only after the laying of the cornerstone that the planning process for the Gesù entered its final stages. At that time, Vignola, consulting with the founder of the church Alessandro Farnese, the Jesuit fathers, and their own *consiliarius aedificiorum* Giovanni Tristano, elaborated the definitive version of his idea for the church. Approved by all in March of 1569, this plan, executed in a wooden model was supposed to serve as the basis for the new construction. In 1571, however, Cardinal Farnese decided to entrust the construction to a younger architect, Giacomo Della Porta, who presented an essentially new project for the facade of the church.

As a consequence of this change, Vignola had a copper-plate engraving made which showed his own—already supplanted—design for the facade (Cat. 89). The engraving was intended to serve as a record of an architectural work that was never realized. A line added to this later reprinting (ca. 1684) of the original engraving reads "this facade was not realized due to the death of the architect."

Thanks to this engraving we can identify the changes, not always striking but nevertheless decisive, wrought by the new architect of the Farnese Cardinal. As in the present edifice—derived from a model of Sangallo—a facade of two orders was foreseen, with the narrow upper part contained by lateral elements and crowned by a tympanum. The front is rhythmically broken by pilasters which only at the flanks of the central axis are replaced by columns in three-quarters which, on the lower order, are joined in the motif of an aedicula. This aedicula, in the form of a broken tympanum acts as the framing of the portal as well as the base for the Farnese coat of arms. The coat of arms of the order—the monogram of the name of Jesus—decorates the center of the large upper tympanum.

The striking focus of the entire composition towards its center is reinforced by three gradual projections. In these the same rhythm of the bays and the same division of niches and doors is clearly repeated.

It is largely from this almost uniform repetition that the very rigorous and consistent hierarchical arrangement springs. It is perhaps the most significant element of the entire composition.

The Regnard engraving (Cat. 90) furnishes a complete idea of the edifice as built, depicting on the left side the plan and elevation of the facade and on the right the transverse section and a perspectival view of the interior.

The facade is the one designed by Della Porta and begun in 1571. Starting from the same typological model on which Vignola's project was based, the younger architect substituted for Vignola's gradual crescendo of the bays a much livelier and richer play of tensions which is concentrated in the structrually differentiated organization of the vertical articulations.

At the center, the composition thickens into a double aedicula with tympana nested one inside the other. More strikingly than in the design of Vignola, here the openings of the facade are concentrated towards the central portion of the facade. Doors, windows, and niches are no longer aligned horizontally but are coordinated vertically, thus contributing to a more marked vertical effect.

The same effect produces a more vigorous articulation of the wall supports which, thanks to the introduction of tall pedestals in the lower order, produce a lighter feeling. All of the pilasters are paired. Those flanking the tripartite central body

Questa facciata nō fu messa in opera per la morte del architetto.

CAT. 89

(which correspond to the first projection) are isolated from the horizontal context by the projected trabeation indicating the superimposition of the two orders. With the large tympanum of the facade, the pilasters are linked to the structure of a great aedicula two storeys high which supports the framing of the entire central section. It is due to the compactness of the external divisions of the first order, as well as to the heavy lateral volutes that, inspite of the dynamic lightness of the orders, the facade maintains that imposing composure that contributes so much to its monumentality.

Recent studies (based on an analysis which begins with an altimetric comparison of the two projects for the facade and their relationship with the nave) clarify the fact that Della Porta also modified the interior architecture of the church. In order to obtain a perfect congruence between the roof of the nave and the new and more slender proportions of the facade, he introduced an attic between the trabeation and the barrel-vault of the nave, intersecting in the groins of the windows (in our engraving still lacking the seventeenth-century decoration).

This change profoundly affected the general appearance of the church. The vast aula, previously heavily enclosed by the half-cylinder resting directly on the line of the walls, now acquires vertical spaciousness. We do not know whether Vignola had already foreseen the subdivision into two floors of the areas which laterally flank the nave, or whether this also derives from the changes realized after 1571. It is possible, in fact, that Della Porta introduced the *coretti* located over the lateral chapels which permitted the Jesuits to attend religious functions in the church in a non-official manner in a space separated from the nave. In fact, only the raising of the first order of the facade allowed for the disposition all along the length of the nave of those low and narrow choirs under the generous vault of the single, spacious corridor over the chapels.

RB

156

FACIES EXTERNA CVM PROSPECTV INTERIORIS TEMPLI AB ALEXANDRO
CARDINALI FARNESIO SOC. IESV ÆDIFICATI .

PARS EXTERIOR *Iacobo de la Porta Architecto* . PARS INTERIOR *Iacobo Barotio à Viniola Architecto* .

Scala palmorum

20

CAT. 90

157

91. Ciro Ferri, *St. Francis Xavier*, Fire-gilded bronze, 86 cm., ca. 1687-1689
Rome, Church of the Gesù, Sacristy

92. Ciro Ferri, *St. Francis Borgia*, Fire-gilded bronze, 86 cm., ca. 1687-1689
Rome, Church of the Gesù, Sacristy

These two statues are part of two groups of four statues each which were formerly placed on the altars of St. Ignatius and St. Francis Xavier in the Gesù. For the altar of the founder of the Society of Jesus, the saints represented are Teresa of Avila, Filippo Neri, Francis Xavier, and Isidore the Farmer, all of whom were canonized in the same ceremony with Ignatius in 1622. For the altar of the Apostle of the Indies the saints chosen were Francis of Assisi, Francis de Sales, Francis di Paolo, and Francis Borgia.

Paid for in part by the superior general of the Congregation of the Oratory Cesare Massei, the statues provide additional examples of Ciro Ferri's activity as a designer of sculpture. This artist, whose name is engraved on the base of each statue, provided the designs and oversaw their execution. Based on the evidence of the minutes of July 21, 1673 of the Congregation of the Oratory ("About the tabernacle [on the high altar of the Chiesa Nuova] whose design Sig. Ciro Ferri is preparing and modelling in clay..."

in Libro VII dei Decreti), Galassi Paluzzi first proposed that Ferri may actually have provided designs and clay models for the Gesù statues. Comparing the statues to the tabernacle, Galassi Paluzzi pointed out the stylistic similarity between the draperies in the two works. The saints, represented according to their official iconographies, are sculpted with a plastic sensitivity far removed from the exaggerations of the mature baroque. Galassi Paluzzi proposed dating the statues between 1687 and 1689, pointing out that they were paid for in part (400 *scudi*), by a bequest from Cesare Massei (†1687); the remaining 200 *scudi* were provided by Cesare's brother Giuseppe, a Jesuit (Galassi Paluzzi, p. 122, n.1). Ferri's death in 1689 provides the *terminus ante* for the statues.

MPD'O

AA.VV., *Tesori*, 1974, p. 118; GALASSI PALUZZI, 1922

CAT. 91

CAT. 92

159

Cat. 93

160

93. *Chasuble*, Embroidered silk, 106 x 79 cm.
Rome, Church of the Gesù, Rectory

This exquisite chasuble is a further testimony to the bonds between the Farnese family and the Society of Jesus. It appears in the inventory of the sacristy of the Gesù of 1685, and in an inventory of 1701 it is described as "a white silk chasuble of his Eminence Farnese entirely done in needle-point (*a punta d'ago*) with scenes from the life of the Madonna." The Farnese coat of arms on the back identifies the donor as Cardinal Alessandro Farnese.

The vestment is richly decorated on both sides, embroidered with satin stitching and petit-point with gold, silver, and colored silken threads. The theme is the Life of the Virgin Mary. The central panels front and back contain scenes of the *Annunciation*, the *Marriage of Mary and Joseph*, the *Visitation*, the *Nativity of Jesus*, and the *Presentation in the Temple*, all individually framed with overlapping angels and masks. On the lateral panels, a florid plait of acanthus leaves intertwines around angels who carry symbols of classic Marian iconography, the Tower of Ivory, the Mystical Rose, the House of Gold etc. Some of the scenes were partially lost in an early restoration.

According to a tradition that is not well documented, the chasuble could bear an impressive attribution: it could be the work of the famous "Pellegrina," Ludovica Antonia Pellegrini, who was active at the end of the sixteenth and at the beginning of the seventeenth centuries. Given, however, that the donor Alessandro Farnese had died in 1589, this attribution is dubious.

The design, and in particular certain details such as the grotesque masks and the playful chromatic ranges with their delicate tonalities, make this piece a rare example of mannerist taste in the applied arts.

MPD'O

PECCHIAI, 1952, p. 341

94. Anonymous, *Gregory XIII and the construction of the Collegio Romano,*
Oil on canvas, 192 x 282 cm., 1655
Rome, Pontificia Università Gregoriana

95. Anonymous, *Gregory XIII approves various Jesuit colleges,*
Oil on canvas, 192 x 282 cm., 1655
Rome, Pontificia Università Gregoriana

Two important but little known canvases which hung in the Collegio Romano until 1870 commemorate Pope Gregory XIII's extraordinary zeal in the establishment of Jesuit colleges and also document two aspects of the Society's architectural practices. Of uncertain attribution and painted by a genial though unsophisticated hand, the paintings, which can now be dated to 1655, formerly hung in the "porteria" and then in the Aula Magna of the Collegio Romano which Pope Gregory paid for and dedicated personally (Cat. 102) in 1584.

An unpublished payment establishes the date and location of these works: "Collegio Romano, conto di fabriche //...scudi 65, per prezzo di altri due Quadri grandi posti nella Porteria dall'una el'altra parte della statua di Papa Gregorio XIII..." (ARSI, F.G. 1343). Although the location of the "porteria" referred to in this document is not clear, it is likely that at this time a new ceremonial entrance to the college was systematized to replace the old "porteria," torn down to make way for the apse of the Church of S. Ignazio. And these new paintings were made to flank a large marble statue of Gregory XIII (see fig. at p. 88 in Rinaldi, 1914) which stood in the old "porteria." These paintings and the unattributed statue were known to Rinaldi and Villoslada, but were thought to have been part of the decorations executed for the dedication in 1584.

The first canvas (Cat. 94) depicts the pope's visit to the site of the new and grandiose Collegio Romano, a work attributed by Baglione to Bartolomeo Ammannati but probably designed by either or both the Jesuit architect Giuseppe Valeriano and Giacomo Della Porta (see Cat. 96-98). The pope had visited the building site on June 18, 1582 and ordered that the simple rubble walls being constructed be demolished and replaced with walls of fired brick ("laterizi"). In the background workmen are demolishing nearby houses to make room for the new edifice. The *Annuae Litterae* of 1582 (letters of general information that circulated among the Jesuits) also recounted that during that visit, a gentleman neighbor of the college knelt before the pope to present a property claim against the Jesuits. Pope Gregory, still astride his horse, called the rector, heard the testimony of both sides, and judged in favor of the Jesuits (*Annuae*, 1584, pp. 7-10).

This account appears to have informed the artist's representation, however he has substituted the kneeling "neighbor" with the architect, who presents his design for the facade of the Collegio Romano. The representation of a young layman as the architect may help unravel the problem of the authorship of the college's design.

In the second painting, the seated pontiff receives emissaries who present plans for new Jesuit colleges and seminaries. Three of the Gregorian foundations are named: "Iaponicum," "Illiricum," and "Vilnense." In Japan Gregory largely underwrote the expenses of the seminaries of Arima and Ansukimono, both founded by Jesuit Giuseppe Valignano, as well as the new Jesuit college at Funai and the novitiate at Iquinseque.

Valignano sent an embassy of the first Japanese Catholics to the pope. They received a festive and solemn reception on their arrival in 1585. Gregory XIII also founded the Collegio Illirico in Loreto, entrusting it to the Jesuits in 1580. By this initiative he intended to contribute to Catholic formation on the far shore of the Adriatic (modern Yugoslavia, Albania, and Greece). The region suffered a serious shortage of priests, and the church there was threatened by the Turks, schismatics, and heretics. Vilnus, capital of Lithuania, was the most important Jesuit center in the Kingdom of Poland. At the request of King Báthory, Gregory XIII founded a Jesuit academy there in 1579 and in 1582 he founded the Pontifical Seminary of Vilnus.

In this painting the pope presents the emmisaries with the plans for their new colleges and seminaries which they examine closely. The plans are provided by the Jesuits (to the right of Gregory), thus documenting the central control the Society exercised over the design of buildings outside of Rome. Thus these two paintings document two types of architectural practices: the use of outside architects hired by prestigious patrons for important buildings and the dissemination of designs for lesser buildings from the Roman headquarters.

EL

RINALDI, 1914, p. 105; VILLOSLADA, 1954, pp. 153-154

COLLEGIVM ROMANVM HVMILITER
INCHOATVM DIRVI ET MAGNIFICENTIVS
EXTRVI IVBET

Cat. 94

PLVRA SEMINARIA ET COLLEGIA
CONDIT INTRA ET EXTRA EVROPAM

Cat. 95

163

96. Anonymous, *Plan of the first site of the Collegio Romano*, Pen and ink, 44 x 58.5 cm., ca. 1581

Rome, Archivium Romanum Societatis Iesu, Armadio 5

97. Anonymous, *Hexagonal Plan for the Collegio Romano*, Red chalk, 44 x 60 cm., ca. 1581

Rome, Archivium Romanum Societatis Iesu, Armadio 5

98. Anonymous, *Ground floor of the Collegio Romano*, Pen and ink and wash, 44.5 x 63 cm., ca. 1581

Rome, Archivium Romanum Societatis Iesu, Armadio 5

Until a few years ago, studies of the planning of the Collegio Romano fell between two points of reference: data furnished by the traditional literature of the art historians (based on Baglione and Baldinucci who attributed the design of the college to Bartolomeo Ammannati), and direct consultation of written sources available at the Archivium Romanum Societatis Iesu, Rome (which lead, rather, to hypothesize a definite participation of architects Giacomo Della Porta and Jesuit Giuseppe Valeriano). Today a new starting point— original graphic materials recently come to light—has made the discussion more complex and intriguing. This starting point exists thanks to late Father Edmond Lamalle's discovery of a series of preparatory and alternative projects for the Collegio Romano, probably drawn in 1581.

These sheets (Cat. 96, 97, 98 as well as others in the ARSI), drawn by various hands, are unfortunately not signed and are still awaiting an in-depth study (which had been promised by the late Fr. Lamalle). Impossible in this present context, this work will have to be based on close graphic and stylistic comparisons with autograph drawings of the architects linked to the succession of projects (Ammannati, Valeriano, and Della Porta).

We display here three drawings which present the most important phases of the genesis of the monumental complex whose construction began January 11, 1582.

On the site of the Church of the Annunziata (obtained in 1560) the Jesuits had constructed their church, but their residence and the classrooms were adapted provisionally from pre-existing buildings. Quite early, however—precisely after the founda-tion by Gregory XIII—it became clear that the future development of the college would require not only a radical transformation of the buildings, but also a definitive enlargement of the building site. Cat. 96 illustrates this first moment in the historical course of events. It presents a plan for the total reconstruction of the edifices on the existing site. The author of the drawing expressed his opinion that the solution is inadequate due to the restrictiveness of the site. In fact, he adds this annotation: "This drawing is made for the same site which the *Collegio* occupies. There would be scarcely 100 rooms on three floors. The lecture halls below and above would number only eleven. But everything is tight and crowded, and there is a great lack of rooms and library space so it is clearly impossible to accommodate the *Collegio* adequately in such a small space."

It was decided to encapsulate the entire nearby block, expanding the area of the college to reach modern-day Piazza del Collegio Romano. Relocating the classrooms in the part of the new acquisition south of the Church of the Annunziata, the entire pre-existing site was reserved as residence for the fathers. Almost all the projects agree with this decision: they locate the principal facade on the south side. Among these, the most surprising is Cat. 97, extraordinary in its inventive conception of the floorplan. An axis of symmetry divides the edifice beginning at the principal entrance which—in order to guarantee the governing regularity of the edifice—is shifted slightly towards the left. Following this axis one first crosses the school buildings, arranged with large lecture halls around a rectangular courtyard of five and six arcades. Passing through an internal portal, one enters the cloister, which is de-

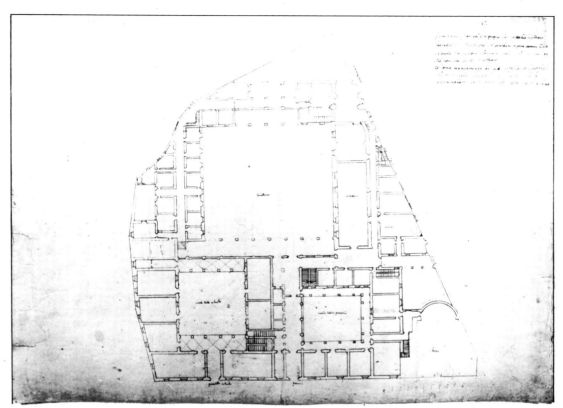

CAT. 96

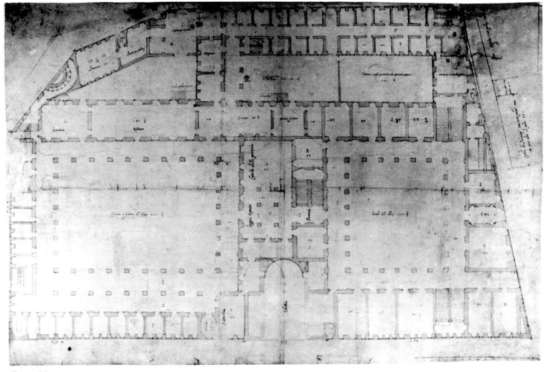

CAT. 98

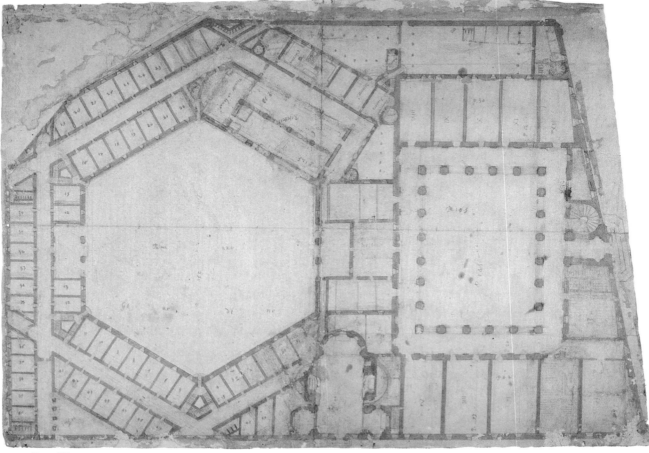

CAT. 97

veloped on an hexagonal plan around a large garden. This extravagant polygonal arrangement is explained not only as a careful search for a particular solution in the mannerist vocabulary, but also as an intelligent compositional appraisal of the topographical factors which conditioned the planning process. The invention, in fact, corresponds to the obtuse angles of the northeastern boundaries of the block. The perfect geometrical balance at work in the hexagon of the garden is underscored even more by the compositional reference to the arrangement which unifies the interior of the college: the crossing of the symmetrical axis is highlighted by three open arcades at the center of two sides of the polygon. Finally, one notices a detail in the drawing of the Annunziata: in the project, the simple rectangular space is transformed into a tri-lobed floorplan.

Cat. 98 shows the floorplan in a project very similar to the definitive solution, a plan strictly conceived according to a system of rectangular coordi-

nates. Both of the large courtyards are rectangular and appear noticeably shifted towards the west. Parallel to the axis of the courtyards is a second line of reference which catches a very long unitary piece of building which traverses the entire block. On the upper floor (not shown here) is the principal corridor of the college which runs its entire length. The entire eastern side was designed for various support services. In this preparatory project one sees in a particularly convincing way the results of the genesis of one of the most unique aspects of the final solution: the bipolar structure on which the compositional tension of the actual facade is based.

RB

BENEDETTI, 1984, pp. 67-104; BÖSEL, 1985, I, pp. 180-211; BELTRAME QUATTROCCHI, 1956; FOSSI, n.d., pp. 140ff.; PIRRI, 1932; PIRRI, 1943; PIRRI, 1970, pp. 52-74, 260-285

166

99. Christophorus de Madrid, *De Frequenti Usu Sanctissimi Eucharistiae Sacramenti*, Rome, 1557

Vatican City, Biblioteca Apostolica Vaticana, Stamp. Barb. V. XIV. 42

A sign of Ignatius' practical imagination is his decision during the last six months of his life to obtain a printing press for the Collegio Romano. Having a press at the college served several different ends: it allowed for the publication of works by Jesuit authors and in-house publications of the Society (like its *Constitutions*), it made books available to poorer students at reduced rates, and it allowed the fathers to edit and emend the texts of classical literature which they judged inappropriate for their students.

When an attempt to obtain an unused press from Cosimo de'Medici failed, Ignatius began a long series of negotiations with the Jesuits in Venice, the printing capital of Italy, for the purchase of a press and type. Ignatius himself rejected the first fonts sent because they were too small and difficult to read, and insisted that they be changed even at greater expense (*EppIg* . XI, 6470). In the meantime, seven days before the death of Ignatius, his secretary Polanco had found a supplier in Rome who furnished "at a good price, capitals and lower case, round and italic letters" (*Lainii*, I, pp. 414-415). Eventually the order to Venice was cancelled.

In its first years the Collegio Romano Press ("in aedibus Societatis Iesu") produced a number of important books, including the *Constitutions* of the Society of Jesus and their explanatory *Declarations* (Cat. 62, 63), the *Ratio Studiorum* (Cat. 66), editions of Erasmus and Martial edited by Andrea Frusio, and Cristobal de Madrid's *De Frequenti Usu Sanctissimi Eucharistiae Sacramenti,* shown here. De Madrid's treatise is both polemical and devotional. It condemns the Protestant understanding of the meaning of the Eucharist, and strongly advocates for all the reception of the Sacrament every eight days, as is prescribed for Jesuits in the *Constitutions* and Rules of the Society.

TL sj

CASTELLANI, 1932, pp. 11-16; *Chron* VI, p. 33; *Lainii*, 1912-1918, I, pp. 414-415

100. Anonymous, *Unfinished line drawing of the facade of the Collegio Romano,*
Pen and ink and pencil, 43.5 x 64 cm., after 1581
Rome, Archivium Romanum Societatis Iesu, Armadio 5

101. Giuseppe Vasi, *Prospetto Principale del Collegio Romano,* Engraving in:
Delle magnificenze di Roma antica e moderna, Rome, 29 x 41.5 cm., 1747-1761
Rome, Archivium Romanum Societatis Iesu, Armadio 5

The architecture of the Collegio Romano had two scopes. As the residence of the Jesuits, the edifice had to present an exterior devoid of sumptuousness, an *opus rude et simplex* in accord with the order's principles of programmatic poverty. But it was also the testimony to grandiose papal patronage, and, as such, the herald of the glory of its founder.

The facade, in fact, presents the most direct interpretation of such semiological requirements. In the facade, the abstention from the use of a rich architectural vocabulary opens the way to a monumentalism based in a compositional exaltation of the functional elements. An intelligent arrangement of the wall openings composed according to the variety of open spaces behind them and their rhythmical grouping within sober framings of wall produce an altogether unique physiognomy. The structural organization of the imposing wall masses finds its focal points in the axes of the two portals which dominate the lateral sections of the central section. This center, heightened by the addition of a third floor above the cornice, gathers together in a richly tensile array the most variegated elements: pairs of windows, the small windows of the mezzanine, a niche, an inscription, and the coat of arms of the founder as well as the circular clockface. Two sundials and a small bell tower crown the ensemble. The lower lateral wings have a much simpler arrangement with groups of three, one, and three windows.

The rhythmical scansion of the wall areas and the linear play of relief in the subtly stratified surfaces are much more important than the formal articulation of the individual architectural elements. These are the very elements which the unfinished drawing on display (Cat. 100) best highlights, as it only sketches out the building's most essential general lines.

The Vasi engraving (Cat. 101), rather, throws light on the urban context of the facade which fills the entire northern side of the immense rectangular *piazza* before it. The result of the expansion of the pre-existing Piazza di Camilliano (on the left-hand side of the view), the *piazza* was already conceived of at the time of Gregory XIII, but was realized only in 1659 thanks to the direct intervention of Pope Alexander VII.

RB

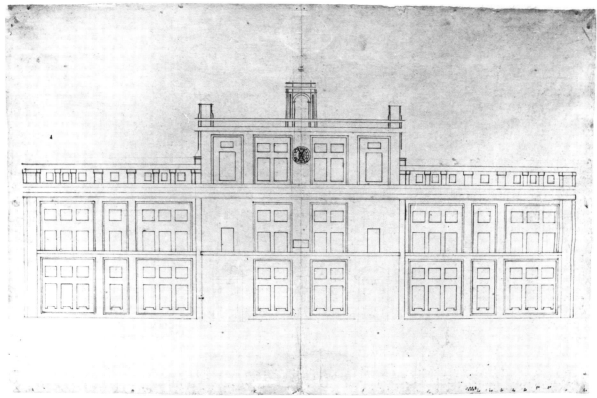

CAT. 100

CAT. 101

169

102. Anonymous, *Notice of the dedication of the Collegio Romano*, in: *Avvisi di Roma*, fol. 452r, October 31, 1584

Vatican City, Biblioteca Apostolica Vaticana, Urb. Lat. 1052

This manuscript is one of the so-called "Avvisi," hand-written fliers, the ancestors of modern daily newspapers. They were most freqently penned by *letterati*, scholars, and secretaries of princes and prelates, particulary on behalf of ambassadors and those who were involved in politics. They diffused fresh reliable news about public events, court intrigues, and the gossip of the nobility.

The author of this *avviso* in his entry "From Rome, on the last day of October, [15]84" wrote as follows about the dedication of the Collegio Romano which his Holiness Gregory XIII had blessed for the Jesuits on October 28, 1584:

"On Sunday the Pope, returning from Monte Cavallo to take up residence at S. Pietro, stopped to see and to bless the edifice of the new Gregorian College, and he was pleased to listen to an oration by the Sicilian Jesuit Stefano Tuccio, a very worthy display of his training and of his imagination. The abstract points illustrated with various oratorical ornaments were principally these: the very great indebtedness which the fathers have to his Holiness for his visit, their gratitude for the other and divine blessings they have received, but in particular this memorable visit, because in this case the condescension of the Pontifical Dignity has greatly added to the honor of this Society; an enumeration of the generosity of the Pope towards the Society, which, because of him, is now diffused throughout all parts of the world; their true way of winning mastery over nations, and extending over all peoples which in appearance seems a combat with a leaden sword but is in fact waged with the arms of Divine Providence and Pontifical Authority; the particular grace [granted by the pope] of entrusting to the Society the ministry of teaching the children of so many nations; their gratitude which cannot match their obligation, but which will endure as long as this edifice, as well as in their studies and teaching of the arts in every city and place; their obligation to celebrate the name of His Holiness, for whom they would not hesitate to give their very lives."

AD

CASTRONOVO, 1976, pp. 6-13, 62-63

103. Anonymous, *General Plan of the Collegio Romano*, Pen and ink and wash, 65 x 90 cm., second half of the 17th century

Vatican City, Biblioteca Apostolica Vaticana, Mss. Chigiana P. VII. 9, fol. 130v-131r

This anonymous plan drawn between 1645 and 1685 shows the block of the Collegio Romano in its final organization, achieved with the construction of the Church of S. Ignazio. Begun in 1626 and funded by a large foundation established by Cardinal Ludovico Ludovisi, the vast edifice which replaced the sixteenth-century Church of the Annunziata is the work of Jesuit architect and mathematician Orazio Grassi (who developed designs by Domenichino, Maderno, and Borromini in his project).

Located on the northwestern corner, the *Tempio Ludovisiano* occupies about one quarter of the entire block. Its interior, based on the model of a Latin cross, is rather similar to the prototypical Church of the Gesù. An unusual feature is the organization of the intercommunicating lateral chapels which practically form independent naves. Supporting the arches are columns which scenographically divide the spatial sequence of the lateral areas and which in their own way enrich the appearance of the central internal space. As our plan clearly shows, the edifice was built in two phases: until 1645 the body of the nave arose, closed provisionally with a wall. Only after 1685 were the crossing and its "arms" built under the direction of Andrea Pozzo.

The construction of the seventeenth-century church required the radical transformation of the arrangement of the entire complex, for the church arose where the fathers' residence had been planned. The site was later enlarged: the irregular northeastern corner was finally perfectly squared. The cloister, also designed by Grassi, arose to the east of the church, in an area scarcely sufficient and much narrower than had been originally planned.

RB

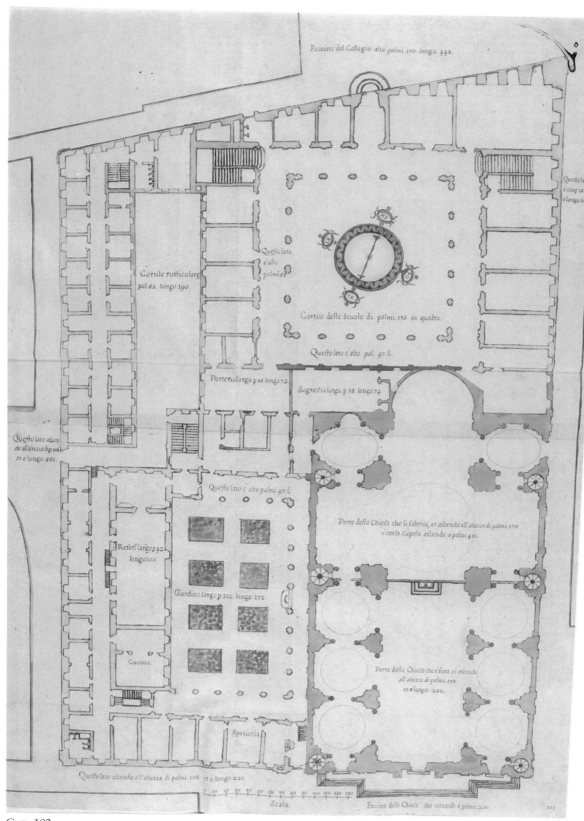

Facciata del Collegio alta palmi. 170. longa. 448.

Questo lato
e alto p. 126.
e longo 656.

Questo lato
e alto
palmi 87.

Cortile rustico largo
pal. 82. longo 190.

Cortile delle Scuole di palmi. 155. in quadro.

Questo lato e alto pal: 97 ½.

Porteria larga p. 56. longa 72.

Sagrestia larga p. 58. longa 74.

Questo lato ascen-
de all'altezza di p. 106.
et e longo 261.

Questo lato e alto palmi. 97 ½.

Parte della Chiesa che si fabrica, et ascende all'altezza di palmi. 370.
e con la Cupola ascende a palmi. 411.

Refet. largo p. 42.
longo 100.

Giardino largo p. 102. longo. 172.

Cucina.

Parte della Chiesa che e fatta et ascende
all'altezza di palmi. 170.
et e larga. 200.

Spetieria.

Questo lato ascende all'altezza di palmi. 106. et e longo 220.

Scala.

Facciata della Chiesa che ascende a palmi. 205.

CAT. 103

171

104. After Peter Paul Rubens (?), *The foundation of the Collegio Germanico,* Engraving in: *Vita Beati Patris Ignatii,* fig. 64, 1609

Florence, Biblioteca dell'Istituto Stensen, Armadio A

Ignatij in Septemtrionis res apprime intenti studio, ac precibus Iulius III Pont Max Collegium Germaniæ iuuentutis non minori Ecclesiæ Romanæ ornamento, quam Germaniæ præsidio Romæ condit.

64

Among the educational initiatives of St. Ignatius, the foundation of the German College ranks among the most important. In 1552, with the encouragement of his friend Cardinal Morone and to the delight of the reigning pontiff Julius III, Ignatius founded a college in Rome to prepare seminarians from German-speaking countries for the priesthood. His goal was consistent with the order's focus on the ministries of the word and service to the pope: Ignatius' Collegium Germanicum sought to prepare future preachers and teachers—pastors and bishops—who could address directly the Protestant revolt against papal authority in the German-speaking world.

The foundation of the Germanicum in Rome is emblematic of the same centripetal vision which inspired the foundation of the Roman College. Although Ignatius himself approved the opening of important colleges in Cologne, Vienna, Ingolstadt, and Prague (Cat. 79, 80), he recognized the importance of preparing some of the best German-speakers in the Roman milieu.

The students followed the same curriculum of languages, arts, and scripture as their confrères at the Roman College, and in the earliest years lived almost next door on Via del Gesù. They also shared the same rigor and simplicity of life imposed by the extreme poverty of the foundation. Ignatius himself spent much of his energy in the last four years of his life seeking alms to support the students of his Roman schools. Financial security for the institutions would only come during the reign of Gregory XIII.

TL sj

Dalmases, pp. 197-198; *Chron* II, pp. 421-422; Ravier, 1973, pp. 155, 268

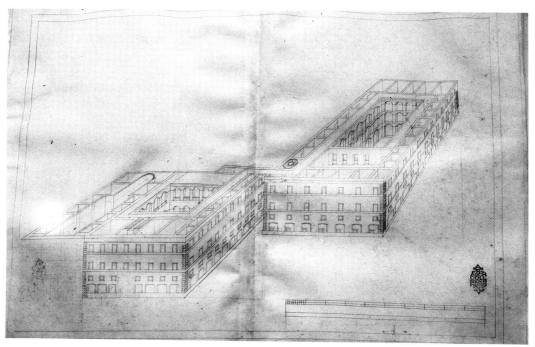

105. Benedetto Molli, *Plan of the Collegio Germanico*, Pen and ink with wash,
61.5 x 63.5 cm., dated February 10, 1632
Rome, Archivio del Pontificio Collegio Germanico-Ungarico, Disegni 10

106. Anonymous copy after Benedetto Molli, *Perspective of the Collegio Germanico
as planned in the 17th century*, in: *Libro del Catasto dei Beni di Roma*,
Pen and ink on parchment: fol. 29v-30r, 1666-1671
Rome, Archivio del Pontificio Collegio Germanico-Ungarico, Admin. 2

The Collegio Germanico's financial stability and its physical placement in the center of Cinquecento Rome was due to the active commitment of Pope Gregory XIII, who undertook a serious "refoundation" of the institution. A bull of January 5, 1574 granted to the college the Medieval basilica of S. Apollinare and two connected buildings: the palace of the titular cardinal immediately adjacent to the church and its rustic outbuildings located on a nearby block and directly connected by an arched passageway over the intervening street.

More than a mere reconstruction of the church (provisionally restored shortly after 1580; see Cat. 117), it was necessary to impose a unitary architectural organization to the college's residence, significantly renovating the primary edifice next to the church and enlarging the secondary site in order to construct there an entirely new, perfectly rectangular block.

Corresponding to this ambitious program is the view of the Collegio Germanico shown in the drawing of Cat. 106, contained in the Libro del Catasto dei Beni edited by Fr. Galeno, procurator of the college from 1666 until 1671. This design is a copy of the project elaborated around 1630 by Paolo Maruscelli in collaboration with the Jesuit Benedetto Molli. In fact, it is possible to identify a most unique mode of architectural rendering that is peculiar to the drawings of this Jesuit architect and "faber murarius:" a kind of *vue cavalière* combined—according to a method sometimes used in military perspectives—with a plan which is superimposed on the roofs of the buildings seen in perspective. The two blocks—both three storeys high and uniformly delineated in their severe external appearance—arise around large quadrilateral courtyards, with a very regular arrangement of rooms, public spaces, and corridors. On the extreme left we see the church, which also shows a new project for its architectonic organization. A single nave flanked by four chapels on each side flows into a narrow, deep apsidal choir. The facade of the church is shown sketched out with chalk lines.

In conformity with this project, construction began in 1631 with the realization of the western wing of the secondary block, and also a new connecting archway.

Except for a few very limited building projects, construction was suspended until the middle of the eighteenth century. In 1742, work resumed with the construction of the present church according to a plan furnished by Ferdinando Fuga. In 1748, the reorganization of the college building next to the church was begun. Construction on the second block was resumed in 1773 according to plans drawn by Luigi Vanvitelli, Ermengildo Sintes, and Pietro Camporesi. Thus, the completion of this vast architectural complex occurred after the suppression of the Society (by Clement XIV, 1773), once the buildings of the Germanico had been entrusted to the secular clergy.

RB

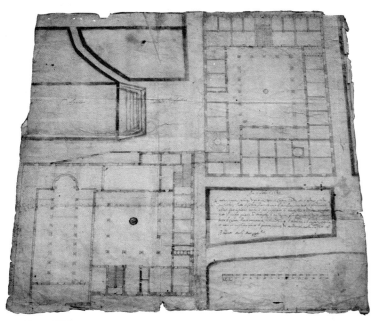

CAT. 105

BÖSEL, 1985, I, pp. 228-242; BÖSEL and GARMS, 1981; CORDARA, 1770; MANCINI, 1967; STEINHUBER, 1906

107. Orazio Grassi, *Elevation of the interior of a church*, Ink with watercolor washes, 27 x 42.7 cm.

Rome, Archivium Romanum Societatis Iesu, F.G. 1238, 5, 4, now in Armadio 5

108. Orazio Grassi, *Project for the facade of a church*, Pen and ink and wash, 41 x 27.8 cm.

Rome, Archivium Romanum Societatis Iesu, F.G. 1238, 5, 3, now in Armadio 5

Among the many Jesuits who worked—whether exclusively or part time—as architects and building superintendents, Fr. Orazio Grassi (1583-1654) held a position of eminence: in general for the cultural range of his singular erudition, and in particular for the artistic quality of the singular architectural works he created.

Professor of mathematics at the Collegio Romano from 1616, Grassi wrote discourses on a wide range of subjects more or less related to his discipline, from the construction of unsinkable boats to Galileo's theory on the nature of comets. It was, perhaps, in the field of architecture that his gifts best converged. As early as 1612 he was charged with founding for the order an architectural academy based on solid theoretical principles to prepare a new generation of Jesuits architects. Although this at-tempt was shortlived, Grassi continued to be considered the foremost Jesuit expert in the field of construction. From 1617 to 1624 and again in 1627-1628, he served as *consiliarius aedificiorum*, the official censor and judge of architectural projects sent to the general curia for approval.

Indubitably his most celebrated work is the *Tempio Ludovisiano*, the Church of S. Ignazio in Rome. Required to show himself equal to the task of inventing a celebration of papal glory and an exaltation of papal nepotism, Grassi sought a solution which was not only magnificent but also artistically sensational. More in line with his function as an architect of the order, however, were his more modest creations for various Jesuit establishments in Italy. In addition to his most important contribution to the construction of the large college in Genoa, it is worth recalling the churches of the colleges of Siena (1626) and Aiaccio (1628) where the architect developed an almost purist stylistic language. In his search for dignified yet ostensibly "poor" formulations, Grassi found his appropriate vocabulary by renouncing the classical orders. His walls are conceived as simple enclosures of space, divided according to functional needs, yet their planar modulation always displays tasteful "graphic" and chiaroscuro shading.

Grassi's particular style, which refers back to a "pauperistic" tradition of the early Cinquecento, is well captured in one of the two drawings displayed here.

The interior elevation of a church (Cat. 107) is rhythmically divided by the alternation of lateral chapels with niches designed for confessionals. The pulpit is placed in the central wall interval. The whole is reduced to pure linearity by the subtle stratification of the walls. Only the arcades recall orthodox classicism.

The architecture of the facade (Cat. 108) is more richly articulated. This drawing betrays the strong stylistic influence of Roman architects of the period around 1600 (one thinks of Giacomo Della Porta). As opposed to Cat. 107 which accurately represents a theoretical study, this second drawing, shows evidence of having a particular design premise: the inconsistency between the orientation of the external facade in relation to the nave behind it. This evidence indicates that the drawing attempted to resolve a particular practical situation which has yet to be identified.

RB

BENEDETTI, 1984, pp. 67-104; BÖSEL, 1985, I, pp. 192-199, 281-290; BRICARELLI, 1922; COSTANTINI, 1966; LAMALLE, 1960, pp. 403ff.; SOPRANI and RATTI, 1769, pp. 9-11; VALLERY-RADOT, 1960, pp. 29*, 22, 96

CAT. 108

109. Andrea Sacchi and Jan Miel, *Pope Urban VIII's Visit to the Church of the Gesù at the Inauguration of the Society's Centenary Celebration (October 2, 1639),* Oil on canvas, 321 x 248 cm., 1639-1641

Rome, Galleria Nazionale d'Arte Antica, Inv. 1445 (on loan to the Museo di Roma)

This painting was commissioned from Sacchi by Antonio Barberini to record both the historical event celebrated here and the Barberini's sponsorship of the decorations for the occasion. Amongst the enormous crowd that fills the church the light falls upon Urban VIII and his entourage of Cardinal Nephews being greeted by the Jesuit General Mutio Vitelleschi. The figures in the immediate foreground (painted by Miel) show us the scene just outside of the church where the crowd, the horses, and the Barberini dwarf may have enjoyed the fireworks display that was put on in the *piazza.*

Historians have been most interested in this painting for the information it provides about the original decoration of the nave, cupola and apse of the church. Clearly visible is Giacomo Della Porta's high altar tabernacle, dismantled in the nineteenth century (Mashek, 1970), with Muziano's *Circumcision* crowned by the IHS, statues, and a Crucifix. The rest of the apse is covered with tapestries lent by the patron. From the cupola still hangs the banner with Sts. Ignatius and Francis Xavier that was brought in procession from S. Pietro to the Gesù on the day following the canonization (Cat. 114). Andrea Lilio's *Doctors of the Church,* the original frescoes in the pendentives are visible, as are the *Virtues* and painted ornaments in the drum. Any decorations that might have enlivened the nave are all but obscured by the tapestries from the Barberini collection.

A recent study, which emphasizes Giacomo Della Porta's initiation of a new approach to the decoration of the nave, has revised our perception of the Society's aims and actual interventions in the interior of the sixteenth-century church (Kummer). Kummer emphasizes both the effect of walking through undecorated and decorated sections of the church as well as the evidence that the large spaces were not meant to remain undecorated.

EL

Fagiolo dell'Arco and Carandini, 1977-1978, I, pp. 111-113; Haskell, 1980, p. 55; Kummer, 1986, pp. 185-203; Pietrangeli, 1971, pp. 69-70

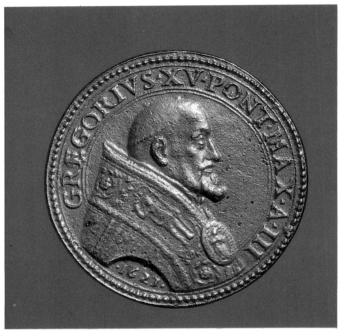

CAT. 110b, OBVERSE   CAT. 110b, REVERSE

110a-b. *Two Medals from the Canonization of Sts. Ignatius and Francis Xavier,*
              Obverse: Gregory XV facing right,
                    "GREGORIUS • XV • PONT • MAX • A • III"
              Reverse: Scene of the Canonization Consistory,
                    "QUNIQUE • - • BEATIS • COELESTES • HONORES • DECERNIT • = • 1622"
              a: Bronze (unfinished, with two appendices top and bottom), 31.1 mm., 1622
              b: Gilded Bronze (finished), 30.75 mm., 1622
Vatican City, Biblioteca Apostolica Vaticana, Numismatica

111. *Soggetto D. Ignatio in Monserrato, overo Mutatione d'Armi,* Rome, 1623
Vatican City, Biblioteca Apostolica Vaticana, Stamp. Chig. IV, 2185, 3

The play *D. Ignatius at Montserrat, or the Change of Arms* is one of a number of dramas performed at the Collegio Romano to celebrate the canonization of Sts. Ignatius and Francis Xavier in 1622. Typical of the elaborate Jesuit productions of the era, its emphasis is triumphalistic and its structure highly conventional: choruses alternate with verse recitatives and flamboyant "production numbers" (including here a pitched battle between Heaven and Hell, allegories of the Four Continents paying homage to the Church Militant, and an international pageant of the Jesuit order).

As early as the mid 1560s comedies were performed at the Collegio Romano and Collegio Germanico, and quickly the practice of theatrical performances spread to the other colleges of Europe. The Jesuits used them both as a means of indoctrination and instruction, and as means of combatting the excesses of the secular theater, especially during the carnival season (Gnerghi, p. 5). During the period between 1570 and 1590 when Counter Reformation sensibilities closed Roman theaters, the Jesuit colleges provided the city with its only dramas.

From the earliest sketches of the *Ratio Studiorum* (Cat. 66), drama played an important role in the Jesuit curriculum. Immense effort was required to produce these spectacles, and rules limiting the number of annual performances and the subject matter were formulated in the final edition of the *Ratio* (1599). Female characters were excluded. Around 1600 classical dramas modeled on Seneca's plays came into vogue, though musical melodramas and intricate allegories dominated the Jesuit stage in Rome throughout the seventeenth century.

TL sj

BJURSTRÖM, 1972; GNERGHI, 1907; TACCHI VENTURI, 1922, pp. 109-110

SOGGETTO
D IGNATIO
IN MONSERRATO,
ouero Mutatione d'Armi.
ATTIONE TRAGICOMICA,
Che da giouani del Seminario Romano si rappresenta in Collegio Romano della Compagnia di GIESV.

Disteso in Atti, e Scene dal Signor Don Girolamo Cao Sardo Conuittore del medesimo Seminario.

IN ROMA,
Appresso Alesandro Zannetti. MDCXXIII.
Con licenza de' Superiori.

112. *Missa S. Ignatii Confessoris*, 1675

Rome, Archivium Postulatoris Generalis Societatis Iesu, 22

MISSA
SANCTI IGNATII
CONFESSORIS
SOCIETATIS IESV
FVNDATORIS

A Sac. Rituum Congregatione recognita,
& approbata Die 2 1. Ianuarij 1 6 7 3.

Die 3 1. Iulii.

IN FESTO

S. IGNATII

CONFESSORIS.

INTROITVS.

 N nomine Iefu omne genufle-
ctatur, cæleftiú, terreftrium, & infernorum, &
omnis lingua confiteatur, quia **Dominus Iefus Chriftus in gloria eft Dei Patris.**
Pfal. Gloriabuntur in te omnes, qui diligunt nomen tuum, quoniam tu benedices iufto.
℣. Gloria Patri, &c.

Oratio.

Eus, qui ad maiorem tui nominis gloriam propagandam, nouo per Beatum Ignatium fubfidio militantem Ecclefiam roborafti: concede, vt eius auxilio, & imitatione certantes in terris, coronari cû ipfo mereamur in Cælis. Per Dominum, &c.

Lectio Epiftolæ B. Pauli Apoftoli ad Timotheum.

Arifsime; Memor efto Dominum noftrum Iefum Chriftum refurrexiffe á mortuis ex femine Dauid, fecundum Euangelium meum, in quo laboro víque ad vincula, quafi male operans, fed verbum

Although St. Ignatius was canonized in 1622, this text for his mass "proper" was only formally approved in 1673 and published for the Universal Church during the Holy Year 1675.

The texts reflect basic elements of Ignatius' own experience and the Jesuit vocation. The entrance antiphon or "introit" taken from the ancient hymn in St. Paul's letter to the Philippians is a reminder of Ignatius' devotion to the holy name and decision to call his new Society "the Companions of Jesus": "At the name of Jesus, every knee must bend in heaven, on earth, and under the earth, and every tongue proclaim, to the glory of God the Father, that Jesus Christ is Lord" (Phil. 2:10). The epistle (2 Timothy 2:8-10, 3:10-12) tells of the trials of those who preach the Gospel of Christ. The gospel is St. Luke's account of the sending of the 72 disciples "to every city and place" to proclaim that the Kingdom of God is at hand. The text underscores the Jesuit missionary vocation of preaching and teaching, and of readiness to go to any place to further the work of the Kingdom. Finally, the communion antiphon is the verse from Luke 12 which Andrea Pozzo used as his theme for the vault of the Church of S. Ignazio (Cat. 136), and which clearly expresses Ignatius' own "zeal for souls": "I have come to cast fire on the earth; would that it were already kindled!"

TL sj

113. *Medal of the Holy Year 1625 with the five saints canonized in 1622*

Obverse: Large central crucifix with (left to right) St. Peter, The Virgin
Mary, St. John the Baptist, and St. Paul beneath a crescent moon and star,
"• 1625•"

Reverse: The Virgin Mary on a cloud with the Child Jesus, St. Teresa,
St. Ignatius, St. Isidore, St. Francis Xavier, and St.Philip Neri
"ST [...], FR • S • FI • = [...] IDO"

Silver with raised border, 40.1 mm., 1625

Rome, Church of the Gesù, Sacristy

114. *Notice of the canonization of Sts. Ignatius and Francis Xavier,* in:
Diario di Giacinto Gigli, fol. 50

Vatican City, Biblioteca Apostolica Vaticana, Vat. Lat. 8717

Saturday March 12, 1622 in the midst of great celebrations five *beati* were canonized: Isidore the Farmer, Ignatius Loyola, Francis Xavier, Teresa of Avila, and Philip Neri. For the ceremony in S. Pietro four large standards were prepared with the images of the new saints: Ignatius and Francis Xavier were depicted on the same banner. This banner was, on the following day, solemnly carried to the Church of the Gesù (Cat. 109), and the other standards were carried in procession to S. Giacomo degli Spagnoli, to Santa Maria della Scala, and to the Chiesa Nuova.

Roman Giacinto Gigli (1594-1670), an alumnus of the Collegio Romano, had from his youth kept a record of the public events that took place in his native city. He entitled his diary *The Memorial of Giacinto Gigli, of the events which occurred in his times, beginning from his fourteenth year, which was the year of our Lord 1608, and the fourth year of the Pontificate of Pope Paul V.*

When the canonization banner of Ignatius and Francis Xavier was transferred from the Gesù to the Collegio Romano, Giglio wrote in his *Diary*:

"On the sixth of April 1622 with great solemnity the standard of Sts. Ignatius and Francis was carried in procession from the Church of the Gesù to the Annunziata of the Collegio Romano. The procession departed from the Gesù towards the Cesarini straight on to the [Piazza del] Pasquino, and then to the Madonna dell'Anima at Torre Sanguina, on [Via della] Ripetta as far as the Borghese [Palace], and then returned down the Corso as far as S. Marco, where it turned on the street which leads to the Collegio Romano. There were 1500 torches of white wax carried by the Collegio Salviati in the procession, and by an immense number of students of the Collegio Romano, and the English and Maronite Colleges and the fathers of the Society, who at the end carried the banner, whose arrival was welcomed by three bishops, and torches carried by a multitude. It was received with music and the blare of trumpets, drums, and firecrackers, and that evening there were diverse fireworks and great rejoicing."

AD

GIGLI, 1958, pp. 1-18, 63.

115. Raphael Sadeler after Federico Zuccari, *Annunciation,* Engraving, 29.3 x 45 cm., 1580

Rome, Archivium Historicum Societatis Iesu, Armadio 4

The Church of the Annunziata at the Collegio Romano, constructed between 1561 and 1567 according to the designs of Giovanni Tristano, was the first church to be built and decorated by the Society in Rome (see fig. on p. 39). Although torn down in 1650 (Pirri, p. 30) to make way for the Church of S. Ignazio, from written descriptions and this engraving of the apse decoration we can reconstruct the general appearance of the interior.

The Annunziata was typical of churches being decorated in the mid-sixteenth century with a flat ceiling, brick floor, paintings limited to the altars set back along the nave, and a more elaborate fresco program in the apse (Lewine). We know that the four nave altars were dedicated to S. Sebastiano, the Virgin, the Crucifixion, and S. Francesco; the latter had a painting (now lost) of the *Stigmata* by Girolamo Muziano (Baglione [1642], 1935, p. 50). There is conflicting evidence concerning the size and form of the original side chapels (apparently only 1.5 m. deep) and later changes that may have been made with the construction of the college (cf. Cat. 97; Pirri, p. 29; Lewine, p. 157; Bösel, I, p. 182, and II, fig. 122-125).

The high altar chapel was decorated by Federico Zuccari upon his return to Rome in early 1566. Vasari writes (1568) that Taddeo Zuccari had arranged for his younger brother Federico, "a chapel to paint in fresco in the church of the reformed priests

Opus quod in æde Virginis Deiparæ Annunciatæ Collegii Romani societatis IESV. Federicus Zuccarus S. Angeli in Vado ad Ripas Mitauri perfecit æneis tabellis expressum. Ioannes sadeler: excud: Coloniæ Agripp: A·D· CIↃ IↃ LXXX·

CAT. 115

of the Gesù at the 'guglia' of S. Mauro [Macuto], and to this Federico immediately put his hand" (Milanesi [ed.], VII, p. 101). The dedication of the church to the Annunziata (hence the image on the high altar) was dictated by its patroness, the Marchesa della Valle. Although Zuccari's fresco was destroyed with the church, its design is preserved in several engravings.

A drawing in the Uffizi, identified as a preparatory sketch for the composition, shows that at some point the program underwent significant expansion. In the earlier drawing, the monogram of Christ, the IHS that figures so prominently in the seventeenth-century decorations of the Society's churches, appeared below the Holy Spirit and thus combined the Annunciation scene with that of the Immaculata (Körte, pp. 525-526, fig. 5). In the final composition this reminder of the Society was eliminated and other figures were added such as the shadowy souls of purgatory, and Adam and Eve in the spandrels. Moreover, the whole scene was expanded to include Kings and Prophets who foretold the coming of Christ, a landscape with Marian symbols, and a host of musical angels (Weil).

In 1571, Cornelis Cort, who subsequently engraved Federico's most important works, made a two-plate engraving of the Annunziata fresco (Körte, p. 525). Cort's engraving was extremely popular as evidenced by the five, or possibly six, copies made by other engravers in the 1570s (Bierens de Haan). This engraving by Raphael Sadeler is particularly faithful to Cort's version. However it is reduced in size and there are slight variations in the arrangement of the inscriptions on the tablets.

EL

BAGLIONE (1642), 1935, pp. 121-122; BIERENS DE HAAN, 1948, pp. 49-51; BÖSEL, 1985, I, pp. 181-182, II, fig. 122-125; KÖRTE, 1919-1932, pp. 524-529, fig. 4-7; LEWINE, 1960, pp. 153-161; MILANESI [ED.], 1907, VII p. 101; PIRRI, 1955, pp. 27-30; RINALDI, 1914, pp. 93-98; VILLOSLADA, 1954, pp. 53-55; WEIL, 1974, pp. 227-228

116. Giovanni Battista de Cavallieri after Nicolò Circignani, *Edmund Campion and Companions Dragged to Execution,* Engraving in: *Ecclesiae anglicanae tropaea,* fig. 32, Rome, 1584

Vatican City, Biblioteca Apostolica Vaticana, R.I., II, 954

The sixteenth-century decorations of St. Thomas of Canterbury, the church of the English College, were destroyed when the church was razed in the nineteenth century. The only element of decoration that has survived is the high altar painting representing the *Trinity with Sts. Thomas of Canterbury and Edward* by Durante Alberti (completed in 1580) that presently adorns the high altar wall of the Gothic Revival church erected on the same site in 1866 (Lotti and Lotti, pp. 37, 125-127).

According to a plan of the church from 1630 (Lotti and Lotti, p. 81), the small three-aisled church had two altars flanking the high altar, and two altars in the side aisles to the left and right of the entrance. Around 1583 the walls between the altars were painted by Nicolò Circignani with thirty-five scenes of the martyrdoms of English saints from the Middle Ages up until 1581 (Monssen, p.131). With figures also painted above the nave columns, the decoration of the church as a whole, which may have included a fictive architectural framework, seems to have resembled the later frescoes commissioned by Baronio for SS. Nereo and Achilleo.

The original appearance of Circignani's cycle is known through a set of engravings published in 1584 by Giovanni Battista de Cavallieri (the paintings behind the *matronei* of the nineteenth-century church described incorrectly as the original frescoes in Strinati, 1979 and Fagiolo and Madonna, 1985a were copied from Cavallieri's engravings in the nineteenth century). This cycle is the second of three sets of frescoes of martyrdoms after Circignani published by Cavallieri between 1583 and 1586 (Vannugli, 1983, p. 102).

The frescoes were commissioned from Circignani by George Gilbert, a zealous admirer of the English martyrs and a resident at the English College at the end of his short life (Buser, pp. 429-430). A eulogy written by the rector of the college to the general of the Society, Aquaviva, explains Gilbert's commission: "[Gilbert] showed a very great venera-

tion for the martyrs, on account of the ardent desire which he entertained to become their companion in torments and death. Hence the holy youth took great pains to learn the names of all the English martyrs of former and modern times, and caused their acts of martyrdom to be represented in paintings, with which he adorned the whole church of this College in the way that your paternity has seen, placing also the holy confessors alternately with the martyrs over the capitals of the columns. This cost him seven hundred scudi, having collected for the purpose contributions from several of his English friends" (Buser, p. 430).

Buser has demonstrated that Circignani's frescoes were based on a set of engravings that accompanied William Allen's *Historia del glorioso martirio di sedici sacerdoti* (Macerata, 1583), an account of the sufferings of sixteen martyrs, including the Jesuit Edmund Campion and his companions. This publication, in turn, was probably produced in response to the Protestant John Foxe's *Acts and Monuments of these Latter and Perillous Days* (1563, 2nd ed. 1570), a history that emphasized and graphically illustrated the martyrdoms of recent reformers.

Unlike the other cycles painted by Circignani for Jesuit college churches in this period, this cycle depicts both martyrdoms of remote times and the torture of contemporary men. Jesuit Edmund Campion was a figure of particular importance to the Jesuits in Rome, having resided in their own college before his martyrdom in 1581. His sufferings occupied three bays of Circignani's cycle. In this engraving he and his companions are shown being carried "from the Tower to Tiburn" on hurdles while Protestant ministers argue their point of view in vain.

EL

Buser, 1976, pp. 427-433, fig. 6-8; Fagiolo and Madonna, 1985a, p. 194; Herz, 1988a, pp. 65, 67; Lotti and Lotti, 1978, pp. 125-128; Mâle, 1932, pp. 109-111; Monssen, 1981, p. 131; Röttgen, 1975, pp. 106-115; Strinati, 1979, p. 11

Qui Summi Pontificis primatum Reginæ in Anglia negant tribui posse,
tanquam Læsæ Maiestatis rei damnantur, et ad supplicii locum Cratibus
impositi, ministris interim hæreticis ad fidem Catholicam deserendam
adhortantibus, per mediam Vrbem ignominiosè raptantur Sic Edmundus
Campianus cum socijs, alijque Catholici tum Sacerdotes tum laici ad
mortem tracti sunt Anno Domini 1581. 1582. 1583.

CAT. 116

S. APOLLINARIS MARTYRIO PERFVNCTVS PROPE RAVENNAM
SEPELITVR.

CAT. 117

117. Giovanni Battista de Cavallieri after Nicolò Circignani, *The Burial of St. Apollinarius,* Engraving in: *Beati Apollinaris Martyris Primi Ravennatum Epi Res Gestae,* fig. 13, Rome, 1586

Vatican City, Biblioteca Apostolica Vaticana, Cicognara VI, 2008

S. Apollinare, a seventh-century church, was given to the Collegio Germanico by Gregory XIII in 1574. Restored by the Society in the ensuing years, the church was soon damaged by the devastating flood (1598) that also ruined the Casa Professa. Several plans for a new church were proposed over the course of the seventeenth century although construction on a design by Fuga only materialized in the 1740s (see Cat. 106).

In a guide to Rome published in 1588, the newly restored church was described at length: "This church has three naves supported by columns, ...pilasters, and walls... The floor was all done in beautiful inlay work with much variety in the stones employed, a good part of which is still there... Under the pontificate of Gregory XIII...the Church of S. Apollinare was very well restored by the Fathers of the Gesù, and brought to that beauty and splendor that is seen today...the ceiling has been painted and gilded, and the tribune, with the middle nave beautifully painted with the history of St. Apollinarius, and the choir above and below, and the organ, and the altars, the high altar as well as the others, all has been renovated with admirable order and ornament.

So that whereas before this church was hardly even known, at the present it is visited by many, and honored" (Ugonio).

The main feature of the new decorations was a fresco cycle by Circignani depicting the life of St. Apollinarius with an emphasis on his torture and martyrdom. Probably executed in 1582, the same year as the frescoes in S. Stefano Rotondo (Monssen), this lost cycle is preserved in a set of fifteen engravings also published by Cavallieri. The frescoes in S. Apollinare were probably larger in scale than the longer cycle in St. Thomas of Canterbury and, as described above, painted on the walls of the nave and in the tribune. In Cavallieri's publication, there are twelve scenes from the life of St. Apollinarius as well as three allegorical scenes of Life, Death, and Sin.

EL

Bösel, 1986, I, pp. 228-229; Herz, 1988a, p. 53; Mâle 1932, p. 113; Mancini, 1967, pp. 16, 84, n. 70-72; Monssen, 1981, p. 131; Röttgen, 1975, pp. 106-115; Ugonio, 1588, pp. 285v-286r

118. *The Church of San Vitale,* Engraving in: Louis Richeome, *La Peinture Spirituelle,* p. 682, Lyon, 1611

Vatican City, Biblioteca Apostolica Vaticana, Stampe Barb. T,VII, 61

In 1595 Clement VIII assigned S. Vitale, a fifth-century church (restored in 1475 by Sixtus IV but in ruinous condition) to the Jesuit Novitiate house at S. Andrea a Montecavallo. Located on the far side of the garden of the house, S. Vitale was put to use immediately by the community of novices. In this view of the nave the Jesuits are shown engaged in the activities of preaching, confession, and providing food for the poor. Some are instructing smaller groups; given the differences in their dress we may suppose that what is represented here is the weekly occasion at which,

according to Richeome (p. 784), members of various foreign communities in Rome were addressed in their native languages.

A report on the renovation of the church from 1597 recorded the following work in progress that year: "The restoration continued and the portico, painted inside and out, was finished, and the painting of the church was begun, and the ornamentation of the ceiling with paintings, large rosettes, leaves, and other decorations which, although not costly, render the church very beautiful and worthy of respect. The tribune is being rebuilt from the foundations" (Zuccari, 1984b, p. 160).

The painted decorations, executed according to a scheme by G.B. Fiammeri chosen by General Aquaviva, were begun in 1596 and continued at least until 1603 (Pirri, p. 12; Huetter and Golzio, p. 46). Both the two scenes of the *Stoning* and *Martyrdom* of the titular saint in the presbytery by A. Ciampelli, and the apse fresco representing *The Way to Golgotha* by A. Commodi, were highly praised by Baglione ([1642], 1935, pp. 320, 334). The nave and entrance wall frescoes representing prophets and scenes of martyrdom were painted by Tarquinio Ligustri.

Although the martyrdom scenes in San Vitale are similar to what we know of those painted by Circignani in the college churches, in some ways they mark a departure from the cycles of the 1580s. Unlike the one surviving Circignani cycle at S. Stefano Rotondo, here a fictive architectural system extends from the entrance wall to the apse, and from the pavement to the vault, thus uniting the entire interior. And, although the Commodi martyrdom scenes are as explicit as any of Circignani's, the nave cycle differs entirely from the earlier type. In Ligustri's works the figures have been drastically reduced in scale and set in lush landscapes. And, most of the accompanying text characteristic of the cycles by Circignani has been eliminated. The new emphasis on landscape may reflect the "new Christian optimism" that infused the writings of Federico Borromeo and Bellarmino around 1600 (Jones, 1988).

San Vitale is remarkable for being one of two Early Christian churches renovated by the Jesuits at the end of the sixteenth century whose decoration survives almost intact. It has been suggested that the renovation of this church may have served as a model for Cardinal Baronio and Clement VIII's much more well-known restorations of the Early Christian churches of SS. Nereo and Achilleo and S. Cesareo around the same time (Herz, p. 59).

EL

682   L'EGLISE DE SAINCT VITAL.

HERZ, 1988a, pp. 53-54, 59, 64-65, 67; HUETTER and GOLZIO, 1938, pp. 44-63; MÂLE, 1932, pp. 113-114, 118-120, 124; PIRRI, 1952, pp. 11-12, 39-42; STRINATI, 1979, p. 17; ZUCCARI, 1981b, pp. 174, 176, 184; ZUCCARI, 1984b, pp. 141-147, 159-165

119. Wierix after Giovanni Battista Fiammeri, *Christ Nailed to the Cross*, Engraving in: Jerome Nadal, *Evangelicae Historiae Imagines*, fig. 127, Antwerp, 1593

Rome, Biblioteca Institutum Historicum Societatis Iesu, Armadio F. 14

According to Nadal's companion, Jiménez, the author of the preface to this publication, Nadal was asked to compose the *Evangelicae Historiae Imagines* by St. Ignatius himself (Buser, p. 425). As the only known work of art commissioned by Ignatius, this set of meditations on images provides key evidence of the ideas concerning the use of art for private and public devotion espoused by Ignatius and his early followers. The emphasis that Ignatius placed in the *Spiritual Exercises* on "composition of place" has received much attention by art historians who have seen in his popular method the roots of the Jesuits' use of art in a vivid or persuasive way.

The *Evangelicae historiae imagines* was in preparation long before its publication in 1593. A first set of drawings recently discovered in the Biblioteca Nazionale in Rome (Wadell, 1985, pp. 31-42) and attributed to Agresti, were executed sometime between 1555 and 1562 and therefore may have been commissioned by Ignatius. Agresti's drawings, however, were not ultimately used, and were subsequently given by the General Charles de Noyelle (1681-1686) to Andrea Pozzo (Wadell, 1980, p. 282). The Jesuit G.B. Fiammeri reworked Agresti's compositions around 1579-1582, changing the format from horizontal to vertical and radically altering the style. These drawings were then used as the basis for a set of precise ink drawings (from which the engravings were made) executed by Bernardino Passeri after 1587 (Wadell, 1980). Finally, Martin de Vos reworked eight of the compositions. Christopher Plantin was involved closely with the supervision of the printing by the Wierix brothers in Antwerp (Mauquoy-Hendrickx, pp. 28-34).

Both the format and specific images in Nadal's publication may have had a significant impact on the decoration of Jesuit churches in Rome and elsewhere. Hibbard pointed to the image of "Christ Nailed to the Cross" as a source for Gaspare Celio's painting of the same subject (1594) in the Chapel of the Passion in the Gesù (Hibbard, p. 44, fig. 29a-b). Two plates were also copied in the wood reliefs on the doors of S. Vitale and other examples of the engravings being used as compositional sources in Italy and other countries have been noted (Pirri). Although Nadal's publication did not appear until 1593, the drawings were undoubtedly known to artists working for the Jesuits before then. The format of text and image may have served as a model for the martyrdom cycles painted by Circignani in the Jesuit college churches in the 1580s (Cat. 116, 117).

EL

Buser, 1976, pp. 424-433; Hibbard, 1972, p. 44, fig. 29a; Mauquoy-Hendrickx, 1976; Monssen, 1981, p. 133; Nadal (1593), 1975, fig. 127; Pirri, 1952, p. 37; Wadell, 1980; Wadell, 1985

CRVCIFIGITVR IESVS.

Matth. xxvij. Marc. xv. Luc. xxiij. Ioan. xix.

.127
c

A. *Peruenitur ad Golgotha.*	D. *Crucifigitur.*
B. *Dabant illi vinum myrrathum cum felle mistum, & cum gustasset, noluit bibere.*	E. *Pilati iussu titulus in summa cruce præfigitur.*
C. *Parant quatuor milites vt crucifigatur.*	F. *Crucifiguntur duo latrones.*
	G. *Fit eclipsis Solis vniuersalis.*

120. Gian Lorenzo Bernini, *Plan for the Novitiate of S. Andrea al Quirinale, signed by Pope Alexander VII*, 1658

Vatican City, Biblioteca Apostolica Vaticana, Mss. Chigiana P. VII. 13, fol. 41

This plan is the project presented by Gian Lorenzo Bernini for the construction of the church of the Novitiate of the Jesuit fathers on Monte Cavallo in Rome. This early project, of October 26, 1658, shows the church within an enclosure with two entrances to the street. The elliptical form of the plan, already used by Bernini in other churches, would be maintained in spite of later modifications to the cupola of the church. In this early drawing of the elevation of the church (which a contemporary hand attributed to Bernini himself) the interior features a dome with no lantern, lit by oval windows.

The elegant calligraphic text of the license signed by Alexander VII reads: "Considering the application of the Fathers of the Society of Jesus of the Novitiate of S.to Andrea at Monte Cavallo to be granted a license to construct and erect a new church on the same site under the title of the same saint, and an enclosure that will extend from their Novitiate towards the street that passes from Our Apostolic Palace towards Quattro Fontane; and having Ourselves seen and studied the plan and the design made of this same church, Our Apostolic Authority concedes to these same aforementioned Fathers permission to have built and erected the aforementioned church on the said site in conformity with and in the way indicated in the appended plan drawn in yellow, and governed by the subscribed scale of 200 *palmi*, approving and confirming this design, and the said plan, and we command that no magistrate nor any other person whatsoever may impede or interfere with its execution: such is Our expressed will and desire. Given at Castel Gandolfo this twenty-sixth day of October, 1658, Alexander Papa VII."

A number of passages in the Chigi pope's *Diary* attest to his interest in the project. The first entry is dated August 9, 1658: "I spoke with Cav. Bernini about Our feelings and those of the Fathers concerning the construction of S. Andrea at the Novitiate." Here the pontiff is probably referring to his desire not to have an imposing edifice constructed which might compete with the nearby Apostolic Palace. An earlier and grandiose project for this site by Borromini was rejected for precisely these motives.

On September 2, the pope wrote: "Cav. Bernini came to Us with the plan of the Novitiate of S. Andrea. We shifted the church more within [the complex and ordered] that he bring two more plans." The architect returned to the pope on September 15 "with the oval of the church of the Jesuits' Novitiate" and again on September 29 "with the model for the Jesuits."

On the 26th of October Alexander VII signed this license which permitted the beginning of work. On November 3 the cornerstone was laid.

The plan conserved in the Chigi codex provides evidence of an early stage of elaboration in the planning of the work, and one which later underwent important modifications.

The most notable revision concerns the lantern of the cupola. Two sketches conserved in Chigi a.I.19, fol. 12r-v document the original idea of crowning the dome with St. Andrew's cross, an idea later abandoned in favor of the present lantern.

In the realization of this work, which he himself considered his masterpiece, Bernini dedicated a great deal of attention to the interior, which stands in startling and notable contrast to the essential simplicity of the exterior. The artist himself felt a particular affinity with this work. A telling anecdote was published in his son Domenico's *Vita del Cavalier Gio Lorenzo Bernini* (1713, pp. 108-109).

"It happened one day that his son, who writes this present work, devoutly entered this church, and there he found the Cavaliere his father retired in a corner, gazing with pleasure over all the parts of that small temple. He respectfully inquired 'What are you doing here, alone and silent?' and the Cavaliere responded 'My son, only from this work of architecture do I feel some particular satisfaction in the depths of my heart, and often to lighten my burdens I come here to console myself with this work of mine.' This was a new emotion for the Cavaliere, who never knew any satisfaction from the many works he had accomplished, judging them all much inferior to the true beauty he knew and understood in his mind."

GM

BERNINI, 1713, pp. 108-109; BORSI, 1980, pp. 106-115, 328; KRAUTHEIMER and JONES, 1975; MORELLO, 1964

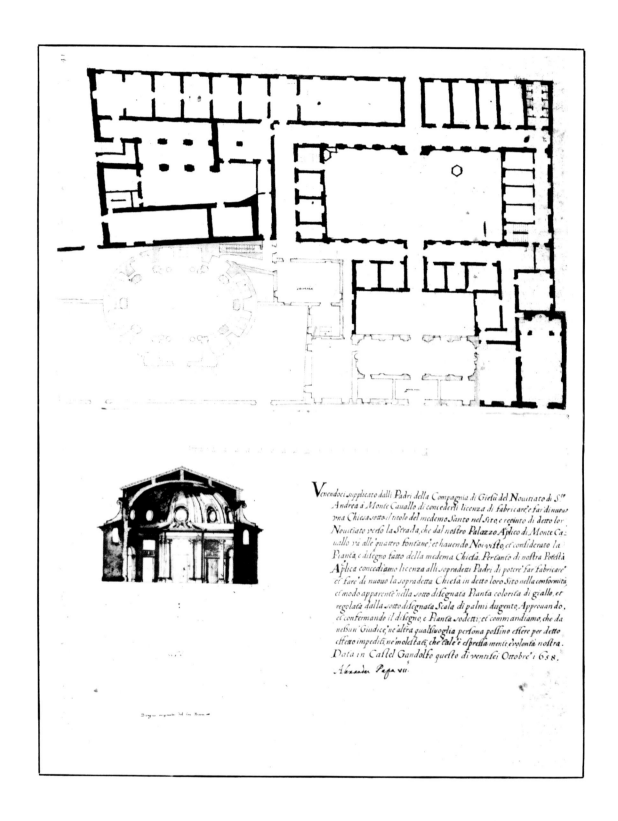

Venendoci supplicato dalli Padri della Compagnia di Giesù del Nouitiato di S.to
Andrea à Monte Cauallo di concederli licenza di fabricare, e far di nuouo
vna Chiesa sotto il titolo del medemo Santo nel Sito, e recinto di detto lor
Nouitiato verso la Strada, che dal nostro Palazzo Aplico di Monte Cauallo va alle quattro fontane; et hauendo Noi visto, et considerato la
Pianta, e disegno fatto della medema Chiesa. Pertanto di nostra Potestà
Aplica concediamo licenza alli sopradetti Padri di potere far fabricare,
et fare di nuouo la sopradetta Chiesa in detto loro Sito nella conformità,
et modo apparente nella sotto disegnata Pianta colorita di giallo, et
regolata dalla sotto disegnata Scala di palmi dugento, Approuando,
et confermando il disegno, e Pianta sodetti; et commandiamo, che da
nessun Giudice, ne altra qualsiuoglia persona possino essere per detto
effetto impediti, ne molestati, che tale è espressamente euolontà nostra.
Data in Castel Gandolfo questo di ventisei Ottobre 1658.

Alexander Papa VII.

121. Giovanni Battista Gaulli, *Musical Angels*, Oil on canvas, 49 x 98 cm., 1672

Vatican City, Pinacoteca Vaticana, Inv. 752

This painting was originally identified as a *bozzetto* for a group of angels in the cupola of the Gesù by Enggass (1957, p. 52, fig. 19-20). The *bozzetto* should be dated to 1672, the year in which Gaulli signed a contract for the entire decorative project (Tacchi Venturi, 1935) and began to paint the cupola. The focus of this heavenly dome is the Father and Holy Spirit below whom appear Christ and the Virgin Mary in their intercessory roles. Between the viewer and the Divinity appears another ring of figures (Jesuit saints alongside of Old Testament figures) who act as both the recipients of divine favor and as intercessors on our behalf.

Most discussions of the cupola scene have centered on the hypothesis, first proposed by Lanckoronska (1935, p. 75), that before the *duplex intercessio* theme was established, Bernini and Gaulli had planned to represent the *Sangue di Cristo* (for a summary of the literature on the problem see Macandrew and Graf, 1972, pp. 253-255). Since then, the drawings upon which Lanckoronska based her hypothesis have been convincingly connected to Gaulli's project for the cupola of the Baptistry Chapel at S. Pietro in Vaticano (Canestro Chiovenda, 1966, pp. 176-177), and the idea of a change in program has been largely discarded.

As a result of the interest aroused by a possible change in program, less attention has been devoted to the theme actually represented. The *duplex intercessio* developed from its discussion in a popular religious text composed in the early 14th century, the *Speculum humanae salvationis* (Meiss, 1954, p. 306; Lavin, 1972, pp. 169-170). Especially important in the fifteenth century, the scene usually represents the Virgin showing to Christ the attributes of her motherhood, and Christ showing his wounds to the Father. However, the most important precedent for its use in the Gesù was the *duplex intercessio* of Christ and the Virgin of the Assumption, frescoes then recently completed by Pietro da Cortona in the cupola and apse of the Chiesa Nuova (Ronen, 1989).

The choice of this theme for the cupola of the Gesù may have seemed part of a more unified iconographic program had it served as the prelude to *Joshua arresting the Sun*, the theme originally planned for the semi-dome of the apse (Cat. 127). Joshua (from whose Hebrew name Jesus' name can be transliterated), stopped the sun, like Christ who puts off the day of judgment to save souls. With the nave representing the *Adoration of the Name of Jesus* and the high altar the giving of the name (*Circumcision*), a whole program would have unrolled through the church centering on the saving power of the name of Jesus, of Jesus himself, and of the Old Testament predecessor to his name.

EL

BANFI, 1959; DREYER, 1981; ENGGASS, 1957, pp. 49, 51-52; ENGGASS, 1964, pp. 153-154, fig. 56; FERRARI, 1990, p. 132; GRAF, 1973, pp. 163-165; HASKELL, 1980, pp. 82, 399; LANCKORONSKA, 1935, pp. 74, 77; OSTROW in LAVIN, 1981, pp. 310-315; MARQUES, 1981

122. Giovanni Battista Gaulli, *Adoration of the Name of Jesus,* Oil on canvas, 120 x 179.5 cm, ca. 1676

Rome, Galleria Spada (see p. 52)

According to one tradition, Ignatius chose the name of Jesus for the Society because of his devotion to his namesake, Ignatius of Antioch, at whose death the monogram of Jesus' name was found emblazoned on his heart. Another tradition maintains that Ignatius and his companions chose the name "Company of Jesus" even before they arrived in Rome in 1537, "given that they had for themselves no other superior but Jesus Christ" (*FN* I, p. 204; see also Cat. 30, 31). In Rome, the IHS monogram immediately became the recognizable symbol of the Jesuits (Cat. 61) and the Circumcision, as the occasion on which Jesus received his name, became a standard adornment of high altars in Jesuit churches. It is

CAT. 121

widely known that the IHS was a Franciscan symbol popularized in the first half of the fifteenth century by the Sienese preacher, St. Bernardino. However, only recently has it been suggestively pointed out that in one of the two churches that stood in the sixteenth century on the site of the Gesù itself, there was a Bernardine chapel dedicated to the name of Jesus (Herz).

Gaulli's *Adoration of the Name of Jesus* places the IHS monogram at the light-filled apex of a vast opening to the heavens. According to the inscription held aloft by angels at the entrance end of the church, the scene is inspired by a line from Paul's Letter to the Philippians (2:10-11): "...at the name of Jesus every knee shall bend, in heaven and on earth and under the earth..." Groups of the elect (the Magi, the Farnese, etc.) float on clouds upwards toward the name. Closest to the frame, naked figures of Vices (Heresy, Avarice, Pride, etc.) are cast downward into the space of the worshipper. The impetus for the Gesù nave decoration may have been the approval (1673) and the new edition (1675) of Ignatius' mass proper (Cat. 112). The entrance antiphon to the mass provided the verse from Philippians that is the subject of the vault (Cat. 112).

The iconography, illusionism, and use of glories of light as the dramatic and thematic focus of the Gesù frescoes also tie them closely to the themes and techniques of ephemeral decorations. Weil has demonstrated that the figures that populate the frescoes in the nave, cupola, and apse, as well as the stucco allegories along the nave, had appeared previously in the Gesù in Forty Hours *apparati*. The relationship between the temporary and permanent decorations was clearest in the case of the apse. There the theme originally planned had appeared as a Forty Hours decoration in 1671 (Cat. 127) and the final subject, the *Adoration of the Lamb* (Cat. 123), was the Forty Hours theme in 1675 (Weil, pp. 238-239).

This painting is a refined *modello* that was probably used as a presentation piece for the patron. Gaulli omitted the gilded vault (for the execution of which he was also responsible) in order to make clear the massing of the figures and the relationship between the light-filled heavens and the darkened space of the damned.

EL

CANESTRO CHIOVENDA, 1962; CANESTRO CHIOVENDA, 1966; ENGGASS, 1964, pp. 31-74, 135-141, fig. 67-72; FERRARI, 1990, p. 137, fig. 21; HASKELL, 1980, pp. 80-83; HERZ, 1988a, pp. 66-67; LANCKORONSKA, 1935, pp. 73-78; TACCHI VENTURI, 1935; WEIL, 1974, pp. 235-240

123. Giovanni Battista Gaulli, *The Adoration of the Lamb*, Oil on canvas glued to a wooden support, 140 x 200 cm., ca. 1679

Rome, Church of the Gesù, Galleria dei Marmi

Among the *bozzetti* executed by Gaulli for the fresco in the semi-dome of the Gesù apse, this painting represents the final version of the *Adoration of the Lamb*, a subject which ideally compliments and completes the cycle of the nave vault, the *Adoration of the Name of Jesus*. The painting, inspired by the text of Revelations 5:20-40, is congruent with the text. In the fresco the artist represents the Lamb who guards the book of the seven seals being adored by the twenty-four elders bearing the golden censers of the prayers of the saints, surrounded by a festive jubilation of angelic creatures belonging to the various heavenly choirs.

The colors, used in light tonalities in a refined chromatic relationship, are rarefied towards the center; the dynamic is one of ascending convergence on the symbolic throne. In the fresco the effect is more evident than in the *bozzetto*: after the recent restoration executed by the *Soprintendenza per i Beni Artistici e Storici di Roma*, one can experience the very explosion of light spreading illusionistically over the space as it reveals paradise. Gaulli's surface, 190 square meters, painted from six different levels of scaffolding and in 55 *giornate*, is a chorus of pastel colors: pinks, greens, and blues follow one another in an harmonious contrast of ever lighter tones which evanesce into an increasingly transparent yellow.

The composition is developed with a predominance of sinuous and serpentine lines which recall Gaulli's debt to Bernini, and the chromatic sensitivity anticipates the delicate color usages of the Rococo.

MPD'O

ENGGASS, 1964; FAGIOLO, 1980; STRINATI, 1984, p. 431

124. Giovanni Battista Gaulli, *The Death of St.Francis Xavier*, Oil on canvas, 64.5 x 46 cm., ca. 1675

Vatican City, Pinacoteca Vaticana, Inv. 1489

This painting is the only known *bozzetto* by Gaulli for his altarpiece in the Chapel of St. Francis Xavier in S. Andrea al Quirinale (for two other paintings of this subject attributed tenuously to Gaulli cf. Canestro Chiovenda, fig. 3-4). Executed shortly after the unveiling of the dome fresco in the Gesù (1675), the *Death of Francis Xavier* (Enggass, 1964, fig. 35) was in place in July of 1676. Gaulli and Maratti's paintings of Xavier's death, practically contemporaneous works (the latter in the Gesù), mark the first appearances of this subject on Jesuit altars in Rome (Schaar, p. 262).

Although by 1672 the Pamphili Prince had stated his intention of donating 20,000 scudi towards the completion of the four side chapels of the church, the funds arrived sporadically and the decoration of the chapels stretched out into the early eighteenth century (Hood, pp. 38-39). Gaulli eventually painted the two flanking canvases for the same chapel (*Francis Xavier Preaching in the East* and *Baptising an Eastern Queen*) that have been dated to the last years of the artist's life (Enggass, 1964, p. 141, fig. 135-136).

Four painters were originally employed in the side chapels of S. Andrea. Three of those chosen, Maratti, Brandi, and Gaulli were on General GianPaolo Oliva's famous list for the Gesù frescoes (Pascoli, 1730, I, p. 200), and the fourth was Ludovico David (Haskell, pp. 87-88). Of all the artists who executed altarpieces, it is Gaulli who works most closely with Bernini's architecture, who is most responsive to Bernini's choice of marbles and the quality of the stones. The somewhat unusual density and saturation of the color in this painting was determined by the relatively dark space of the chapel. The quick shifts of folds and strokes of color jostling each other juxtaposed to the rich variegated marbles enliven the space.

This *bozzetto* is extremely close to the executed altarpiece although the artist has still not resolved the position of the saint's legs. In the final work, the expression in his rolled back eyes and his inert body make the saint seem even closer to death. The border

of the *bozzetto* is not repeated in the altarpiece, in which the saint's body presses even closer to the edges than it did in the *bozzetto* before the border was added.

EL

CANESTRO CHIOVENDA, 1977; ENGGASS, 1964, pp. 25-26, 141; FERRARI, 1990, pp. 260-261; GIACHI and MATTHIAE, 1969, pp. 51-61; GRAF, 1976, I, p. 101, II, fig. 347-348; HASKELL, 1980, pp. 87-88; HOOD, 1979-1980, pp. 38-39, 42-45; SCHAAR, 1968, pp. 262-264

125. Jean Valdor after Andrea Sacchi, *Catafalque for the Benefactors of the Society of Jesus at the Church of the Gesù*, Engraving, 39 x 16 cm., 1640

Rome, Archivium Romanum Societatis Iesu, Rom 131 II, fol. 505

In 1639 the Jesuits opened their centenary year celebration with a series of events for which the churches and colleges were decorated. In September of that year Antonio Barberini had his preferred painter, Andrea Sacchi, decorate the Gesù for the inauguration (Cat. 109). Two months later Sacchi erected a funeral catafalque in the same church to honor all of the Society's deceased benefactors. The catafalque is known through this engraving and a descriptive pamphlet, both published by Antonio Gerardi. Sacchi's introduction of the obelisk, the central element of his design, to catafalque decoration would prove influential for both funeral *apparati* and permanent tombs (Fagiolo dell'Arco and Carandini, II, p. 25).

To create an appropriate ambience for the occasion, Sacchi covered the church with black drapery, leaving the white pilasters visible. The catafalque, placed in the crossing, measured 12 meters across and 13 meters deep. In the engraving we see four obelisks (painted to appear like granite) whose flames have been snuffed out. The central core of the monument features a mausoleum on whose base is a chiaroscuro painting of Gregory the Great in oration

for the Souls of Purgatory. As Gerardi notes, Gregory's 30 "suffragij" or masses for the dead said on successive days for the soul of a brother, made this subject appropriate for the occasion. Above him are shown two fictive bronze figures of Adam and Eve held in bondage by a skeleton. On the altar side of the catafalque were Mortality and Immortality. The two skeletons holding the inscription and playing with a stone above are described as a symbol of the facility with which death plays with human hopes. Not shown in the engraving were the four skeletons between the piers of the crossing. These figures held trophies symbolizing four aspects of worldly accomplishment conquered by death: ecclesiastical office, political power, victories won by war, and material possessions (Gerardi, 1639).

EL

Fagiolo dell'Arco, 1975, p. 143, fig. 23; Fagiolo dell'Arco and Carandini, 1977-1978, I, pp. 116-118, II, pp. 25, 27; Gerardi, 1639; Haskell, 1980, p. 55; Mâle, 1932, pp. 218-219

126. Dominique Barrière, *Catafalque for Prince Nicolò Ludovisi and Costanza Pamphili at the Church of S. Ignazio*, Engraving, 62.4 x 41.6 cm., ca. 1665

Rome, Archivium Romanum Societatis Iesu, Armadio 5

In 1664 the Jesuits erected a catafalque in the unfinished Church of S. Ignazio for the joint funeral of their patrons Nicolò Ludovisi († Dec. 1664) and his wife Costanza Pamphili (last will Feb. 1665; Borsi, 1972, p. 71). A pamphlet describing the catafalque (ARSI, Rom 134 I, fol. 131-134), the text of the funeral oration (dated 1667; Rom 134 I, fol. 135-147), and a large engraving of the decorations were printed and dedicated to the deceased couple's son, Giovanni Battista.

Barrière's catafalque gave primary importance to the virtues and the political and ecclesiastical

offices of Nicolò. Glory stands on top of the urn holding portraits of the Prince and Costanza. The Prince's four primary virtues, Religion and Magnanimity (facing the door) and Prudence and Magnificence (facing the crossing) sit on the cornice between burning lamps. Chiaroscuro paintings between them represent the States of the Prince of Fiano and of Venosa. On the lowest register two chiaroscuro scenes ("Roma Regnante che comparte al Prencipe cariche, e governi Ecclesiastici consignandoli bastoni di comando, e standardi" facing the entrance, and "la Spagna sul trono, che dà il bastone di commando al

CAT. 125

CAT. 126

medesimo Prencipe significandosi li honorati governa da quella commessigli," facing the altar) are flanked by portraits of the couple's children. Six emblems, two inscriptions, and two further scenes behind the catafalque completed the program (ARSI, Rom 134 I, fol. 131-134).

As the prefect of the church pointed out to the Ludovisi heir in the pamphlet, the Church of S. Ignazio had only been completed up to the crossing at the time of the funeral. The high altar was set against a temporary wall put up at the end of the nave (Cat. 103). In the engraving, the crossing, with decorated pendentives and the drum supporting a

cupola that would never be executed (Cat. 135), are invented. In a thinly veiled effort to keep the Ludovisi heirs interested in supporting the church founded by their Cardinal uncle and supported by their parents, the Jesuits described the church as "One of the most noble and best studied modern temples that can be seen today in Europe."

EL

FAGIOLO DELL'ARCO and CARANDINI, 1977-1978, I, pp. 210-211; ARSI, Rom 134 I, fol. 131-134

127. *Victory of Joshua over the Amorites*, Engraving in: Giovanni Domenico Roccamora, *Parte seconda delle cifre dell'eucaristia*, Rome, 1670

Vatican City, Biblioteca Apostolica Vaticana, St. Chigi IV, 233 (2)

Roccamora's *Cifre dell'eucaristia* is devoted to the description and commentary on various Old Testament episodes and allegorical themes which relate to the eucharist. Illustrated with engravings executed by three artists, these inventions are conceived in the form of Forty Hours *teatri. Il Sol Guerriero*, or, *The Sun stopped by Joshua*, appeared here one year before it became the subject of a Forty Hours apparatus erected by Giovanni Maria Mariani at the Gesù (1671). This engraving probably served as a partial visual source for Mariani's apparatus, which notably expanded the scene with figures of the Father, the Holy Spirit, and "blessed spirits" in the upper zone. Below, in the background, Mariani included Priests carrying the Ark of the Covenant through the stilled waters of the Jordan river. In the foreground, rather than emphasize the battle, Mariani's apparatus focused on the halting of the sun (Fagiolo dell'Arco and Carandini).

General GianPaolo Oliva may have been trying out his idea for the permanent decoration of the Gesù when this apparatus was erected. Until the death of Giacomo Cortese in 1676, Oliva had hoped to entrust the Jesuit battle painter with the decoration of the apse of the Gesù with a fresco of this subject, which was ideally suited to his talents (Pascoli [1730], 1933, I, p. 121; Haskell, p. 79).

The name "Jesus" is a transliteration of Joshua's Hebrew name into Greek. A fresco of Joshua halting the sun would have provided an Old Testament precedent for the name of Jesus (the giving of which occurred at the circumcision, the subject of Muziano's painting on the high altar) and likened the saving power of the sun with the saving power of Christ and the eucharist.

EL

Fagiolo dell'Arco and Carandini, 1977-1978, I, pp. 283-284; Noehles, 1978, pp. 96-99; Weil, 1974, pp. 239-240

Sol contra Gaba
ne movearis,
stetitque Sol,
donec ulcisceretur se gens de
inimicis suis.
Ios. c. 10.

128. Andrea Pozzo, *Tuscan Column*, Pen and Ink, 42.5 x 28 cm., before 1693
Rome, Archivio del Pontificio Collegio Germanico-Ungarico, Disegni 316

129. Andrea Pozzo, *Tuscan Column*, Engraving in: *Perspectiva pictorum et architectorum*, Vol. 1, fig. 36, Rome, 1693
Vatican City, Biblioteca Apostolica Vaticana, Cicognara VIII, 854, I

In their recent catalogue of drawings in the Archive of the Collegio Germanico-Ungarico, Bösel and Garms (1983) discovered several preparatory drawings (and early states of engravings) for Pozzo's treatise on perspective.

The drawing exhibited here next to the final engraving is one of two preserved preparatory drawings for the same plate. With one of the inscriptions reversed, it is clear that this was intended to be used by the engraver preparing the plate, but since it lacks other inscriptions that appear in the engraving, it seems that this was not the definitive sheet.

De perspectiva pictorum et architectorum was intended to instruct painters and architects in perspective. Beginning with the fundamentals of perspective and the orders of architecture, the plates illustrate primarily Pozzo's own painted ceilings (Cat. 136), altars (Cat. 138), Forty Hours *apparati*, and proposed (Cat. 130) and realized architectural projects in Rome.

This publication, widely distributed in Europe, appeared immediately in several languages including Chinese (1729). Immensely successful as a model book, Pozzo's treatise (especially the designs for altars), was used well into the eighteenth century by artists and architects in Central Europe and elsewhere.

EL

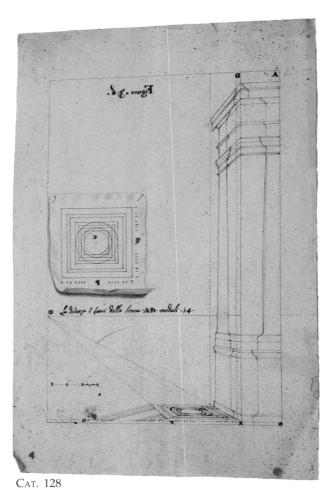

CAT. 128

BÖSEL and GARMS, 1983, pp. 267-268; KERBER, 1971, pp. 207-208

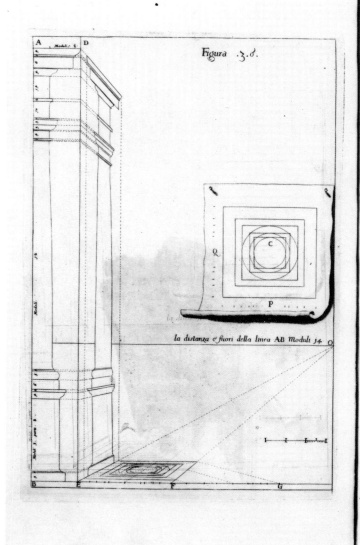

Figura .3.6.

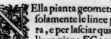

la distanza è fuori della linea AB Moduli 14 O

FIGURA TRIGESIMASEXTA.

Præparatio ad figuram 37.

IN vestigio geometrico C, & in ejus elevatione AB, præcipuas tantum lineas adnotavi, ne figuram confunderem, & ut studiosorum industriæ aliquid relinquerem. Linea plani EG habet divisiones latitudinis P, & longitudinis Q vestigii geometrici C. Expunctis latitudinis ducentur more solito visuales ad O punctum oculi; ex punctis longitudinis fient occultæ ad punctum distantiæ, quod extra lineam AB protenditur modulis quatuor decim: & ubi occultæ ex divisionibus longitudinis secant visualem FO fiunt parallelæ ad lineam plani, adhibitis sectionibus talium parallelarum cum visualibus, ad complendam deformationem vestigii.

Eædem lineæ quæ in vestigio deformato sunt parallelæ ad EF, prolongantur usque ad visualem EO, & continuantur cum aliis parallelis ad perpendiculum DE. Fiunt quoque visuales ad punctum oculi ex divisionibus elevationis AB translatis in perpendiculum DE; adhibitis sectionibus talium parallelarum cum visualibus, ad complendam deformationem longitudinis elevationis.

FIGURA TRENTESIMASESTA.

Preparatione della figura 37.

NElla pianta geometrica C, e nella sua elevatione AB ho messo solamente le linee più principali, per non confonder la figura, e per lasciar qualche cosa all'industria degli studiosi. La linea piana EG contiene le divisioni della larghezza P, e della lunghezza Q della pianta geometrica C. Da i punti della larghezza si fanno al solito le visuali al punto O dell'occhio. Da i punti della lunghezza si fanno le linee occulte al punto della distanza, il qual si dilunga moduli quattordici dalla linea AB: e dove le linee delle divisioni della lunghezza segano la visuale FO, si fanno le paralelle alla linea piana EF, adoperando i segamenti di tali paralelle con le visuali, per finir di digradar la pianta.

Le medesime linee le quali nella pianta digradata sono paralelle a EG, si prolungano sino alla visuale EO, continuandole con altre paralelle al perpendicolo DE: si fanno altresì le visuali al punto dell'occhio, dalle divisioni dell'elevatione AB trasportate nel perpendicolo DE; ad operando i segamenti di tali paralelle con le visuali per finir di digradare la lunghezza della elevatione.

Figura 37.

130. Andrea Pozzo, *Project for the High Altar of the Church of the Gesù*, Engraving in: *Perspectiva pictorum et architectorum*, Vol. 2, fig. 73, Rome, 1700

Vatican City, Biblioteca Apostolica Vaticana, Cicognara VIII, 854, (2)

This is one of two projects for a new high altar for the Gesù included by Pozzo in his treatise. Although the apse was furnished with Giacomo Della Porta's impressive aedicula (Masheck), throughout the seventeenth century the Jesuits considered the apse, whose walls were bare, an unfinished project. The Farnese, official patrons of the high altar, had originally set aside a large quantity of antique marbles for its completion. In the 1670s and 1690s the Jesuits negotiated fruitlessly with the Farnese heirs for financing of the project (Tacchi-Venturi, 1929a; Pecchiai, 1952, pp. 109-126). The first step towards completing the decoration was taken when the Farnese agreed to allow Gaulli to paint the semi-dome (Cat. 123) and vault of the apse in the 1670s and 1680s. Only in the nineteenth century would the apse be completely decorated.

In this engraving Pozzo represents a simplified version of Gaulli's *Adoration of the Lamb* in the semi-dome and proposes a completely new arrangement for the altar. Here, as in the apse of the Church of S. Ignazio built according to his design (fig. on p. 55), Pozzo practically negates the architectural presence of the altar. No longer projecting out into space, this aedicula, in the form of an arch, asserts itself by breaking through the cornice.

As Pozzo himself notes, the most courageous element of his design is his extension of the apse behind the arched opening. According to the plan and section in figure 74 of his treatise (Bjurström, fig. 64b), the wall would be broken through to an existing corridor space behind the altar. A painting or relief would be set several feet behind the arched opening, and two windows (hidden from view) would light the image from both sides. The *Circumcision* is set in an apse-like space that echoes the form of the real apse and illusionistically extends the space. Pozzo's high altar design, like his famous Forty Hours inventions, would have captivated the worshipper by the use of brilliant light and through the illusionistic extension of space.

EL

BJURSTRÖM, 1972, p. 110, fig. 64a

Figura 73.

131. Vincenzo Mariotti after Andrea Pozzo, *The Chapel of S. Ignazio in the Church of the Gesù*, Engraving, 62.6 x 37.8 cm., 1697

Rome, Archivium Romanum Societatis Iesu, Armadio 4

In 1695, as the design for the Chapel of S. Ignazio was being developed, Vincenzo Mariotti, one of the engravers employed by Pozzo for the preparation of the first volume of his perspective treatise, was contracted to execute this engraving. Although the contract (ARSI, Rom 140, fol. 273) specified that he was to complete the plate by the end of the year, the work was allowed to stretch out until 1697 so that the print could be an accurate reflection of the continuously evolving design. This fully rendered engraving, intended to convey the idea of the chapel as a whole, includes both the new elements and the frescoes and reliefs above the cornice that were executed in an earlier campaign of decoration.

Pozzo's design encompassed the new aedicula, the side walls verneered with marbles, and the marble groups above the side doors. The decoration of the existing organ was modernized and a vestibule to the left of the altar was redecorated. Numerous sculptors, several just starting their careers, were employed in the chapel. Pierre Legros executed his first public commissions in Rome for this project: the silver statue of the saint and *Faith Trampling Heresy*, to the right of the altar. To the left of the altar is Theodon's *Religion Trampling Paganism*. Above these allegorical groupings (symbolizing the goals of the Ignatius' missions) are two historical reliefs that celebrate moments of papal approbation: the *Confirmation of the Society by Paul III* by A. de'Rossi and the *Canonization of Ignatius by Gregory XV* by B. Cametti.

The movemented aedicula of *verde antico* is supported by four travertine columns verneered with lapis lazuli, a rare and costly stone that had never before been used on such a scale. In Mariotti's engraving a temporary model of the Trinity group is represented since the form and materials in which it was to be executed would not be finalized until decades later. Both below the niche and above the cornice of the church, episodes from Ignatius' life are illustrated with an emphasis on his visions and miracles. Below the altar is conserved the urn containing the remains of the saint (Cat. 134).

A silver statue of the saint provided a reliquary-like centerpiece for the ensemble (see fig. on p. 4). It is unfortunate that the statue represented in this engraving (completed before the design for the statue was finalized) does not reflect the statue as executed (see also Cat. 132) as the silver components of the original statue by Legros were melted down in the late eighteenth century. The reconstruction in 1804 (March) with stucco head, hands, and legs around the original chasuble was likely to have been based on the disposition of the original structural supports and the later, more accurate illustration of the statue in Pozzo's treatise (fig. on p. 58).

EL

KERBER, 1971, pp. 152, 159-161, 164, 171, 173, 175, 178; MARCH, 1934; PECCHIAI, 1952, pp. 163, 358; ARSI, Rom 140, fol. 273-277

IMAGO SACELLI QVOD S. IGNATIO DE LOYOLA.
Conditori Societatis Iesu erectum est
in templo Domus Profeßæ Romanæ eiusdem Societatis,
in quo Sacra eius oßa uenerantur.
M.DC.XCVII.

132. Anonymous, *Medal of the Chapel of S. Ignazio in the Gesù,*
Obverse: The Chapel of S. Ignazio,
"*ARA•S: IGNAT•LOYO• SACRA•ROMAE 1697*"
Reverse: Portrait of St. Ignatius,
"*S•IGNAT•LOYOL•SOC •IESU• FUN•*"
Bronze, 45 x 35 mm., 1697
Rome, Archivium Romanum Societatis Iesu, Medaglie dei Santi e Beati

In 1697, less than halfway through construction of the Chapel of S. Ignazio in the Gesù, the Jesuits launched a multi-media publicity campaign for their new project. Mariotti's engraving (Cat. 131) was finally completed, and a 5-page pamphlet (and a broadsheet version) describing the chapel in detail was printed in Italian and Latin. In addition, this medal, which was unknown to scholars who have studied the chapel previously, was struck. Two other exemplars are known: one illustrated recently without discussion (collection unidentified, see Gallamini, 1990) and another, very close to this version in the fineness of detail, in silver-plated brass (British Museum, London, 582.31.3).

The motive for this flurry of activity may have been the pope's visit to the chapel on August 3 (ARSI, Rom 140, fol. 20r). On that occasion the scaffolding was completely dismantled, the work executed thus far was evaluated, and changes were made. The medal, together with Mariotti's engraving and documents that outline the changes requested by *periti* and observers inform us of the state of the design up until 1697 (Kerber, 1971, p. 158).

Like Mariotti's engraving, the medal reproduces an idea for the pose of the statue of the saint that was never executed. Further ornament and figures were requested for the frieze and the Trinity group, which are here simpler than in the final version. In addition, the fine detail of the relief on the medal allows us to make out a very different arrangement of narrative reliefs on the bases. Four of the five reliefs shown on the top row seem to be single figure compositions that could be visions of the saint. On the bases of the aedicula appears an additional row of four more reliefs that seem to represent miracles of Ignatius.

Unfortunately, it is difficult to account for the arrangement of the narrative cycle shown in the medal in spite of extensive documentation of the various phases of the chapel's design. By the summer of 1697, the seven bronze reliefs were already completed. Indeed, a second narrative cycle was made in the form of a silver *scalino* which no longer exists. Due to their small dimensions (ARSI, Rom 141, fol. 237r-239v), the six reliefs on this *scalino* (usually placed above the altar mensa), already contracted in March 1696, could not be represented here. A payment in May 1697 to Lorenzo Merlini (the sculptor who executed the central bronze relief) for a wax model of Ignatius performing an exorcism (Kerber, 1965a, p. 500), may however refer to a plan for a second band of reliefs that was subsequently abandoned.

The chapel documents are curiously silent about the manufacture and distribution of this medal. Bonacina, the administrator of the project, never mentions it in his narrative accounts of the chapel's construction. Nor have any payments to a medallist come to light thus far. The only written evidence of its existence is a payment of 14 *scudi* for "una medaglia d'oro della Capp.a" (ARSJ, F.G. 2056, fol. 281) that was given to Pierre Legros towards payment for his work on the large model of the silver statue. It is ironic that the Jesuits were compensating his work with this medal, which shows the statue in a form never executed. It may reflect Legros' winning entry in the competition for the statue, a lost design which showed off his skills enough to win the competition, but had to be altered (Pecchiai, 1952, p. 181). In spite of the differences between the medal and the chapel as built, the mold was reused for a new issue of the medal in 1699 which now showed on the reverse, the newly constructed Chapel of Luigi Gonzaga (Ashmolean Museum, VI.8.91).

EL

GALLAMINI, 1990, pp. 99, 121, fig. 101

133. Girolamo Frezza after Sebastiano Cipriani, *Project for the Chapel of S. Ignazio in the Gesù*, Engraving, 63.7 x 39.5 cm., 1696

Rome, Archivium Romanum Societatis Iesu, Armadio 4

This engraving is the only surviving visual testimony of the controversial architectural competition for the Chapel of S. Ignazio in the Gesù. When the Society's longstanding desire to build a new, more noble chapel for the saint finally began to take on form at the end of 1694, Andrea Pozzo was asked for design ideas. Although Pozzo had already executed important projects for the Society, objections were raised to his appointment.

As a result, at least two other architects submitted plans: G.B. Origone, who came recommended by the Cardinal of San Sepolcro, and Cipriani (c. 1660 - c. 1740), a student of G.B. Contini, who was supported by Agostino Chigi (Pecchiai). This engraving was produced as a result of what seems to have been a heated controversy between Pozzo and Cipriani, and between Chigi and the Jesuits. Skillfully avoided by Bonacina in his accounts of the design proceedings, the controversy was based on Cipriani's claim not only that the Jesuits and *periti* fairly chose his design over Pozzo's and then reneged, but also that Pozzo then plagiarized his design.

Cipriani's plan had indeed been given a formal critique by the committee (ARSI, Rom 140, fol. 52v-53r; Kerber, pp. 147-148). Based on these criticisms, it is doubtful that the Jesuits ever seriously entertained building Cipriani's project at all, although perhaps they thought that they could count on Agostino Chigi to fund the project if they chose his architect. However, the critique adds further complications to the problem since the plan that the critics had before them differs from the engraving. One of the principle reasons for rejecting Cipriani's design was that the urn of the saint above the altar, "the best feature" of his design, could not be executed (see Cat. 138). The engraving must represent a later design because the urn has been put back below the mensa, and the altarpiece is a concave relief representing *Ignatius'*

Vision of the Trinity.

The similarities of Cipriani's plan to the chapel finally built reveal elements of a program that must have been given to the architects. Like Pozzo's chapel, Cipriani's plan called for four lapis columns, a lapis frieze, and an aedicula of green marble. Both artists feature versions of Ignatius' *Visions of the Trinity*, but Cipriani combines the narrative with allegories of Heresy and Paganism. The narrative and allegories would be separated by Pozzo in whose design the Vision at La Storta occurs across space, and heresy and paganism pertain to independent allegorical groups. There are only two other narratives in Cipriani's plan: the *Vision at La Storta* on the right and the *Confirmation of the Society* on the left. Pozzo may have taken the idea for his marble reliefs flanking the aedicula from Cipriani, although the narrative structure received further clarification in his plan.

What is striking about Cipriani's plan is the relative simplicity of the program and its lack of clarity. In the central image narrative is combined with allegory and in the side reliefs two different types of episodes (a vision versus the historical event that marked the official beginning of the Society) are represented. But beyond the content of the chapel's imagery, one senses that the Jesuits— singlemindedly pursuing magnificence—were not moved by Cipriani's idea for the chapel. His plan lacked the kind of inventiveness and dazzling effect that could make the viewers of Pozzo's chapel stand "for hours and hours, immobile, like statues" (see p. 56).

EL

Bösel, 1985, I, p. 172, II, fig. 120; Hager, 1981, p. 762; Kerber, 1971, pp. 146-149, 152, fig. 80; Pecchiai, 1952, pp. 151, 154, 156-160, 172; ARSI, Rom 140, fol. 52v-53r

All' Ill.mo et Ecc.mo Sig.re Principe
D. Agostino Chigi

Torna allo Sguardo dell'Ecc.a V.ra il disegno dell'Altare del Glorioso Patriarca S. Ignazio da erigersi nel Sontuoso Tempio del Giesù di Roma, che trà gli altri di più matura consideratione, e vaghezza fu esposto alla censura di molti Sig.ri Qualificati, quali per la chiarezza del loro sublime intendimento mostrorono essere uniformi nel voto dell'Ecc.a Vostra, che fù anche prima gradito dalli R.R.P.P. di quella Compagnia con riportarne dà essi cò mio rossore piena approuatione. Benche estimeri poi siano stati gli applausi, se nell'ammirarlo fù raputo Onde Io per non sogiacere alla sorte, che lo condannaua all'oblio, hò uoluto, che con i gemiti delle pressure sueglasse la Fama de suoi difetti per aualesarli al mondo. Chi dà uerne ha Giuditio, e chi hà Giuditio mostra d'esser prattico nell'estimatione. Sò, che questo mio parto uerrà rauiuiato da un Sole, cioe dall'Ecc. V.ra, che è l'Apollo delle Virtù, quale sà scaltare li Pitoni, che con l'alto pestifero tentano affuscare il bello di quelle. Basti il dire, che queste mie linee anno per accendere il Sole, da cui sempre à me deriuano benigni gl'Influssi, e resto con farle profend. Inchino. Roma li 4 ottobre 1696.

D. V.ra Ecc.a

134. Alessandro Algardi, *St.Ignatius and the Early Jesuits*,
Terracotta with traces of gilding, 29 x 51 cm., c. 1629-1637
Rome, Museo di Palazzo Venezia

Early sources are strangely silent about the appearance of the sixteenth- and seventeenth-century tombs of St. Ignatius. This terracotta *bozzetto* was a preparatory model for the relief on the urn of the saint, the only component of his earlier tomb to have been reused in Pozzo's chapel (1695) in the Gesù.

Prior to Ignatius' canonization, his remains were preserved in a simple wood box to the right of the high altar (Pecchiai, 1952, p. 130). In 1622, they were transferred, in a new marble urn, to the Savelli Chapel of the Crucifixion in the left transept, henceforth the Chapel of S. Ignazio. Seven years later, a new bronze urn, a more appropriate container for the remains of the founder was commissioned.

Although Algardi is not mentioned in any of the documents for the new urn, his hand in the work is confirmed by a later tradition for the attribution, a preparatory drawing (Neumann, fig. 4), and its style (Montagu). Neumann hypothesized that the relief was not cast until the 1730s or 1740s when a new *paliotto* was completed and the urn was re-gilded. Although Montagu convincingly dismantles Neumann's hypothesis, some doubt remains that the relief was placed on the urn in the seventeenth century. It is not described in guidebooks, and it appears in neither engravings of the chapel (Cat. 131, 133) nor in Pozzo's fresco of angels adoring the urn in the vault of the Corridor in the Casa Professa.

Ignatius, holding his traditional iconographic attribute (the Rules of the Society), occupies the center of the relief. To his right is Francis Xavier, who, in the final bronze stands with his left foot on a skeleton. Next to him is Roberto Bellarmino who hung the first image of Ignatius above his tomb giving rise to his official cult. Bellarmino was also involved with the beatification proceedings for Luigi Gonzaga who kneels beside him. To Ignatius' left is Francis Borgia (canonized in 1671) holding a monstrance before which kneels Stanislas Kostka. Other figures have been identified (Pecchiai, pp. 263-264) as the three Jesuits martyred in Japan (holding crosses), and Ignazio de Azevedo (holding a copy of the icon at S. Maria Maggiore which accompanied forty Jesuits martyred en route to Brasil). An early photograph showing this relief before it was damaged and somewhat clumsily restored, shows some of the missing attributes of the saints that appear on the bronze cast (Neumann, fig. 2).

In later tombs of Jesuit saints Luigi Gonzaga and Stanislas Kostka, the scenes of their deaths are represented on the urns themselves. Algardi's relief, which groups important figures (not all saints) of the Society's early history and its first *beati* and saints, is an early example in Rome of the Society's self-commemorating imagery. In retrospect, it seems like a somewhat hesitant beginning. As the decoration of the urn of a saint, the subject seems rather anomalous. Focusing on neither the after-life of Ignatius nor the miracle-working capabilities of his relics, this relief above all exalts Ignatius as founder in the company of illustrious Jesuits.

EL

MONTAGU, 1985, II, pp. 387-389, fig. 13-14; NEUMANN, 1977; PECCHIAI, 1952, pp. 131, 193, 199, 262-264, tav.24

135. Andrea Pozzo, *Fictive Cupola in the Church of S. Ignazio,*
Engraving in: *Perspectiva pictorum et architectorum,* Vol. 1, fig. 91, Rome, 1693
Rome, Biblioteca della Provincia Romana della Compagnia di Gesù, XVIII GG 192 A

Andrea Pozzo's fictive cupola in the crossing of the Church of S. Ignazio provided an ingenious decorative solution to an architectural and urbanistic problem that had vexed the Jesuits for decades. Construction of the church designed by Orazio Grassi was supervised by Antonio Sassi, who, perhaps on the orders of Nicolò Ludovisi, raised the height of the nave and facade by 4.4 meters (Habel, 1981, p. 36). If a cupola, which the Jesuits desperately wanted on the Roman skyline, were to be seen at all, it would have to be enlarged. But construction of a cupola of such large dimensions above walls of increased height posed structural problems, threatened the entrance of air and light into the attached college, and would still have been difficult to see from the small *piazza* in front of the church. For all of these reasons, it was never built.

It is likely that Pozzo, who had already executed fictive cupolas in the churches of S. Francesco Saverio in Mondovì (1676-1679; Kerber, 1961, p. 46) and in the Gesù in Frascati (1681-1684; Kerber, 1971, pp. 47-48), suggested this solution for the church of S. Ignazio. Executed in 1684-1685, the painting is illustrated in two plates in the *Perspectiva*, a line drawing and this rendering which provided the model for a restoration of the damaged painting (1961-1963).

While Pozzo's "cupola" gave the interior of the church its desired architectural and pictorial unity, the exterior still remained without its crowning element. It is interesting to note that in the 1727, in a debate over the definition of the terms of Costanza Pamphili's legacy to the Jesuits, the pope officially determined that the money left for the completion and decoration of the church could be applied to a new *piazza* (Habel, 1971, p. 51). The money saved by not building a cupola may have helped move the problem of decoration from the interior of the church out of doors. The creation of one of the most specious fictions in baroque painting may have indirectly given the city of Rome one of her most "theatrical" urban spaces.

EL

BALDINUCCI, 1975, p. 325; BÖSEL, 1985, I, p. 199; DE FEO, 1988, pp. 13-14, fig. 13-14; KERBER, 1971, pp. 91-93; MARTINETTI, 1967, pp. 54-58; MONTALTO, 1934; MONTALTO, 1962

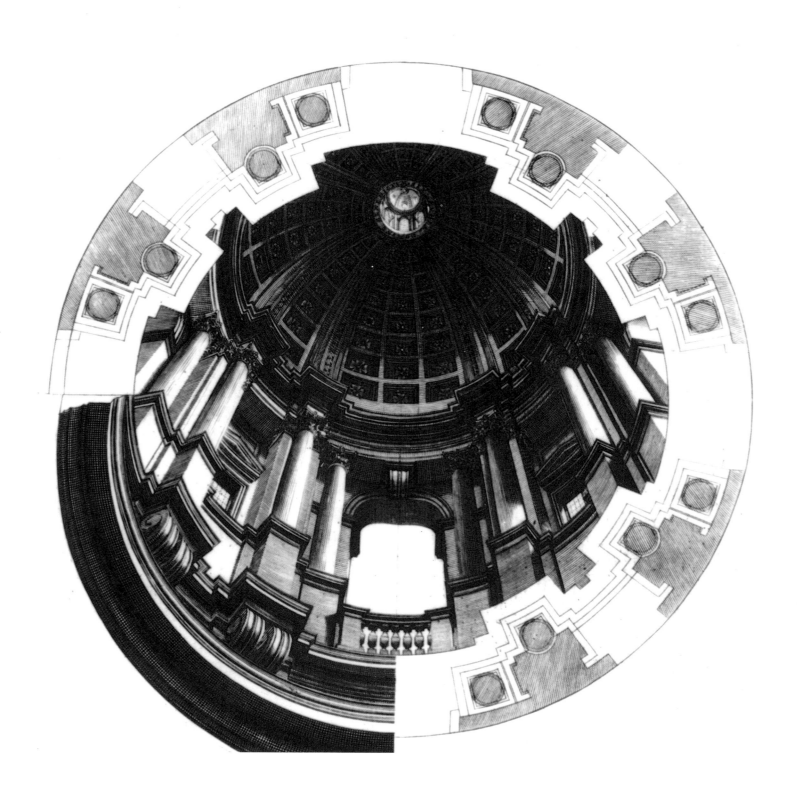

136. Arnould van Westerhout and Girolamo Frezza after Andrea Pozzo, *Vault of the Church of S. Ignazio*, Engraving, 66.5 x 31 cm., 1702 (loose sheet in Andrea Pozzo, *Perspectiva pictorum et architectorum*, Vol. 1, 1693)

Vatican City, Biblioteca Apostolica Vaticana, Cicognara VIII, 854

The meaning of Andrea Pozzo's frescoes in the vault of the Church of S. Ignazio (1693-1694) hinges on the association of Ignatius and the Jesuit mission with the power of light and fire. Depicted at the center of the field, high above the four parts of the earth, the saint is struck by rays of light emanating from Christ's wounded side, a variation on the theme of the *sangue di Cristo*. From the heart of Ignatius, as from a mirror, light issues to the four corners of the earth. The converting power of this light or flame is mediated by the Jesuit saints who travelled to the four continents as missionaries. The sending of the missionaries and the spreading of fire on earth are taken from the gospel and communion antiphons, respectively, of Ignatius' mass proper (Cat. 112).

The ceiling marks the grandiose culmination of a Jesuit imagery that had been expressed in Rome in smaller projects (like the sacristy of the same church) throughout the century. The themes of the four continents, the vanquished heretics and the converted heathen, and the glory of the saint were well-tried themes in baroque art. However, what makes the iconography of the vault particular to the Jesuits—other than the Jesuit saints who act as intermediaries to the world-wide Catholic mission—is a significant play of words, of the names Jesus and Ignatius. Here Pozzo develops a dialectic between the name of Jesus, chosen for the Society by the saint, and "ignis," fire, a pun on the name of Ignatius. The saint's famous phrase "Incendite et inflammate," ("Kindle and enflame") appears at one end of the vault, and Christ's "ignem veni mettere in terra" ("I have come to bring fire to the earth"), on the other end. Both are sources of burning fire. And Ignatius was fire "both in name and in reality" (Picinelli [1694], 1975, Lib. 2, ch. 1, 6).

Set within a grandiose fictive triumphal architecture, the scene is ideally viewed from a spot midway up the nave. One justification for painting the vault was that through Pozzo's *quadratura* the architectural defects of the space could be corrected. The idea that fictive architecture can be so real as to not only mask but correct a real space lies at the origins of several of Pozzo's fresco commissions. It reminds us that the resolution of one problem did not exclude the willful creation of a whole host of others. It did not seem to bother those who criticized the architectural design of the church that if one progresses along the nave too far and looks back, the fictive architecture collapses.

EL

FERRARI, 1990, fig. 25-27, pp. 208-209; HASKELL, 1980, pp. 90-91; KERBER, 1971, pp. 69-74; SCHADT, 1971; WILBERG-VIGNAU, 1970

Fig. 100.

DELINEATIO PICTURÆ IN FORNICE TEMPLI
S. IGNATII

Quod pictum seruat Roma, hoc cœlauit in ære:
Non una incidit; pinxit at una manus.

Arnoldus uan Westerhout Fig. Sculpsit   Andreas Puteus Sr. Iesu Inuen. et Pinx   Hieronymus Frezza Architect Sculpsit 1700.

217

137. Andrea Pozzo, *St. Ignatius Receives St. Francis Borgia*, Oil on canvas, 75 x 39.5 cm., ca. 1697-1701

Rome, Church of S. Ignazio, Rectory

St. Ignatius Receives St. Francis Borgia is a *bozzetto* for Pozzo's fresco to the right of the high altar in the Church of S. Ignazio. The apse was the last part of the church to be decorated, having undergone a change in design and program between the frescoes in the semi-dome begun 1685, and a second phase of work in 1697-1701. Pozzo's earlier plan, known through an engraving by Dorigny (1689, discovered by Kerber, 1965b, fig. 2), shows only one image below the cornice, the *Vision at La Storta*. On either side of the altarpiece the apse opened to *coretti* above and passages to a false ambulatory below. According to Pozzo (*Perspectiva,* II, 1700, fig. 81), he originally executed this idea with perspectives on canvas. In the final plan two paintings of Ignatius (*Sending Francis Xavier to India* on the left and the image exhibited here on the right) were substituted for his fictive *coretti* and ambulatory.

In this scene, Francis Borgia, the Spanish nobleman who would become the third general of the Society, accompanied by his son, is welcomed to Rome and into the Society by Ignatius and an allegorical figure of Religion (Kerber, 1971). Symbols of worldly power (the crown) and wealth (his son's plumed hat) are left behind as Ignatius, accompanied by two Jesuits, indicates Borgia's entrance into religious life.

Between the *bozzetto* and the final work minor changes were made in the drapery, in the distribution of colors, and in the use of light. Due to a minor change in the composition, the *bozzetto* must have been painted after Pozzo prepared his plate of the apse in the second volume of his perspective treatise (fig. on p. 55). It should therefore be dated sometime between the start of the new campaign of work in 1697 and the documented execution of the fresco in the apse in 1701.

EL

KERBER, 1965b; KERBER, 1971, pp. 68-69

CAT. 139

138. Andrea Pozzo, *The Chapel of S. Luigi Gonzaga*, Engraving in:
      Perspectiva pictorum et architectorum, Vol. 2, fig. 62, Rome, 1700
Rome, Biblioteca della Provincia Romana della Compagnia di Gesù, XVIII GG 192 B

139. Andrea Pozzo, *S. Maria Maddalena dei Pazzi's Vision of S. Luigi Gonzaga*,
      Oil on canvas, 53.5 x 84 cm., ca. 1697
Rome, Church of S. Ignazio, Sacristy

The chapel containing the tomb of St. Luigi Gonzaga was designed by Andrea Pozzo for the right transept of the Church of S. Ignazio. Distinguished by its four solomonic columns verneered with *verde antico*, this chapel is in many ways complementary to the Chapel of S. Ignazio in the Gesù. Concave rather than convex, the movemented aedicula and twisted columns create a complex play between object and ground. Legros' relief of the saint in glory floats indeterminately between the viewer and a space beyond the wall opened up by the aedicula.

Although construction of this chapel began in 1697, two years after that of the Chapel of S. Ignazio, there are two reasons to date its design either to the same year or even before the founder's chapel. First, in early designs for both chapels Pozzo placed the urn of the saint above the altar, a location rejected in deliberations on the design of the Chapel of S. Ignazio on the grounds that only the host should be placed above the altar. Pozzo included one such design for the Chapel of S. Luigi in his treatise noting that it could not be executed (Pozzo, II, 1700, fig. 65; De Feo, fig. 37). It is unimaginable that after the conceit was rejected for the Chapel of Ignatius he would repeat it in a design for Luigi's chapel. Secondly, in a letter commenting on Pozzo's early designs for the Chapel of S. Ignazio (Feb. 27, 1695), a dissatisfied critic (P. Antonio Baldigiani) urged Pozzo to provide alternative designs: "I do not doubt...that F. Pozzo can produce other designs that are equally good, and better, and in fact his design painted in the Church of S. Ignazio for the Chapel of B. Luigi is much better, and will be judged so by Professors [of design], which F. Pozzo himself did not deny, when I told him so" (ARSI, Rom 140, fol. 149v). It seems that Pozzo had already painted a mock-up of the Chapel of Luigi Gonzaga, perhaps full-scale, like the one we know he painted in the left transept Chapel of the Annunciation (Kerber, 1971, p. 69, n. 137; Montalto, 1958, p. 670, tav. 117, fig. 2). Therefore its design, preferred by Pozzo himself, may have been established by 1695.

The *bozzetto* exhibited here (Cat. 139), a study for the vault fresco in the same chapel, represents a saint's vision of Luigi (1600) that served as testimony for his beatification (1605). The right transept was the last part of the church vault to be frescoed by Pozzo (1697).

In contrast to recent representations of saints in glory such as those of St. Andrew (S. Andrea al Quirinale), Ignatius and Francis Xavier (the Gesù), in this vault Pozzo introduced a saintly witness to Luigi's beatitude. The design of the fresco is related to the vault in Antonio Gherardi's Chapel of St. Cecilia in S. Carlo ai Catinari which was constructed between 1691 and 1699 (Pickrel, 1987, p. 237). Rather than simply open the vault to a heavenly glory, Gherardi created a real intermediary space in which musical angels dangle their legs over the rim of the vault opening, like Pozzo's angels here, providing a transition between the interior space and the open sky.

Though loosely painted with details indicated summarily, the *bozzetto*, which has been squared for enlargement, represents a final stage of design. Only the most distant figures, Luigi and the angels surrounding him, would receive further definition in the executed work.

EL

DE FEO, 1988, pp. 21, 54-57, 107-109; FERRARI, 1990, fig. 28, p. 208; HIESINGER, 1980, pp. 11-12; KERBER, 1971, pp. 68-69, 181-186; LAVAGNINO, 1959, pp. 183-191; MONTALTO, 1958, pp. 181-186

Figura 26.

SACELLVM B. ALOYSIO GONZAGÆ. SOC IESV ERECTVM IN TEMPLO COLLEGIJ ROMANI EIVSDEM SOC ANNO

CAT. 138

140. Jacob Frey, *Notices of the Chapel of St. Ignatius located at La Storta*
("Notizie della Cappella di S. Ignazio, Situata in mezzo della Storta"),
Engraving, 22.7 x 33.4 cm., ca. 1700

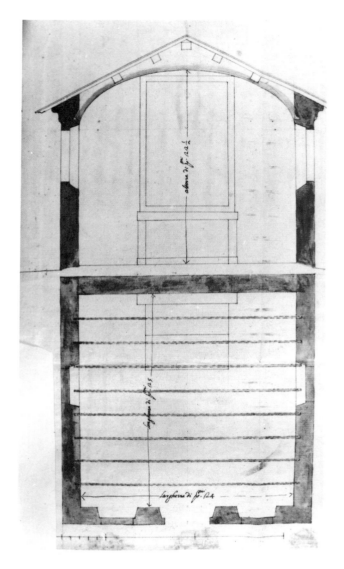

ANONYMOUS DRAWING, PLAN AND ELEVATION OF THE CHAPEL AT
LA STORTA, 1699, ARSI, ROM 136, FOL, 324

Frey's engraving records the renovation undertaken by the Society in 1700 of the Chapel at La Storta, the site of the most frequently depicted vision of Ignatius. The original chapel was represented variably as a modest structure in illustrations of the vision. Although we know nothing about the appearance of the building until 1700, it is likely that the Jesuits had done some work on the structure and it

decorations sometime around Ignatius' beatification or canonization.

The work on the chapel (whose total cost amounted to 296 scudi) was directed by Carlo Mauro Bonacina, the Milanese Jesuit brother who also administrated construction of the chapels of Sts. Ignatius and Luigi Gonzaga in the same years. The renovated chapel, a small aisleless space 5.3 by 5.6 meters and 5 meters high, is illustrated in an unpublished drawing (pen and ink and wash, 41.9 x 27.9 cm.) conserved with several documents describing the project (ARSI, Rom 136, fol. 324).

A summary of the work by Bonacina records the following renovations: the walls were repaired and painted, the roof was enlarged and a vault made, new lamps, candelabras, a *paliotto*, two confessionals and the two windows on the facade were installed. There were nine paintings already in the chapel and these were retouched and their frames regilded. Lastly, the document records the payment of 31.50 scudi for a new altarpiece: "For the large painting, that is the altarpiece, conceived and begun by our brother Cesare Agostino Bonacina, because of whose death, finished by Sig. Carlo Francesco de Angelis, with its frame 16 palmi high and 11 palmi wide" (ARSI, Rom 136, fol. 315r).

The chapel, almost completely destroyed during World War II, was reconstructed after the war. The only remnant of the seventeenth-century chapel is the inscription plaque over the door (for pre-war photographs cf. Fonck, fig. 10-14).

De Angelis' altarpiece was probably the image of the vision illustrated in the engraving (it is highly unlikely that the very badly painted image reproduced in Fonck, fig. 14, identified as the original altarpiece, is the painting by de Angelis). With Ignatius represented in pilgrim's garb, his hat and walking stick on the ground before him, the pilgrim must have felt the special blessing of Christ on his own stay in the Eternal City.

EL

FONCK, 1924; KÖNIG-NORDHOFF, 1980, p. 312, fig. 4; ARSI, Rom 136, fol. 314-324

NOTITIÆ DE SACELLO S. IGNATII, SITO IN MEDIO STORTÆ,
in quo datur commoditas celebrandi Missam.
NOTIZIE DELLA CAPPELLA DI S. IGNAZIO, SITUATA IN MEZZO DELLA STORTA
nella quale si dà il commodo di celebrarui la S.ta Messa.

Inscriptio marmori incisa
supra Portam dicti Sacelli

D. O. M.

IN HOC SACELLO
DEUS PATER
S. IGNATIO ROMAM PETENTI
AD SOCIETATEM JESU INSTITUENDAM
ANNO MDXXXVII.
APPARUIT
IPSUM EJUSQUE SOCIOS
CHRISTO FILIO CRUCEM BAJULANTI
BENIGNE COMMENDANS
QUI SERENO VULTU IGNATIUM INTUENS
HIS VERBIS AFFATUS EST
EGO VOBIS ROMÆ PROPITIUS ERO.
THYRSUS GONZALEZ
PRÆPOSITUS GENERALIS SOCIETATIS
SACELLO REFECTO, ET ORNATO
SANCTO PARENTI
P.
ANNO MDCC.

Iscrizione Latina scolpita in marmo
sopra la Porta della detta Cappella

D. O. M.

IN QUESTA CAPPELLA
L'ETERNO PADRE
APPARUE À S. IGNAZIO
INCAMINANTESI A ROMA
PER FONDARE LA COMPAGNIA DI GIESU
L'ANNO MDXXXVII.
CON BENIGNEMENTE RACCOMMANDARLO
INSIEME CON SUOI COMPAGNI
AL FIGLIOLO GIESU CHE PORTAUA LA CROCE
IL QUALE GUARDANDO IGNAZIO CON LIETO ASPETTO
GLI DISSE TALI PAROLE
IO A VOI SARO FAVOREVOLE IN ROMA.
TIRSO GONZALEZ
PREPOSITO GEN.LE D.A COMPAG.A DI GIESU
RISTORATA ET ABBELLITA LA CAPPELLETTA
VI HA POSTA QUESTA MEMORIA DI DIVOTIONE
VERSO IL SUO SS.MO PATRIARCA
L'ANNO MDCC.

Aspectus
Ejusdem Sacelli
venientibus
ab
Urbe.

LA STORTA

Veduta
della med.ma Cappella
andandoui
da
Roma

Designatio
Viarum
ab Urbe
ad Stortam
Disegno
delle Strade
da Roma
alla Storta

Scala di cinque miglia Italiane

CAT. 140

141. Anthony Van Dyck (?), *Saint Ignatius*, Oil on canvas, 345 x 213 cm., ca. 1623

Vatican City, Pinacoteca Vaticana, Inv. 790, Mag. 40A

This painting, controversial both in its attribution and its original location, is probably the painting placed in the Chapel of S. Ignazio in the left transept of the Gesù after the saint's canonization. The attribution to Van Dyck, first cited by Titi (1674), is made more convincing by the existence of a painting certainly by Van Dyck (Pinacoteca Vaticana) of the same dimensions depicting St. Francis Xavier that supposedly adorned the right transept chapel. However, the awkwardness of both pose and expression of the St. Ignatius, in contrast to the assured movement and more convincing *affetti* of the St. Francis Xavier (König-Nordhoff, fig. 175), has led scholars to question Van Dyck's role in the execution of the St. Ignatius.

There is uncertainty, however, over whether or not this pair actually adorned the transept altars. The existence of an earlier, slightly smaller pair of portraits (König-Nordhoff, fig. 170-171) of the saints, likewise represented in a landscape adoring the name of Jesus, as well as a tradition of attributing a pair of portraits in the Gesù to Rubens, complicate the problem. Even Della Porta's measured plans for the left transept chapel (Ackerman, 1965), do not permit us to establish definitively which pictures belonged on the altar.

The image itself represents Ignatius, outside of Rome, holding a book (inscribed "AD MAIOREM DEI GLORIAM") in his left hand and extending his right hand in adoration of the enflamed monogram of Jesus. Three putti support a banderole with the inscription: "QUID MIHI EST IN COELO ET A TE QUID VOLVI SUP TERRAM." At the saint's feet lies his abandoned suit of armor, and in the background to the left the pilgrim Ignatius kneels before Christ at La Storta. This fluidly executed background scene, in which two *pentimenti* (Christ's cross which has been made to rest more logically on his shoulder and Ignatius' staff which he originally held) can be discerned, exhibits more of Van Dyck's characteristic handling than the figure of Ignatius in the foreground. Ignatius is represented as a man converted to the arms of Christ, both illuminated from within and by the name of Jesus. The prominence of the armor and the vision in the background suggests that this image was inspired by the play "D. Ignatio in Monserrato over Mutatione d'Armi," performed at the Collegio Romano in 1622 as part of the canonization festivities (Cat. 111).

EL

KÖNIG-NORDHOFF, 1986, pp. 76-80, 87-89, 244-245, fig. 174; REDIG DE CAMPOS, 1936-1937

Bibliography

AA.VV. *Tesori d'Arte Sacra*. Rome, 1974.

ACKERMAN, J.S. "Della Porta's Gesù Altar." In *Essays in Honor of Walter Friedlaender*, pp. 1-2. New York, 1965.

ACKERMAN, J.S. "The Gesù in the Light of Contemporary Church Design." In *Baroque Art: The Jesuit Contribution*. Edited by R. Wittkower and I. Jaffe, pp. 15-28. New York, 1972.

Acta Sanctorum Julii. Vol. 7, Venice, 1749.

ALMAGIÀ, R. *Planisferi, carte nautiche e affini dal sec. XIV al XVII esistenti nella Biblioteca Apostolica Vaticana* (Monumenta Cartografica Vaticana, 1). Vatican City, 1944.

ANGELI, D. *Sant'Ignazio di Loyola nella vita e nell'arte*. Lanciano, 1911.

Annuae Litterae Societatis Iesu, 1582. Rome, 1584.

ARGAN, G. *The Renaissance City*. New York, 1969.

BAGLIONE, G. *Le vite de' pittori, scultori et architetti dal pontificato di Gregorio XIII. del 1572. in fino a' tempi di Urbano Ottavo nel 1642* (Rome, 1642). Edited by V. Mariani. Rome, 1935.

BALDINUCCI, F.S. *Vite di artisti dei secoli XVII-XVIII. Prima edizione integrale del Codice Palatino 565*. Edited by A. Matteoli. Rome, 1975.

BANFI, F. "Il *Paradiso* del Baciccia." *L'Urbe*, 22, 1959, pp. 4-10.

BANGERT, W. *A History of the Society of Jesus*. St. Louis, 1972.

BASILE, A. "Le due grandi cappelle della crociera nel Gesù l'anno della canonizzazione di Sant'Ignazio e San Francesco Saverio." in *La Canonizzazione dei Santi Ignazio di Loyola e Francesco Saverio*, pp. 116-118. Rome, 1922.

BELTRAME QUATTROCCHI, E. *Il Palazzo del Collegio Romano e il suo autore*. Rome, 1956.

BENEDETTI, S. *Fuori dal classicismo*. Rome, 1984.

BERNINI, D. *Vita del Cavalier Gio Lorenzo Bernini*. 1713.

BIERENS DE HAAN, J.C.J. *L'Oeuvre gravè de Cornelis Cort graveur hollandais 1533-1578*. The Hague, 1948.

BJURSTRÖM, P. "Baroque Theatre and the Jesuits." In *Baroque Art: The Jesuit Contribution*. Edited by R. Wittkower and I. Jaffe, pp. 99-110. New York, 1972.

BLUNT, A. *Guide to Baroque Rome*. New York, 1982.

BORSI, F. *La Chiesa di S. Andrea al Quirinale*. Rome, 1967.

BORSI, F. *Montecitorio. Ricerche di storia urbana*. Rome, 1972.

BORSI, F. *Bernini architetto*. Rome, 1980.

BORSI, S. *Roma di Sisto V: La Pianta di Antonio Tempesta, 1593*. Rome, 1986.

BÖSEL, R. *Jesuitenarchitektur in Italien 1540-1773. Die Baudenkmäler der römischen und der neapolitanischen Ordensprovinz*. 2 vols. Vienna, 1985-1986.

BÖSEL, R. "Typus und Tradition in der Baukultur gegenreformatorischer Orden." *Römische Historische Mitteilungen*, 31, 1989, pp. 239-253.

BÖSEL, R. and J.GARMS, "Die Plansammlung des Collegium Germanicum-Hungaricum, I. Der Gebäudekomplex von S. Apollinare in Rom." *Römische Historische Mitteilungen*, 23, 1981, pp. 225-275.

BÖSEL, R. and J.GARMS, "Die Plansammlung des Collegium Germanicum-Hungaricum. II. Sonstiger alter Bestand." *Römische Historische Mitteilungen*, 25, 1983, pp. 335-384.

BRICARELLI, C. "Il P. Orazio Grassi architetto della chiesa di S. Ignazio in Roma." *Civiltà Cattolica*, 73, 1922, pp. 13-25.

BUSER, T. "Jerome Nadal and Early Jesuit Art in Rome." *Art Bulletin*, 58, 1976, pp. 424-433.

CAMPBELL, T. *The Earliest Printed Maps, 1472-1500.* London, 1987.

CANESTRO CHIOVENDA, B. "Della *Gloria di S. Ignazio* e di altri lavori del Gaulli per i Gesuiti." *Commentari*, 13, 1962, pp. 289-298.

CANESTRO CHIOVENDA, B. "Cristina di Svezia, il Bernini, il Gaulli, e il libro di appunti di Nicodemo Tessin d.y. (1687-1688)." *Commentari*, 17, 1966, pp. 171-181.

CANESTRO CHIOVENDA, B. "*La Morte di S. Francesco Saverio* di G.B. Gaulli e suoi bozzetti, altre opere attribuite o inedite." *Commentari*, n.s. 28, 1977, pp. 262-272.

Canones Congregationum Generalium Societatis Iesu. Rome, 1581.

CASANOVA UCCELLA, L. *Palazzo Venezia: Paolo II e le Fabbriche di S. Marco.* Rome, 1980.

CASTAGNOLI, F. et. al. *Topografia e urbanistica di Roma.* Bologna, 1958.

CASTELLANI, G. "La Tipografia del Collegio Romano." *AHSI*, 2, 1932, pp. 16-18.

CASTRONOVO, V. et al. *La stampa italiana dal cinquecento all'ottocento.* Rome and Bari, 1976.

CEEN, A. *The Quartiere de'Banchi: Urban Planning in Rome in the first Half of the Cinquecento.* Ann Arbor and New York, 1986.

CHARMOT, F. *La Pédagogie des Jésuites.* Paris, 1943.

COFFIN, D. *The Villa in the Life of Renaissance Rome.* Princeton, 1979.

CONNORS, J. *Borromini and the Roman Oratory, Style and Society.* Cambridge, Ma., 1980.

CONNORS, J. "Bernini's S. Andrea al Quirinale: Payments and Planning." *Journal of the Society of Architectural Historians*, 41, 1982, pp. 15-37.

Constitutiones et Regulae Societatis Iesu (Monumenta Historica Societatis Iesu). 4 vols. Rome, 1934-1948.

Constitutions of the Society of Jesus. Translated by G. Ganss. St. Louis 1970.

CONWELL, J. "The Kamakaze Factor: Choosing Jesuit Ministries." *Studies in the Spirituality of the Jesuits*, 11/5, 1979.

CORDARA, J. *Collegii Germanici et Hungarici Historia.* Rome, 1770.

COSTANTINI, C. "Un battello insommergibile ideato da Orazio Grassi." *Nuova Rivista Storica*, 50, 1966, pp. 731-737.

DE FEO, V. *Andrea Pozzo. Architettura e illusione.* Rome, 1988.

DE HORNEDO, R. "La 'vera effigies' de San Ignacio." *Razon y Fe*, 152, 1956, pp. 203-224.

DESTOMBES, M. *Mappemondes, A.D. 1200 - 1500* (Monumenta Cartographica Vetustioris Aevi, Vol. 1). Amsterdam, 1964.

Die Cosmographia des Claudius Ptolomäus: Codex latinus 277. Facsimile ed. Zürich, 1983.

DIERICKX, M. *Het beste portret van St. Ignatius van Loyola.* Amsterdam, 1945.

DIONISI, A. *Il Gesù di Roma.* Rome, 1982.

DONOHUE, J. *Jesuit Education.* New York, 1963.

DREYER, P. "Eine unbekannte Zeichnung von Gianlorenzo Bernini." In *Per A. E. Popham*, pp. 161-163. Parma, 1981.

DUMINUCO, V. "Ignatian Spirituality and Jesuit Education." *Entre-Nous* (Ecole St. Louis de Gonzaga) 249, 1973, pp. 49-57.

EHRLE, F. *Roma al tempo di Giulio III: la pianta di Roma di Leonardo Bufalini del 1551.* Rome, 1911.

EHRLE, F. *Roma al tempo di Urbano VIII: la pianta di Roma di Maggi-Maupin-Losi del 1625.* Rome, 1915.

EHRLE, F. *Roma al tempo di Clemente VIII: La pianta di Roma di Antonio Tempesta del 1593.* Vatican City, 1932.

ENGGASS, R. "Three Bozzetti by Gaulli for the Gesù." *Burlington*, 99, 1957, pp. 49-53.

ENGGASS, R. *The Painting of Baciccio: Giovanni Battista Gaulli 1639-1709.* University Park, Pa., 1964.

ENGGASS, R. *Early Eighteenth Century Sculpture in Rome.* 2 vols. University Park, Pa., 1976.

Epistolae et Instructiones S. Ignatii de Loyola (Monumenta Historica Societatis Iesu). 12 vols. Madrid, 1903-1911.

Exercitia Spiritualia S. Ignatii de Loyola et eorum Directoria (Monumenta Historica Societatis Iesu). Revised edition. Rome, 1969.

FABRE, P. "Un nouveau catalogue des églises de Rome." *Mélanges d'archéologie et d'histoire*, 7, 1887, pp. 432-457.

FAGIOLO, M. "Struttura del trionfo gesuitico: Baciccio e Pozzo." *Storia dell'Arte*, 38-40, 1980, pp. 353-360.

FAGIOLO, M. and M.L. MADONNA, eds. *Roma 1300-1875. L'arte degli anni santi.* Exh. cat. Rome, Palazzo Venezia, 1984.

FAGIOLO, M. and M.L. MADONNA, eds. *Roma 1300-1875. La città degli anni santi. Atlante.* Exh. cat. Rome, Palazzo Venezia, 1985a.

FAGIOLO, M. and M.L. MADONNA, eds. *Roma Sancta. La città delle basiliche.* Rome, 1985b.

FAGIOLO DELL'ARCO, M. *Bernini: una introduzione al Gran Teatro del Barocco.* Rome, 1967.

FAGIOLO DELL'ARCO, M. "Il barocco romano (rassegna degli studi 1970-1974)." *Storia dell'arte*, 24-25, 1975, pp. 125-143.

FAGIOLO DELL'ARCO, M. and S. CARANDINI. *L'effimero barocco. Strutture della festa nella Roma del '600.* 2 vols. Rome, 1977-1978.

FANNELLI, G. *Firenze.* Rome and Bari, 1988.

FERRARI, O. *Bozzetti italiani dal Manierismo al Barocco.* Naples, 1990.

FONCK, L. *"La Storta" Un antico santuario di S. Ignazio di Loiola alle porte di Roma.* Rome, 1924.

Fontes Documentales de S. Ignatio de Loyola (Monumenta Historica Societatis Iesu). Rome, 1977.

Fontes Narrativi de S. Ignatio de Loyola et de Societatis Iesu initiis (Monumenta Historica Societatis Iesu). 4 vols. Rome, 1943-1965.

FOSSI, M. *Bartolomeo Ammannati architetto.* Florence, n.d.

FRANZ, H. *Bauten und Baumeister der Barockzeit in Böhmen. Entstehung und Ausstrahlungen der böhmischen Barockbaukunst.* Leipzig, 1962.

FRUTAZ, A. *Le Piante di Roma.* 3 vols. Rome, 1962.

GALASSI PALUZZI, C. "Quattro statue di Ciro Ferri e una tela di Jacopo Zoboli ignorate nella ven. Chiesa del Gesù di Roma." In *La Canonizzazione dei Santi Ignazio di Loyola e Francesco Saverio*, pp. 119-126. Rome, 1922.

GALASSI PALUZZI, C. "Le decorazioni della sacrestia di S. Ignazio e il loro vero autore." *Roma*, 4, 1926, pp. 542-546.

GALASSI PALUZZI, C. *Storia segreta dello stile dei gesuiti.* Rome, 1951.

GALLAMINI, P. "La medaglia devozionale cristiana: secoli XVII-XVIII-XIX (parte ii , secolo XVII)." *Medaglia,* 18, 1990, pp. 60-124.

GAMRATH, H. *Roma Sancta Renovata.* Rome, 1987.

GERARDI, A. *Relazione del solenne funerale e catafalco fatto dalli Padri della Compagnia di Giesù nella loro Chiesa della Casa Professa. A tutti li loro Fondatori, e Benefattori per tutt'il mondo defonti in questo primo lor secolo.* Rome, 1639.

GIACHI, G. and G. MATTHIAE. *S. Andrea al Quirinale* (Le Chiese di Roma illustrate, 107). Rome, 1969.

GIGLI, G. *DIARIO ROMANO 1608-1680.* Edited by G. Ricciotti. Rome, 1958.

GNERGHI, G. *Il teatro gesuitico ne'suoi primordi a Roma.* Rome, 1907.

GNOLI, D. "Descriptio Urbis, o censimento della popolazione di Roma avanti il sacco borbonico." *Archivio della R. Società Romana di Storia Patria*, 17, 1894, pp. 375-493.

GOETSTOUWERS, J.B. *Synopsis historiae Societatis Iesu.* Louvain, 1950.

GOLDBERG, E.L. *After Vasari. History, Art, and Patronage in Late Medici Florence.* Princeton, 1988.

GRAF, D. "Giovanni Battista Gaullis Ölskizzen im Kunstmuseum Düsseldorf." *Pantheon*, 31, 1973, pp. 162-180.

GRAF, D. *Die Handzeichnungen von Guglielmo Cortese und Giovanni Battista Gaulli.* 2 vols. Düsseldorf, 1976.

GUIDONI, E. "Il significato urbanistico di Roma tra antichità e medioevo." *Palladio*, 22, 1972, pp. 3-32.

GUIDONI, E. "Città e ordini mendicanti. Il ruolo dei conventi nella crescita e nella progettazione urbana nei secoli XIII e XIV." *Quaderni Medievali*, 4, 1977, pp. 69-106.

GUIDONI, E. *La città europea, formazione e significato dal IV al XI secolo.* Milan, 1978.

GUIDONI, E. and A. MARINO. *Storia dell'urbanistica: Il Cinquecento.* Rome, 1982.

HABEL, D. M. "Piazza S. Ignazio, Rome, in the 17th and 18th Centuries." *Architectura*, 11, 1981, pp. 31-65.

HAGER, H. "Sebastiano Cipriani." In *Dizionario biografico degli italiani*, Vol. 25. Rome, 1981.

HAMY, A. *Essai sur l'iconographie de la Compagnie de Jésus.* Paris, 1875.

HASKELL, F. "Pierre Legros and a Statue of the Blessed Stanislas Kostka." *Burlington*, 97, 1955, pp. 287-291.

HASKELL, F. "The Role of Patrons: Baroque Style Changes." In *Baroque Art: The Jesuit Contribution.* Edited by R. Wittkower and I. Jaffe, pp. 51-62. New York, 1972.

HASKELL, F. *Patrons and Painters. A Study in the Relations Between Italian Art and Society in the Age of the Baroque.* 2nd ed. New Haven, 1980.

HELD, J. "Rubens and the *Vita Beati P. Ignatii Loiolae* of 1609." In *Rubens before 1620.* Edited by J.R. Martin, pp. 93-134. Princeton, 1972.

HERZ. A. "Imitators of Christ: The Martyr-Cycles of Late Sixteenth Century Rome Seen in Context." *Storia dell'arte*, 62, 1988a, pp. 53-70.

HERZ, A. "Cardinal Cesare Baronio's Restoration of SS. Nereo ed Achilleo and S. Cesareo de' Appia." *Art Bulletin*, 70, 1988b, pp. 590-620.

HIBBARD, H. *Carlo Maderno and Roman Architecture 1580-1630.* London, 1971.

HIBBARD, H. "*Ut picturae sermones*: The First Painted Decorations of the Gesù." In *Baroque Art: The Jesuit Contribution.* Edited by R. Wittkower and I. Jaffe, pp. 29-49. New York, 1972.

HIESINGER, U.W. and A. Percy, eds. *A Scholar Collects. Selections from the Anthony Morris Clark Bequest.* Exh. cat. Philadelphia, The Philadelphia Museum of Art, 1980.

HOLLSTEIN, F.W.H. *Dutch and Flemish etchings, engravings, and woodcuts ca. 1450-1700*, Vol. 27. Amsterdam, 1983.

HOLT, E.J. "The British Museum's Phillips-Fenwick Collection of Jacques Courtois's Drawings and a partial Reconstruction of the Bellori Volume." *Burlington*, 108, 1966, pp. 345-350.

HOLT, E.J. "The Jesuit Battle-Painter Jacques Courtois (le Bourguignon)." *Apollo*, 89, 1969, pp. 212-223.

HOOD, W. "Ciro Ferri's *Pensiero* for the Altarpiece of the Blessed Stanislaus Kostka in Sant'Andrea al Quirinale." *Bulletin. Allen Memorial Art Museum*, 37, 1979-1980, pp. 26-49.

HUETTER, L. and V. GOLZIO. *San Vitale* (Le Chiese di Roma illustrate, 35). Rome, 1938.

Imago Primi Saeculi Societatis Iesu a Provincia Flandro-Belgica eiusdem societatis repraesentata. Antwerp, 1640.

Inscriptiones Epistolarum S.I. Rome, 1988.

INSOLERA, I. *Roma*. Rome and Bari, 1985.

JONES, P.M. "Federico Borromeo as a Patron of Landscapes and Still Lifes." *Art Bulletin*, 70, 1988, pp. 261-272.

KERBER, B. "Designs for Sculpture by Andrea Pozzo." *Art Bulletin*, 47, 1965a, pp. 499-502.

KERBER, B. "Zur Chorgestaltung von S. Ignazio in Rom." *Pantheon*, 23, 1965b, pp. 84-89.

KERBER, B. *Andrea Pozzo*. Berlin, 1971.

KÖNIG-NORDHOFF, U. "Die Christus-Vision des P. Diego Ledesma S.I. Zu einer Zeichnung des Matthias Kager aus dem Bereich der Stortaikonographie." *Achivium Historicum Societatis Iesu*, 49, 1980, pp. 311-322.

KÖNIG-NORDHOFF, U. *Ignatius von Loyola. Studien zur Entwicklung einer neuen Heiligen-Ikonographie im Rahmen einer Kanonisationskampagne um 1600*. Berlin, 1982.

KÖRTE, W. "Verlorene Frühwerke des Federico Zuccari in Rom." *Mitteilungen des Kunsthistorisches Institutes in Florenz*, 3, 1919-1932, pp. 518-529.

KRAUTHEIMER, R. *Rome: Profile of a City 312-1308*. 2nd ed. Princeton, 1983.

KRAUTHEIMER, R. and R.J. JONES, "The Diary of Alexander VII." In *Römisches Jahrbuch für Kunstgeschichte*, 15, 1975, pp. 199-233.

KUMMER, S. *Anfänge und Ausbreitung der Stuckdekoration im Römischen Kirchenraum (1500-1600)*. Tübingen, 1987.

KÜNSTLE, K. *Ikonographie der Heiligen*. Freiburg im Breisgau, 1926.

Lainii Monumenta, Epistolae et Actae Patris Jacobi Lainii (Monumenta Historica Societatis Iesu). 8 vols. Madrid, 1912-1917.

LAMALLE, E. "L'Inventaire des plans des Archives Romaines de la Compagnie." In Vallery-Radot, *Le Recueil de Plans d'édifices de la Compagnie de Jésus conservé a la Bibliothèque Nationale de Paris*. pp. 387-505. Rome, 1960.

LANCIANI, R. *Storia degli Scavi di Roma*. 4 vols. Rome, 1902-1912.

LANCKORONSKA, K. *Dekoracja Kosciola "Il Gesù"*. Lwów, 1935.

LAVAGNINO, E., G.R. ANSALDI, and L. SALERNO. *Altari barocchi in Roma*. Rome, 1959.

LAVIN, I. "Bernini's Death." *Art Bulletin*, 54, 1972, pp. 158-186.

LAVIN, I. *Bernini and the Unity of the Visual Arts*. Oxford and New York, 1980.

LAVIN, I., ed. *Drawings by GianLorenzo Bernini from the Museum der Bildenden Künste Leipzig, German Democratic Republic*. Exh. cat. Princeton, Princeton University Art Museum, 1981.

LAVIN, I. "Riflessioni su 'La Morte di Bernini'," In *Le immagini del SS.mo Salvatore. Fabbriche e sculture per l'Ospizio Apostolico dei Poveri Invalidi*, pp. 259-264. Exh. cat. Rome, Castel Sant'Angelo, 1988.

LEWINE, M.J. "The Roman Church Interior, 1527-1580." Ph.D. dissertation, Columbia University, 1960.

LEWINE, M.J. "Roman Architectural Practice During Michelangelo's Maturity." In *Stil und Überlieferung in der Kunst des Abendlandes. Akten des 21. internationalen Kongresses für Kunstgeschichte in Bonn 1964*, 2, pp. 20-26. Berlin, 1967.

Litterae Apostolicae quibus institutio confirmatio et varia privilegia continentur Societatis Iesu. Rome, 1578.

LOTTI, L. and P. L. LOTTI. *La Comunità Cattolica Inglese di Roma. La sua Chiesa e il suo Collegio*. Rome, 1978.

LUCAS, T. *A Guide to the Rooms of St. Ignatius*. Rome, 1990.

LUZIO, L. *I globi Blaviani* (Catalogo dei globi antichi conservati in Italia, fasc. 1). Florence, 1957.

MACANDREW, H. and D. GRAF. "II. Baciccio's Later Drawings: A Re-discovered Group Acquired by the Ashmolean Museum." *Master Drawings*, 10, 1972, pp. 231-259.

MÂLE, E. *L'art religieux après le Concile de Trente*. Paris, 1932.

MANCINI, C.M. *S. Apollinare. La chiesa e il palazzo* (Le Chiese di Roma illustrate, 93). Rome, 1967.

MARCH, G.M. "Intorno alla statua di Sant'Ignazio di Loiola nel Gesù di Roma." *AHSI*, 3, 1934, pp. 300-312.

MARCONI, P. *La città come forma simbolica.* Rome, 1973.

MARDER, T. A. "The Evolution of Bernini's Designs for the facade of S. Andrea al Quirinale: 1658-76." *Architectura*, forthcoming.

MARQUES, M. B. M. "Un dibujo de G. B. Gaulli para los frescos de la cupola del Gesù." In *Per A. E. Popham*, pp. 205-211. Parma, 1981.

MARTINETTI, G. *S. Ignazio* (Le chiese di Roma illustrate, 97). Rome, 1967.

MASHECK, J.D.C. "The Original High Altar Tabernacle of the Gesù rediscovered." *Burlington*, 112, 1970, pp. 110-113.

MAUQUOY-HENDRICKX, M. "Les Wierix illustrateurs de la Bible dite de Natalis." *Quaerendo*, 6, 1976, pp. 28-63.

MEISS, M. "An Early Altarpiece from the Cathedral of Florence." *The Metropolitan Museum of Art Bulletin*, 1954, pp. 302-317.

MERTEN, K. "St. Salvator im Clementium — ehmals böhmische Jesuitenkirche — und die Wälsche Kapelle in der Altstadt Prag." *Bohemia* (Jahrbuch des Collegium Carolinum), 8, 1967, pp. 144-162.

MILANESI, G. ed. *Le opere di Giorgio Vasari.* 9 vols. Florence, 1906-1907.

MONSSEN, L.H. "*Rex Gloriose Martyrum*: A Contribution to Jesuit Iconography." *Art Bulletin*, 63, 1981, pp. 130-137.

MONTAGU, J. *Alessandro Algardi.* 2 vols. New Haven, 1985.

MONTALTO, L. "Proposta di restauro della cupola finta in prospettiva nella Chiesa di S. Ignazio in Roma." *Bollettino d'arte*, 28, 1934, pp. 224-228.

MONTALTO, L. "Il problema della cupola di Sant'Ignazio da Padre Orazio Grassi e Fratel Pozzo a oggi." *Bolletino del centro di studi per la storia dell'architettura*, 11, 1957, pp. 33-62.

MONTALTO, L. "Andrea Pozzo nella Chiesa di Sant'Ignazio al Collegio Romano." *Studi romani*, 6, 1958, pp. 668-679.

MORELLO, G. "Bernini e i lavori a S. Pietro nel diario di Alessandro VII." In *Bernini in Vaticano*, pp. 321-340. Exh. cat. Vatican City, BAV, 1964.

MORELLO, G. ed. *Memorie melitensi nelle collezioni della Biblioteca Apostolica Vatican*, Exh. cat. Vatican City, BAV, 1987.

MORELLO, G. "I rapporti tra Bernini ed Alessandro VII negli autografi del Papa." In *Atti del colloquio Documentary Culture: Florence and Rome from Grand Duke Ferdinand I to Pope Alexander VII.* Florence, 1990.

MORONI, G. *Dizionario di erudizione storico-ecclesiastica.* Vol. 23. Venice, 1843.

MÜLLER PROFUMO, L. "Orazio Grassi e il Collegio dei Gesuiti a Genova." In *Miscellanea di storia moderna. Studi in onore di R. Cataluccio.* Genoa, 1984.

NADAL, J. *Imagenes de la Historia Evangelica* (Antwerp, 1593). Edited by A. de Ceballos. Barcelona, 1975.

NEUMANN, E. "Das Figurenrelief auf der Urne des Hl. Ignazio im römischen 'Gesù.'" *Pantheon*, 35, 1977, pp. 318-328.

New York. *The Age of Caravaggio.* Exh. cat. New York, The Metropolitan Museum of Art, 1985.

NOEHLES, K. "Visualisierte Eucharistietheologie. Ein Beitrag zur Sakralikonologie im Seicento Romano." *Münchner Jahrbuch der bildenden Kunst*, 29, 1978, pp. 92-116.

Obras Completas de San Ignacio. Madrid, 1982.

ORLANDINI, N. *Historiae Societatis Iesu Pars I.* Rome, 1615.

OSTROW, S. F. "Marble Revetment in Late Sixteenth-Century Roman Chapels." In *IL 60. Essays Honoring Irving Lavin on His Sixtieth Birthday.* Edited by M. A. Lavin, pp. 253-276. New York, 1990.

PADBERG, J. "How we live where we live." *Studies in the Spirituality of Jesuits*, 20/2, 1988.

PANCIROLI, O. *Tesori nascosti nell'alma città di Roma.* Rome, 1600.

PAPI, G. "Le tele della cappellina di Odoardo Farnese nella Casa Professa dei gesuiti a Roma." *Storia dell'arte*, 62, 1988, pp. 71-80.

PARTNER, P. *Renaissance Rome 1500-1559, A Portrait of a Society.* Berkeley, 1979.

PASCOLI, L. *Vite de' pittori, scultori, ed architetti moderni* (Rome, 1730). 2 vols. Facsimile ed. Rome, 1933.

PASTOR, L. *Storia dei Papi dalla fine del Medioevo.* 16 vols. Rome, 1910-1934.

PECCHIAI, P. *Roma nel Cinquecento.* Bologna, 1948.

PECCHIAI, P. *Il Campidoglio nel Cinquecento.* Rome, 1950.

PECCHIAI, P. *Il Gesù di Roma.* Rome, 1952.

PICINELLI, F. *Mundus Symbolicus* (Cologne, 1694). Reprint ed. New York and London, 1976.

PICKREL, T. "L'élan de la musique: Antonio Gherardi's Chapel of Santa Cecilia and the Congregazione dei Musici in Rome." *Storia dell'arte*, 61, 1987, pp. 237-254.

PIETRANGELI, C. *Il Museo di Roma. Documenti e iconografia.* Bologna, 1971.